ALSO BY EDWARD JABLONSKI

The Gershwin Years,
with Lawrence D. Stewart (1958)

Harold Arlen: Happy With the Blues

George Gershwin

The Knighted Skies

The Great War

Flying Fortress

Warriors With Wings:
The Story of the Lafayette Escadrille

Ladybirds: Women in Aviation

Man With Wings:
A Pictorial History of Flight (in progress)

Airwar:
I—*Terror From the Sky*
II—*Tragic Victories*
III—*Outraged Skies*
IV—*Wings of Fire*

Masters of Modern Music:
Schoenberg/Bartok/Stravinsky (in progress)

Atlantic Fever:
The Great Transatlantic Aerial Adventure

Sea Wings

The Gershwin Years (Revised Edition),
with Lawrence D. Stewart (1973)

Double Strike

Double Strike

THE EPIC AIR RAIDS ON REGENSBURG-SCHWEINFURT AUGUST 17, 1943

by Edward Jablonski

1974

DOUBLEDAY & COMPANY, INC., GARDEN CITY, NEW YORK

ISBN: 0-385-07540-5
LIBRARY OF CONGRESS CATALOG CARD NUMBER 73–79678
COPYRIGHT © 1974 BY EDWARD JABLONSKI
ALL RIGHTS RESERVED
PRINTED IN THE UNITED STATES OF AMERICA
FIRST EDITION

For
Diane and Art Hofmeister,
With affection.

A child may ask: "What is war?"
How can you answer that question?
Do you just send him away,
Never to tell him the truth?

Emily
(11 years old)

86076

CONTENTS

INTRODUCTION

The "double strike" mission to Regensburg and Schweinfurt in the summer of 1943 was a qualified disaster; it was unique—the first of its kind and it was costly. The mission had accomplished something and yet there was also something tantalizingly ambivalent about it: it had neither truly failed nor succeeded. Still it was carried out under tremendous handicaps by the men of the United States Eighth Air Force. At the same time, the German Luftwaffe that rose up to attack the American bombers—"viciously," to employ the term most frequently used by crews in postmission reports—failed to stop the American bombers, though they did succeed in destroying a great number of them.

"Regensburg-Schweinfurt was the bloodiest and most savagely fought air battle of the war up to that time," Lieutenant General Ira C. Eaker has written. Its "battlefield was a thousand miles long and five miles above the earth. It was fought in subzero temperatures and the gladiators, friend and foe, wore oxygen masks . . . The flight crews demonstrated a determination and courage seldom equaled and never surpassed in warfare."

Those qualities—determination and courage, to which another, sacrifice, can be added—were not exclusive to any group. The combined deeds, German and American, that day defined the capabilities of human valor under stress.

The American crews who fought and the Luftwaffe pilots who attacked them were driven by a deep faith in their actions as well as the simpler will to survive. The Americans genuinely believed that the success of their mission would truly contribute to a hastening of war's end. The German pilots, who fought predominantly in their own skies, were defending their homeland (however corrupted by Hitler and company) and by extension, their very homes and families. Thus was the political aspect of the battle somewhat tinctured; it was not quite "nazi" versus "democrat," but rather airman versus airman, each battling for valid personal reasons.

But after the skies cleared and the fires extinguished, the damage assessed and the toll reckoned, the truth was that the American objectives had been a vain hope. They had ultimately eluded the brave men who had participated in the mission and had eluded those equally brave men who had planned, agonized over, ordered, and then evaluated the mission.

At this latter day who has the right to point the accusing finger and say that this or that leader had blundered? The fact is that no one had blundered. True there was that one great ubiquitous variable that can never be sufficiently allowed for—human vulnerability. So were certain natural factors, such as weather and all it implies. In other words, there was no one "guilty," no one militarily inefficient, no one who "caused" what occurred in the skies over Germany on August 17, 1943.

Nor could anyone, at the time, predict how it would all turn out. All who worked on the mission hoped for total success, but no one, however optimistic, was unrealistic enough to expect it. Nor did anyone foresee the high rate of American bomber loss. Such foresight is denied all except those who claim it simplistically by looking backward. This is the luxury of the armchair strategist, or hobbyist, pontificating long after the event. But war in the living room and war in the field are dread worlds apart.

During the course of the Second World War and practically ever since there has been argument over the efficacy of that concept of warfare known as "strategic bombardment," the employment of aircraft in the destruction of enemy industries devoted to the manufacture and distribution of materials of war. There are two major arguments associated with this concept, one being that it never actually worked (which is false) and the other that it contributed to the killing of the innocents—the old, women, children—and the indiscriminate ravishment of cities (which is true). Frequently, it was found, war industries were situated near or in cities and towns and thus was modern total war demonstrated with frightful impact. The one argument is technical and the second is moral. But knowing what we do of war, how can morality be a factor? Such phrases as "civilized rules of warfare" are a cruel travesty, and meaningless; indeed, they are self-contradictory. In war the slaughter of innocents along with the "guilty" (are there no innocent soldiers?) and the widespread ruin of cities are mandatory. That is the nature of war as it has evolved into the twentieth century. It is fatuous to expect a desperate people, however dedicated to the observance of the "civilized rules of warfare," not to use every means of saving themselves no matter how inhumane the weapons.

The most annihilative weapons now in existence are those that may be delivered by air—by aircraft or missile. These weapons had their roots in the Second World War, in the dozens of Regensburgs, Schweinfurts, Hamburgs, Dresdens, Londons, Berlins, Tokyos, and their sophisticated (for the time) variants, Hiroshima and Nagasaki. To maintain that those strikes were not effective or decisive is unrealistic; to believe that they could not be repeated, a geometric progression of havoc, is dangerous.

Two lessons emerged from Regensburg-Schweinfurt: one human, the other military. It was an epic of courage and endeavor, and more. It was a portent of things to come once the Allies had—as they then did not have—the means (men, planes, and ordnance). Even though an aircraft factory and a ball-bearing plant were not wiped off the face of the earth, it was not long before that became possible; today it would be a certainty. In the summer of 1943 Allied air leaders honestly believed that they wielded the most potent weapon in history, but various factors—

ranging from political through indeterminate—countered or vitiated that potency. This is not a brief for the concept of strategic bombardment—and certainly not a plea for a second chance to prove its full efficacy. It is unlikely that much of civilization would survive such a demonstration.

But an understanding of what occurred during Regensburg-Schweinfurt, why it was executed without question and what it portended may be illuminating. Military "experts" might dismiss it as a near-failure, those who romanticize war might find in its telling great deeds and plenty of cockpit gore, more than enough to satisfy their blood lust. The non-professional strategist, the collecter of statistics, the list-maker, will find plenty of material to prove his point, whatever it is.

No understanding of Regensburg-Schweinfurt will emerge unless it is properly set in its time, with all of the limitations that affected it (and not recognized until long after the fact) set in focus. All too many critiques of battles written after the events have congealed into objective statistics seem to take all things into account except that there were human beings involved—some even manage to ignore the fact that there was a war on.

In retrospect, looking backward at the war years 1939–45 is a chilling experience. How could "civilized" men have done such things? How could men, unknown to each other, endeavor almost daily to kill each other? Imagine setting out in great aircraft laden with bombs to drop explosives upon factories, or even cities. There is something irrational about these ideas—and yet these things were done and accepted as normal. But given the realities of the time—there *was* a war on—the unreal and the abnormal become commonplace.

The Second World War, an "honest war" in the phrase of a participant who has witnessed later wars, was inevitable once Hitler had unleashed his pattern for Nazi conquest. Stopping him and all he represented was a necessity "at all costs"—and the cost was high. There was no question either of which side represented the forces of good and evil. But once war became a way of life, about mid-1944, the political issues faded to some extent and destruction and death became all. With the turn of the tide it became a matter of survival for the Germans (and the Japanese) rather than the promulgation of an evil political philosophy. The painfully learned lessons, the many Regensburgs and Schweinfurts, were applied to the destruction of Germany. The full import of air power was finally recognized and, fortunately, the war ended before it could be fully exploited. But this could hardly be classified as an advance in civilization.

The purely military function of the Regensburgs and Schweinfurts was not to advance civilization, but to bring the war to as quick an end as possible; this would be salutary to both sides. But the Germans were just as determined to win as the Allies and they were terribly unco-operative. It was not possible to place a call to Hitler and ask him if it was true, as Allied Intelligence had reported, that there was a poison gas works at Dresden; nor could you check with Goering, or better yet with Albert Speer, to learn just how much damage had been done to an aircraft factory and whether or not one more trip would complete the job. As for the Luftwaffe, so far as it was permitted by the inept Goering, it was the greatest problem of all—a point heavily underscored during Regensburg-Schweinfurt. All the planning in the world could not allow for every individual in every plane—he was unpredictable.

Air battles, three dimensional, wide-ranging and subject to more variables than any other form of combat, were the least predictable and most liable to calamity or unexpected success. There was as much possibility for one as the other once the master plan left the paper and came alive in the air. These variables and factors, known and unknown, contributed to the chain of events that made up Mission 84, Regensburg-Schweinfurt. Among these myriad of factors lies the truth about war.

War is, in the view of one historian, that human activity devoted to the solution of political, economic, or social differences by killing and destruction. However patriotically rationalized, these are the ultimate functions of war. Accept war and you must also accept these functions—and their consequences.

E.J.

New York, N.Y.
25 February 1973

I

PRELUDE

Eighty-three official bombing missions of varying intensities and effectiveness preceded the Eighth Air Force's double strike attack upon the Messerschmitt factory at Regensburg and a complex of factories which produced ball bearings at Schweinfurt. In every way this mission was the most complex, the most ambitious, the most superlative-afflicted of all the previous eighty-three. Never before had so many men and aircraft been involved in what, on paper, was in fact a single mission; never before had the Eighth Air Force penetrated so deeply inside Germany; never before had the Eighth attempted a long-distance shuttle mission. Never before would so many men and aircraft be lost.

The strategic reasoning behind the mission was to cripple the Luftwaffe to enable even further destruction of Germany's war industries. This, in turn, would make it possible to establish Allied beachheads in France, hopefully to drive the Germans back to Berlin.

Berlin—and the checkmate of Hitler—was the primary Allied goal. This was agreed upon by Winston Churchill and Franklin Roosevelt in their first meeting following the Japanese attack on Pearl Harbor which served to bring the United States into the Second World War. This act was subsequently followed, within four days, by a declaration of war on the United States by Germany and Italy.

From December 22, 1941, until the turn of the new year the

American President and the British Prime Minister, plus their General Staffs, met in Washington to discuss, argue, and generally agree on several fundamental points. One of the many results of their conference, code-named Arcadia, was to form a Combined Chiefs of Staff, British and American, to simplify and unify Allied strategy for, hopefully, winning the war—first in Europe, then in the Pacific. This unique conception, somewhat like a war-making Board of Directors, may not always have accomplished its purpose but it functioned remarkably well (there was certainly no such co-operation between the German and Italian and Japanese high commands).

To implement the "Germany First" concept, an invasion of Europe (as was being demanded by a beleaguered Russia) was required. But as Hitler, the Luftwaffe, the Wehrmacht, and, to a lesser extent, the German Navy, had demonstrated, crossing the English Channel was no simple task. In fact, the Germans had found it impossible.

Therefore, until the Allies could launch a full-scale cross-Channel invasion, there was only one means of reaching the German war machine: by air. This plan called for a joint effort by the veteran Royal Air Force, whose Bomber Command had been striking at German industrial installations (or more precisely, German industrial towns and cities) since May of 1940, and the untried United States Army Air Force, which would be represented in Britain by the Eighth Air Force. It was hoped that the combined weight of the two bombing forces would cripple Germany's war potential and hasten the close of the war.

Accomplishing this, merely getting it started, was no easy undertaking. There were all but overwhelming problems in training and logistics to solve: transporting men, aircraft, replacement parts, fuel; acquiring bases and establishing housing. There were, briefly, thousands of details to attend to before American airmen could even begin to join Bomber Command in the assault on Germany.

There was also the haunting specter of a victorious Japan raging through the Pacific. Among those who dissented from the "Germany First" policy were American Navy men who saw Japan as the prime, most potent enemy. If the bulk of supplies was shipped off to Europe, what would happen to the men in the Pacific? They could not be abandoned, of course, but what supplies they received, what men were sent to join them, were at the expense of amassing forces in Britain for the opening of the Second Front. Thus did the fortunes of war—not going well so far as the Allies were concerned—necessitate compromises which in turn consumed time.

It was not until the summer of 1942 that the first American heavy bomber (the chosen instrument for the strategic bombardment campaign), a Consolidated B-24 Liberator, arrived in Britain. It was joined shortly after by a Boeing B-17 Flying Fortress. These were the first of the great armada of war-making aircraft that would, in time, burgeon into the powerful Eighth Air Force which had been forming in the United Kingdom since February. Two aircraft could hardly have been expected to wreak much damage upon Nazi Germany. Three days after the arrival of the B-17 American airmen did participate in their first bombing mission to German-held targets. With a characteristic predilection for anniversaries the date selected was July 4; it was not to be a banner day.

To begin with, the Americans had to borrow six bombers from the Royal Air Force since they had not yet been issued any of their own. There were six, American-made (at least) Douglas A-20s, the Boston (later named the Havoc), flown by men of the 15th Bombardment Squadron (Separate) of the 27th Bombardment Group (Light). One of these crews had already flown a mission with the R.A.F., but the Independence Day effort was to be the first of any (if modest) weight. On this mission the 15th Squadron would be accompanied by a veteran R.A.F. unit, No. 226 Squadron, in their own six Bostons.

Their objectives, Luftwaffe airfields, lay in occupied Holland just across the North Sea. The plan was to come in low, to surprise the Germans by eluding their radar, swoop in to bomb and strafe and then get away fast. As it went with so many well-planned missions, the execution did not work out in reality as it had on paper. As the aircraft approached their several targets it became all too evident (obviously they had been spotted by a Nazi ship while crossing the North Sea) that surprise had not been achieved. The flights were greeted with heavy antiaircraft fire—one of the worst, the R.A.F. crews later reported, that they had ever encountered.

Statistically, the first "official" American bombing of German-held targets on that memorable July 4, 1942, was anything but a military triumph. Only two of the six American-crewed Bostons succeeded in striking their assigned targets; two crews and aircraft were lost, victims of the afflictive flak. Of the four American-manned planes that returned one was in very rough shape. But its story initiated a tradition of determination, courage perseverance, toughness of men and aircraft—and just plain luck—that would characterize the exploits of American airmen that would follow that hapless Fourth of July.

In the attack on an airfield near De Kooy, where one of the American Bostons had been shot down, another, piloted by Captain Charles C. Kegelman, was hit in the right engine. It burst into flame and the propeller sheered off and cartwheeled wildly across the field; with the starboard engine burning, the plane veered erratically and perilously near the ground. In an instant a wingtip did scrape the earth and Kegelman fought desperately to keep the plane under control. Trailing flame and smoke, the Boston lurched downward enough so that its aft section, too, scraped the ground. It bounced and Kegelman managed to gain sufficient airspeed and control with his remaining engine to keep the plane airborne.

They were up but not out, for at the farther edge of the field was a flak tower whose guns were training on the stricken, low flying, aircraft. Kegelman turned the plane directly into the tower as all gunners of the Boston concentrated on it until the flak stopped coming at them. Only then were the bombs jettisoned and Kegelman, noting that the destroyed engine had stopped burning, skirted the waves over the North Sea back to the 226th's base at Swanton Morley. (For his part in the mission Kegelman was awarded the Distinguished Service Cross, second only to the Medal of Honor among American decorations.)

Kegelman's Boston was one of the four American-crewed Bostons that had returned from the mission to Holland; one R.A.F. Boston was lost also. Of the four bases selected for attack, one was not bombed at all and the flight to which it had been assigned returned to England with bomb loads intact. Those bases that had been assaulted were hardly put out of operation, so that, in truth, the Fourth of July "first" mission accomplished practically nil tactically. It was little more than a nuisance raid and, at the cost of three aircraft, had hardly been worth the effort. Except that it was, though small, an American contribution (with British help) and that was good for morale as well as prestige. American airmen had finally taken a tentative jab at the Axis and had won the respect of their brother fliers in the R.A.F.

Obviously the Axis would not crack under helter-skelter hit-and-run strikes by a handful of light bombers. It would take the heavies, in massive formations, to provide the smashing blows. The first of these took place in little over a month after the 15th Squadron's "first." The 97th Bombardment Group (Heavy), which had been transporting its men and machines to bases at Polebrook and Grafton Underwood, England, beginning in May of 1942, was pronounced ready for missions early in August.

This moment had not come easily. When the 97th crews arrived in Britain it was quickly evident that many were undertrained. Some gunners had never fired a gun from a moving aircraft; there were pilots who had little practice in formation flying and there were radio operators who were unfamiliar with the Morse code. In the few weeks before August 9 (when combat readiness was announced) the crews of the 97th flew several practice missions over England—again in co-operation with the

R.A.F. whose Spitfires served both as "enemy" aircraft for gunnery practice and as escort. The 97th was equipped with the Boeing B-17E, at the time the very latest of the Flying Fortresses, with an enlarged rudder (for improved high altitude performance) and a new gun position in the tail. Although it was still weak in forward fire power, the B-17E was considered the first of the truly offensive Fortresses.

Once alerted, excitement ran high in the 97th installations. But then one other element was soon introduced into the combat picture—English weather. So it was that the mission which had been "laid on" (a Britishism quickly adopted by the Yanks) the second week of August was canceled out by the weather. During the next week this occurred again—thus supplanting excitement with tension. Finally in the evening of August 16 the 97th was alerted for the third time and the weather held; by the afternoon of August 17, 1942, the Eighth Air Force embarked upon its first heavy bomber combat mission of the war.

Like the 15th Squadron's July 4th strike into Holland, it was not an impressive effort numerically. But unlike the earlier mission it was a success. Only eighteen B-17s were involved along with several escorting squadrons of R.A.F. Spitfires. Six of the Fortresses were dispatched toward the French coast in a diversionary feint to draw off the Luftwaffe from the target area, the Sotteville marshaling yards near Rouen. The remaining B-17s took off soon after and also headed for France. Two flights of six planes each, with group commander Colonel Frank A. Armstrong, Jr., in the first and Major General Ira C. Eaker, head of VIII Bomber Command (not yet officially the Eighth Air Force though popularly called that), in the second. Appropriately the plane in which Eaker flew was named *Yankee Doodle*. Four Spitfire squadrons were assigned to accompany the two little formations to Rouen and back.

The weather, for a change, was perfect. As the planes approached the target, bombardiers could see the complex of tracks, shops, and cars from ten miles away. It was a textbook setting as all Fortresses rode in at an altitude of 23,000 feet and neatly dropped their bomb loads. There was some antiaircraft fire and only two American planes were hit, with little damage to aircraft and none to crews. A rather tentative intrusion by Messerschmitt 109 fighters resulted in an attack by three (again as with the flak, with no or minimal effect) while the others remained well out of the range of the Fortress's guns, as if studying the new large bomber. The bombing was accomplished without serious interference from the enemy or the weather.

Upon dropping their bombs the twelve B-17s wheeled around gracefully and headed back for England where their arrival was awaited by high brass, ground crewmen and newsmen. Mission No. 1 was hailed as a success: all aircraft had taken off, had bombed (if not with vaunted "pickle barrel" precision, at least with reasonable accuracy) and, importantly, all had returned safely. The mission appeared to be a vindication of the American conception of daylight bombing, a technique both the Germans and the British had abandoned as too costly.

2.

Following the raid on Rouen-Sotteville, Air Marshal Sir Arthur Harris, Commander-in-Chief of R.A.F. Bomber Command, sent a lighthearted message to Eaker: CONGRATULATIONS FROM ALL RANKS OF BOMBER COMMAND ON THE HIGHLY SUCCESSFUL COMPLETION OF THE FIRST AMERICAN RAID BY THE BIG FELLOWS ON GERMAN OCCUPIED TERRITORY IN EUROPE. YANKEE DOODLE CERTAINLY WENT TO TOWN AND CAN STICK YET ANOTHER WELL-DESERVED FEATHER IN HIS CAP.

While the response to the bombing was enthusiastic, with the British especially so, the truth was that Harris and most of his colleagues were not convinced that the American way was the answer. There was, in fact, a great deal of theoretical disagreement on this between the two Allied camps. Mission No. 1 had been accomplished within easy flying distance of Britain; the force had been a small one (with a consequent light bomb delivery) and, besides being practically unchallenged by the Luftwaffe, had been heavily escorted during the entire mission, from takeoff to landing. Fighter support was not only a critical luxury, (it was in truth a necessity, but it had not yet been rammed home that the B-17 was not in fact an absolute flying fortress). At that time there were no fighters extant that could fly to Germany and back—and the heart of Nazidom lay there, not in defeated and occupied France and the Low Countries.

Despite Harris's jolly reference to *Yankee Doodle* and the sincerity of his felicitations, he was not at all convinced that the American doctrine of "high altitude daylight precision bombardment" was the answer to the question of how to get Germany First. He believed, and his view reflected the general British attitude, in nighttime area attacks. While such bombings may not have proved as accurate as the daylight attacks (indeed, some in the early days of the war were literally miles off target), they cost less in men and machines because German defenses and night fighters were not then in condition to cope with these techniques.

Such bombings also killed more German civilians, even when the approximate area of the target was hit. Thus when the U. S. VIII Bomber Command was assigned to Britain, it was the host's expectancy that it would join the R.A.F.'s Bomber Command in night bombings of the critical cities in the Ruhr as well as other strategic industrial centers (including Berlin) deeper inside Germany.

General Eaker did not concur. American crews had been trained for daylight operations; just retraining them would consume as much time as had already slipped by since Pearl Harbor. Secondly: American bombers had been designed to operate in daylight also, with the famed and very secret Norden bombsight, at high altitudes out of reach of antiaircraft fire. Theoretically, too, these bombers particularly were considered to be so heavily gunned (thus the "Flying Fortress") that, in formation, they would be capable of a most formidable self-defense. A further theory, cognate to the day-precision concept, was that if a target were sufficiently struck with reasonably high accuracy it followed that it would be eliminated from the war. General area bombings at night were incapable of such concentration, Eaker maintained. In this stance he was joined by a powerful ally, Major General Carl A. Spaatz, who had come to England to command the Eighth Air Force, leaving Eaker free to continue at the head of its bomber command. It devolved upon the able Spaatz to co-ordinate the operations of the VIII Air Support (originally engaged in training, reconnaissance and troop transport and later medium bombing), VIII Fighter and VIII Bomber Commands. He was responsible, too, for a smooth co-ordination of these operations with those of the British. The problem of daylight versus nighttime bombing was a rather delicate one.

Thus from the beginning the feasibility of absolute co-operation between the two Allied Air Forces was at an impasse. But it was also obvious that if anything were to be accomplished there would havc to be some form of related effort. It was agreed, under the polite but firm arguments of Spaatz and Eaker, that the Americans would proceed according to their original plan, with both forces integrating their efforts in attacking German, or German-held, targets. But each would also go its own theoretical way.

American crews, learning their deadly trade in combat, began by striking at nearby—*ergo* under fighter protection—objectives in France and the Low Countries by day while Bomber Command continued to bomb inside the Reich at night. The two forces were co-operating in a sense: they were reaching out together to hit the enemy, but their efforts were not truly co-ordinated—there was no real concentration as anticipated by the Combined Chiefs of Staff.

So firm was he in advocating his point of view that Harris often found himself standing against the Combined Chiefs, the Air Staff, the Secretary of State for Air, and Churchill, if necessary.

He frequently, in fact, chose to ignore their "suggestions," then their pleas and even their orders. Tough-minded, assured, thoroughly the "professional," Harris managed to stop just short of insubordination, though his superiors were remarkably long-suffering and forgiving. But Harris knew his stuff, had built Bomber Command up from practically nothing and was forceful in his views. Having experienced German ruthlessness, he was willing to be ruthless also: he had no compunctions about destroying German cities while attempting to wreck its factories. The rumor was that he had once said, "It takes six months to rebuild a factory, but twenty years to grow a new factory worker." He was a realist in an unreal time, but it made him unpopular even in England where he was frequently called "Butcher" Harris. He believed that the war could be settled by bombing alone and that if the American Air Forces would co-operate—that is, do it his way—the war could be won solely by air power.

As early as June 1942, just two months before *Yankee Doodle* "went to town," Harris had assured Churchill that "Victory, speedy and complete, awaits the side which employs air power as it should be employed." Firm in the belief that he knew how to employ it, he also believed that it was possible, thus, to "knock Germany out of the war in a matter of months . . ." To do this it would mean that Britain should concentrate upon the application of air power, and relegate the Army and Navy to secondary roles—an idea that did not endear Harris to the senior services. In brief, Harris's plan was to eliminate Germany's industries along with the towns and cities that harbored them. In this he hoped he would be joined by the American Air Forces, a hope in which he was frustrated. Even as late as November 1943 he advocated this approach when he wrote to Churchill: "We can wreck Berlin from end to end if the U.S.A.A.F. will come in on it. It will cost between 400–500 aircraft. It will cost Germany the war."

It should be noted that Harris did not invent the tactic of bombing German cities at night, he inherited it when he assumed command of Britain's bomber forces in February 1942. Night bombing was primarily a concession to the high loss rate in Bomber Command and not conceived to bring about the deliberate devastation of German cities. In time, under Harris's leadership, British bombing accomplished that however, whatever the intent of Bomber Command's campaign. Even so, it took intensive training as well as the development of electronic devices before crews were able to find their targets at night with any real accuracy.

Harris's particular *bête noire* was the Ministry of Economic Warfare which was established ostensibly to advise the Air Ministry as to the priority of German target systems based upon its knowledge of Germany's economic conditions. In other words, the Ministry of Economic Warfare was supposed to know just how much destruction of which target would most seriously damage the Nazi war machine. (This is a simplification of the Ministry's function—which was a great deal broader, but is true as it applied to the strategic bombing program.)

The Ministry of Economic Warfare was made up of professorials or industrialists rather than military men and thus, so far as Harris was concerned, well-intentioned amateurs. His suspicion of such dated back to the First World War when certain schemes for dealing with the enemy were suggested by perfectly intelligent, sane, men. One idea was offered to deal with the Zeppelin by harpooning it from an airplane; another suggestion: freeze clouds and mount antiaircraft guns on them.

The Ministry of Economic Warfare did not come up with such screwball ideas, but those they did bring to Harris he found hardly more practicable. One of the favorite target systems was oil—which made sense, except that the pragmatic Harris realized he did not have the numbers—men and aircraft—with which to deal with such targets. Besides oil targets were not so easy to find, nor were they simple to get to, deep inside Germany as they were—and once (and if) found, they were generally a prickly nest of antiaircraft guns. Until he had the means, Harris preferred to send his crews to the Ruhr, the heartland of German industry.

There were pressures from other sources besides the Ministry of Economic Warfare—the Air Ministry, Churchill (whose ear was attuned to the people's voice), the other services and the general day-to-day twists and turns of the war. For example, when German submarines began to make the Atlantic a graveyard for Allied shipping, the cry went out to shift air power to that quarter. Aircraft, and crews, were "borrowed" from Bomber Command for Coastal Command, thus weakening Harris's Ruhr campaign. Certain that he was right, Harris stubbornly fought for his command and, so far as he could, almost to the point of insubordination, he pursued his own plan. He hoped, too, that his American colleagues would share his wisdom.

3.

While the Americans had much to learn about making war, and they could—and frequently did—learn it from their British colleagues, there was a strong determination in the American high command to stick to its strategic guns, so to speak. Both Spaatz and Eaker, backed by the Chief of the U. S. Army Air Force, General Henry H. Arnold, elected to continue with the doctrine of daylight strategic bombardment.

British air leaders, while counseling generally against this, did not seek to interfere officially. It was thought best to let the American crews see for themselves what they could do; they were eager, confident, determined and—who knows?—they may very well have been capable of carrying it off. Meanwhile, the British did all they could to make the crews at home, helped to establish bases, freely shared all their hard-fought-for knowledge and generally tried to make the American transition from peace to war as easy as British experience could make it.

Initially all appeared to be going quite well. True, no really large raids were mounted in the first month of operations but as the green crews acquired combat experience, always within fighter escort range of course, the missions went well. Day after day the Fortresses set out and, as occurred on the Rouen-Sotteville mission, all aircraft returned safely. No less than nine missions were flown before any Fortress fell to enemy guns. This seemed to bode well, although no one pretended that the American planes had run up against truly formidable Luftwaffe opposition.

While the crews accumulated experience in the air, the question of target priority seemed a rather random thing: railroad marshaling yards, airfields, shipyards, various industrial targets, among others. If there was a primary target system that emerged during the first few months of operation by the Eighth Air Force it was determined by circumstances and it was an unpopular and unrewarding one. This was associated with the German submarine menace in the Atlantic which contributed to a most serious supply problem. In bombing the U-boat bases, the most important in France on the Bay of Biscay, the bomber crews ran into heavy, and costly, opposition both from fighters and flak—and, as it was learned, with meager effect. Also such attacks, while they did little damage to the sub pens, frequently killed Frenchmen.

Although formations had not been large during the early missions the bombing was regarded as generally effective and the losses predicted by the British did not materialize. The London *Daily Mail* observed, following the first month's missions: "So remarkable has been the success of the new Flying Fortresses operated by the U.S.A.A.F. from this country that it is likely to lead to a drastic resorting of basic ideas on air warfare which have stood firm since the infancy of flying."

This optimistic view, if premature, was welcome, for the American airmen were anxious to prove themselves. But there was no systematic erasure of strategic targets—nor, ominously, was there, in the first few missions, any real opposition from the Luftwaffe. By September this period of grace came to an end and the American bombers began to suffer from aggressive fighter attacks. Here indeed was good reason for a "resorting of basic ideas on air warfare." The idea that the B-17s and B-24s could venture into German-dominated skies in self-defending formations required drastic revision indeed.

Not that Spaatz, Eaker, and the other commanders were not aware of the need for fighter protection, although it would take time before the aircraft that could provide escort to Germany and back materialized. That the Luftwaffe was a formidable enemy was evident in both the losses of bombers and the claims, generally highly exaggerated, by bomber gunners for German aircraft destroyed and damaged.

Churchill had something to say about this to Roosevelt's presidential assistant Harry Hopkins. "We do not think the claims of the Fighters shot down by Fortresses are correct though made with complete sincerity, and the dangers of daylight bombing will increase terribly once outside Fighter protection and as range lengthens." Churchill, too, was tending toward urging the Americans to switch to night bombings—and for the development of a long-range escort fighter. He explained to Hopkins that he believed "that the very accurate results so far achieved in the daylight bombing of France by your Fortresses under most numerous Fighter escort mainly British, does not give our experts the same confidence as yours in the power of the day bomber to operate far into Germany."

Within a week he made an ominous statement to his own Chiefs of Staff Committee predicting that the Fortress and Liberators flying by day would "probably experience a heavy disaster" once they left the protection of limited-ranged fighters. He hoped that the Americans could be persuaded to switch to night operations and to confine their daylight activities at that time (October 1942) to striking the sub pens in the Bay of Biscay.

Another debilitating factor had arisen to afflict the growing pains of the Eighth Air Force in Britain. This was Operation Torch, the Allied invasion of North Africa which was to begin on November 8, 1942, under the command of Lieutenant General Dwight D. Eisenhower. Eaker lost two of his most experienced

B-17 groups (the 97th and the 301st), four fighter groups as well as a large number of trained men. The remaining heavy bomber groups—seven in all—were expected to make their contribution to Torch by containing the antisub campaign, thus hopefully keeping the shipping and supply lanes free of U-boat packs.

Because of the weather and a growing aggressiveness on the part of the German fighters (which had introduced the technique of attacking the bombers head-on), as well as the fact that the targets were not particularly vulnerable, it was a thankless task.

The misfortunes of the winter of 1942—the aborted missions, the rising toll, even to flak—again raised, in the British camp the question of the wisdom of the American dedication to daylight operations. On the other hand, American air leaders were quite pleased with the accomplishments of their crews, limited as they were by the elements and the demands for men and equipment for other theaters of war—including the Pacific. Studies made by Air Force Intelligence reinforced the belief "in the soundness of our policy of the precision bombing of strategic objectives rather than mass [blitz] bombing of large, city size areas." The implied criticism of British policy in this as well as subsequent statements which eventually came back to them led to some frostiness in the Anglo-American air forces high command in early December.

By the turn of the year (1943), with a foothold in North Africa, it was decided that a very high-level meeting be held at Casablanca, bringing together Churchill, Roosevelt, and their Combined Chiefs of Staff. Not long before he left for Africa, Churchill enumerated certain disappointments for his Secretary of State for Air, Sir Archibald Sinclair. First Churchill was quite concerned because the British bomber force had not been expanded as it was supposed to have been and secondly he voiced a view that was current in Bomber Command: "I note that the Americans have not yet succeeded in dropping a single bomb on Germany."

Thus when he arrived in Casablanca on January 12, 1943, Churchill was determined to speak with Roosevelt about switching the American bomber offensive to nighttime operations. Before Churchill warmed up to the subject he was approached by General Eaker who managed to plead the case for American bomber policy so skillfully that Churchill decided not to press the issue with the President and to "give them [the American bombers] a month or two more and they would come into action on an ever-increasing scale." Persuasively Eaker presented all the arguments he could in favor of day bombing plus night bombing—he used the expression "around the clock" which impressed Churchill—working together against specific targets. All he needed, Eaker argued, was a little more time and a lot more aircraft and crews which so far had not been forthcoming. Impressed, too, by the possibility of an almost constant pressure upon Germany by such a combined effort, Churchill withdrew his opposition and so cleared the way for what would eventually be formulated as the Combined Bomber Offensive.

Meanwhile several critical decisions were made at Casablanca, among them the one to invade Sicily and eventually Italy; there was the hope, too, of invading France some time in 1944, depending upon the state of the German war machine; also the term "unconditional surrender" was used for the first time at Casablanca. Finally, according to Churchill's notes, it was decided too to mount from the United Kingdom "The heaviest possible air offensive against German war effort." To define this offensive the so-called Casablanca Directive was issued; the objective, it stated, was "the progressive destruction and dislocation of the German military, industrial, and economic system, and the undermining of the morale of the German people to a point where their capacity for armed resistance is fatally weakened."

A list of target priorities was included in the Directive with German submarine construction yards leading; second was the German aircraft industry; third transportation, followed by oil plants with, finally, "other targets in enemy war industry." Precisely how to undermine the morale of the German people was not actually elucidated since, in fact, no one knew, or ever would.

The night area bombings, it was supposed, may have contributed to that since undoubtedly they destroyed homes and those who happened to be trapped in them. But, as with the sufferers of London, such destruction and killing served more to stiffen the enemy backbone and the resolve of the survivors.

Three days after the Cassablanca conference ended, and as if to justify some of his argument presented to Churchill, Eaker's heavies struck at a target inside Germany for the first time. On January 27, 1943, some fifty B-17s and B-24s, without escort, bombed Wilhelmshaven's U-boat yards. Despite the city's flak reputation, it was the fighters—an estimated hundred—that took the toll. And even that was remarkably low, two Liberators and one Fortress, a fact that was attributed to the possibility that the more experienced fighters were based in France and not in the homeland (which some German air leaders had never expected would be visited by the American bombers).

However slight the effect by a not very large formation of American bombers may have had on German morale, the first strike on a target on German soil was salutary to the morale of American crewmen. They were reaching, if tentatively and not very powerfully, into the heart of the Reich. But the mission could not have had much effect upon the production of submarines.

And so it continued as Eaker built up his bomber force, no longer being drained off to the African invasion, and his crews accumulated experience. At the same time, of course, the Luftwaffe also gained experience in how to deal with the daylight attacks. No doubt about it, the major obstacle to a strategic campaign against Germany's war industries was the German fighter. Unless the German war machine could be seriously damaged the proposed invasion of Hitler's Europe was little more than a glimmer of hope. And as the daylight missions increased in numbers and impact, German fighters were drawn away from other sectors and based near the western front and in western Germany—this even at the expense of the critical Russian debacle. By the middle of 1943 about a third of the total Luftwaffe fighter strength faced the Eighth Air Force and R.A.F. Bomber Command.

But so was the Eighth Air Force growing, in bomber as well as fighter strength. By May, Eaker had received reinforcements with the arrival of several new groups—". . . a great day for the Eighth Air Force," he informed his chief, General Arnold. "Our combat crew availability went up in a straight line from 100 to 215." The following day (May 14, 1943) no less than two hundred heavy bombers were dispatched to the shipyards at Kiel, plus other targets, in the longest mission to that date in the war, meaning, of course, that a good part of the way into and out of Germany was without escort. Losses for the day, eleven planes, were not regarded as prohibitive considering the numbers involved and distance flown.

Four days later the Combined Chiefs of Staff approved a "Plan for the Combined Bomber Offensive from the United Kingdom" which had been conceived at Casablanca. Within a month the Plan was made official in a directive dated June 10, 1943. The soul of the Plan was the co-operative effort hoped for by Bomber Command and the Eighth Air Force; the heart of the Plan was in target selection.

Weighing several factors, an American Committee of Operations Analysts (counterparts to the British Ministry of Economic Warfare), drew up a target priority list. The selection was based, stated simply, on an evaluation of those industries that should be bombed (and were readily susceptible to bombardment) in order to effect the German war effort at the earliest possible date and at the least necessary cost; the objective ultimately was the invasion of Europe.

Originally called the Advisory Committee on Bombardment, the committee met, consulted with experts in various industries, established subcommittees and eventually issued statements and conclusions. One of the assertions underscored the American doctrine (the members of the committee, of course, were American) when a general statement on target selection was made: "It is better to cause a high degree of destruction in a few really essential industries or services than to cause a small degree of destruction in many industries. Results are cumulative and the plan once adopted should be adhered to with relentless determination."

Although the committee willingly left the ultimate selection of targets to the experts closer to the scenes of action in Britain, a certain priority was suggested, the first on the list being the German aircraft industry (airframes and engines). Next came ball bearings, the destruction of which, it was believed, would cause a great bottleneck in German industry. Third on the list was petroleum; fourth, grinding wheels and abrasives (necessary to the manufacture of metal parts for various machines). Number five was the non-ferrous metals: aluminum, copper, and zinc. In sixth place was the synthetic rubber industry and, curiously, the submarine menace was only seventh in priority. Following were such systems as transport vehicles, the transportation complex (railroads, canals, highways) and so on through coke factories, iron and steel industries, tools and practically every aspect of industry which contributed to the German war effort.

This paper was delivered to Britain where it was further revised by Ministry of Economic Warfare as well as representatives from the Eighth Air Force and the British Air Staff. While all were impressed with the document the priority list was revised with submarines again placed in first place, with the German aircraft industry second, ball bearings third, oil fourth, synthetic rubber and tires fifth, and transport vehicles sixth. Associated with these major systems were some seventy-six objectives or targets which would require a certain number of aircraft with a certain tonnage of bombs to deal with them. These formulas were worked out by a Committee on bombing, appointed by General Eaker, and headed by Brigadier General Haywood S. Hansell, Jr., Brigadier General Frederick L. Anderson, Jr., and with Air Commodore Sidney O. Bufton, representing the R.A.F. Their ultimate study was entitled the "Plan for the Combined Bomber Offensive Operation from the United Kingdom" and was designed as an operational guide for the conduct of the air war through the invasion of western Europe.

Interestingly, although the Primary Objective list was close to that which had preceded their study—with submarines still number one—this, in turn, was preceded by an "Intermediate Objective: German fighter strength." Thus when it appeared again in the Primary Objective tabulation it is as "The remainder of the German aircraft industry." Next in line, as before, was ball bearings.

Fourth primary objective in the more or less final Combined Bomber Offensive plan was oil, after which had been added parenthetically "contingent upon attacks against Ploesti from the Mediterranean."

The plan, though called Combined Bomber Offensive, applied in fact more directly to the Eighth Air Force, since Harris chose to interpret it all rather loosely. Nor did he agree with some of its points—for example, he did not believe that oil and ball-bearing targets would prove any more worthy than the submarine targets. Thus the plan did not work quite as hoped on paper—it never would, but that would not become known until after it had been tried or after the war.

As it affected the Eighth the plan provided for a great accumulation of American bombers in England through March of 1944—no less than 2,702 heavies (B-17s and B-24s) and some 800 mediums. It was hoped, in the spring of 1943, when the Combined Bomber Offensive was drawn up, that the Allies would cross the English Channel into Hitler's Europe on May 1, 1944. Working toward this, the Eighth Air Force bomber strength was to pass through four phases during each of which the distances covered, the bombs dropped and targets attacked would increase proportionately with the increase in the number of aircraft available in the United Kingdom.

Gradually Eaker was able to dispatch larger and larger formations to more distant targets. The larger formations, it was hoped, would counter to some extent the lack of fighter escort to targets deep inside Germany. Through May, June, and July of 1943 formations, ranging at times in the 200 and 300 count, struck at several targets in Germany, without prohibitive losses. It was obvious that the German fighter, however, was the most disruptive obstacle in the way of a return to Europe.

Some of the heavy bomber strength was again siphoned off to Africa when three B-24 groups left late in June for a special mission: more than one hundred planes left the Eighth to join the Ninth Air Force. Despite this deprivation, Eaker was still capable of mounting 200-plus missions. By July formations numbering 300 and more were striking targets inside Germany—a number of them associated with the aircraft industry with attention also given to submarine targets.

By August 1, 1943, the Liberators that had been sent to the Mediterranean, joined by others, were ready to make the first really big strike on one of the primary objectives—number 4—oil. This was to be the low level mission against the Romanian oil fields at Ploesti, the first of several major disasters that would be suffered by the U. S. Air Force between August 1 and October 14, 1943. The Ploesti mission cost more than fifty Liberators, mostly to flak and machine-gun fire. There were other reasons for the losses, among them a tragic human error (a wrong turn made by the mission's lead plane).

Meanwhile from the United Kingdom, in compliance with the Combined Bomber Offensive, the Eighth continued attacking various targets in Germany during the latter days of July. Among these were the U-boat yards at Hamburg which were struck in co-operation with Bomber Command and which produced one of the most catastrophic fire storms of the war. This was followed by a series of missions that, by the end of July, had taken a rather large toll—those missions, for example, of July 25th, 26th, 28th, 29th and 30th, added up to a total loss of eighty-seven heavy bombers (not counting those that returned to their bases so damaged that they would never fly again). So it was that despite the previous accumulation of crews and aircraft, the Eighth Air

Force was depleted by the end of July—the crews were fatigued and the effective bomber strength was down again.

There were no Eighth Air Force missions from July 30 until August 12 as crews rested and more heavy bombers were delivered and damaged aircraft were made battle-worthy again. When the campaign opened again, the Eighth attacked targets in the Ruhr, which must have pleased Bomber Command's Harris (this, too, was a costly mission, losing twenty-five bombers). This mission was followed by two rather heavy attacks on various German airfields in France and Holland. This was a sudden, significant shift from the pattern of operations during late July.

Obviously something was in the offing.

ONE

Now entertain conjecture of a time . . .

The United States, with the turn of 1943, had endured a full year of war. The mood was one of qualified optimism, a happier national frame of mind than had prevailed through most of 1942. But as that year ended—a year of ringing place names: Bataan, Corregidor, Tokyo (the Doolittle raid), Midway, Guadalcanal, and North Africa—*Yank* could report that "Allied troops all over the world were finally getting into position for big and effective offensives. In North Africa, in Russia and in the Solomons, Axis forces were taking a licking and Allied forces were acquiring areas from which they could start real drives toward victory."

This was echoed, even more affirmatively, in January when Franklin D. Roosevelt, in his address to the Congress and the people of the United States, said, "The Axis powers knew that they must win the war in 1942—or eventually lose everything." The President emphasized American production, growing rapidly as the United States geared for war, and he especially dwelled upon the massive growth in the "strength of ships and planes"; that in 1942 "We produced 48,000 military planes—more than the airplane production of Germany, Italy, and Japan put together." He thus substantiated British social scientist D. W. Brogan's keen observation: "To the Americans war is a business, not an art." Shortly after having given his address Roosevelt left for the historic meetings at Casablanca.

If the tide appeared to be turning on the military front, all was not as well as it might have been on the home front. Butter was in short supply and there was a governmental crackdown on non essential driving. A series of strikes, led by a recalcitrant John L. Lewis of the United Mine Workers, produced shortages in the coal supply and also, consequently, in the production of steel. The strikes led also to confrontations between Lewis and the power of the President, and the two-year-old Truman Committee (which investigated every aspect of industries in any way connected with the war). It was Senator Harry Truman who informed Lewis, after the latter had verbally attacked a member of the committee, "We don't stand for any sassy remarks."

The Army paper *Stars and Stripes,* in its Middle East edition, editorialized: "Speaking for the American soldier—John L. Lewis, damn your coal-black soul." The antics of Lewis, not altogether unjustified despite the fact that there *was* a war on, produced the Smith-Connally Act which made it a criminal offense to strike a Government operated (i.e. war) industry.

If the war fronts seethed, the home front was not notable for tranquillity. *Time* magazine reported in August that since Pearl Harbor some 22,500 war workers had died in traffic accidents; in the same period 16,913 soldiers had died in battle zones around the world.

The ugliest news to emanate from the home front was that of a race riot which erupted in Detroit in June. The summer heat plus incendiary human elements—a numerous Negro population and a large influx of Southern war workers; not to mention local hate mongers such as Father Charles Coughlin and the Reverend Gerald L. K. Smith, men of God. These came together over a small incident at Belle Isle, a park-picnic grounds, and led to fist fights, wild rumors and then a spree of killing (perpetrated mainly by whites) which did not come to an end until the Governor of Michigan called for Federal troops. In the smoke and debris lay twenty-five dead black people and nine whites; hundreds were injured and property damages ranged in the millions.

Millions of man-hours of labor were lost in the Detroit war plants also as result of the rioting. There were those who placed the blame on agents of the Axis, but investigations by Attorney General Francis Biddle found no proof of this.

Such was some of the bitter news which reached American servicemen in various parts of the country and the world. It was difficult to rationalize fighting and dying to destroy fascism, one of whose major preachings was racial superiority, with Detroit—and later Harlem—in the headlines. Likewise was labor unrest difficult to explain to a Marine on Guadalcanal who could not take the day off if he did not like the way things were going.

Not all the news from home was depressing, though to the GI it could be bemusing. In the summer of 1943 he would read about the formation of the first military unit composed of women, the Women's Army Corps (originally with the word Auxiliary preceding the Army) formed the year before to relieve men from clerkdom for more active duty. Eventually the Navy (WAVES), Coast Guard (SPARS), and the Marines (no clever initials) followed suit. Women proved to be more than mere substitutes and soon fulfilled many a duty once considered the province of the masterful male (as they did also in factories). In time WASPs (Women Airforce Service Pilots) would be piloting heavy bombers across the Atlantic. These were changes that the man in uniform could not always absorb gracefully. The word play on the acronym WAC caused some hostility, as did the whistles that greeted marching WACs on Army bases.

It was a time for romanticism, if not always romance. Popular songs flourished and although the juke-boxes of southern camps produced the sound of twang and sob, which the northern boys referred to disdainfully as "hillbilly music"; "There's a Star-Spangled Banner Waving Somewhere," "There's a Wreck on the Highway (But I Didn't Hear Nobody Pray)"—there were more sophisticated melodies to haunt the heart. "As Time Goes By" an old

(1931) song that had been revived for the aptly named film, *Casablanca,* was a favorite early in 1943; so was Harold Arlen's "We're Off to See the Wizard" (words by E. Y. Harburg) which was the theme song of Australian soldiers in North Africa. The musical *Oklahoma!* by Richard Rodgers and Oscar Hammerstein 2nd, opened in New York early in the year and provided a treasury of song for juke-box, recordings, and radio: "People Will Say We're in Love," "Oh, What a Beautiful Mornin'," "The Surrey with the Fringe on Top," and the comic "I Can't Say No." Music was an important link with home for the men in the services and for those who did not indulge in romanticism or country music, there was still the music of the big bands, although these were being swallowed up by the services. Such name leaders as Claude Thornhill, Artie Shaw, and Glenn Miller eventually donned uniforms and other name bands—Harry James, Tommy Dorsey, Benny Goodman—played for servicemen all over the country and, in some instances, the world. Most servicemen resented the extreme popularity of an underweight 4-F with the girls, an ex-band singer named Frank Sinatra.

But the songs and bands provided momentary escapism—as did the movies—for the GI. "Don't you know there's a war on?" was a favored refrain as was the explanation for the various shortages afflicting both civilian and serviceman alike: "It all goes to the boys in the serivce [or] overseas."

Airmen in their bases in England took a professional interest in the news from Oklahoma of a student navigator who strayed some 45 miles off course in a practice night mission, then had his bombardier zero-in on some lights they had come upon and dropped six 100-pound practice bombs on the center of Boise City, Oklahoma. No great damage was done, nor was anyone injured, but it did wake up the town to the extent that its newspaper editorialized the next day: "What this place needs are some searchlights and antiaircraft guns." This was not, in fact, true for no further attacks upon Boise City were reported for the duration.

Grimmer word leaked to the press that the Truman Committee

had begun investigating the Curtiss-Wright Corporation, specifically the Wright Aeronautical Corporation of Lockland, Ohio. By early July the Committee made it known that "the Curtiss-Wright Corporation has enjoyed spectacular and unprecedented success in obtaining war contracts" (second only to massive General Motors), but that "the Lockland plant is a glaring example of the concentration of contracts in large plants with inexperienced management trying to get out a large production on a fixed-price contract and ruthlessly slashing quality to maintain production and schedules in the face of excessive production costs caused by poor management. The company has been furnished with the finest plant and machinery available at Government expense.

"By permitting defective materials to be passed and by permitting variations from blueprint tolerances without changing the specification, the Government [namely the Air Force inspection team stationed at Lockland] also maintained the myth of precision manufacture for the benefit of a company which was awarded its contracts because of a reputation it had earned as a result of its prewar production record . . ."

The heart of the matter was that the Truman Committee had found that 25 per cent of the engines produced at Lockland proved defective and that, it appeared, the Air Force inspectors on the scene condoned this. Zealous inspectors who insisted upon compliance with proper standards were shifted to other posts. Obviously the company team and the Air Force team were interested in making a good paper showing in production efficiency and willing to make concessions. According to the Committee's report a "substantial number" of aircraft fitted with engines from the Lockland plant had suffered mechanical failure and crashed (this point was not thoroughly backed up with concrete figures). Still, it was patent that all was not well at the Lockland plant, changes were made and the rather sensational accusations eventually faded from the headlines (although the following year the three-man Air Force inspection team was court-martialed and dismissed from the service).

Such revelations gave airmen pause in their overseas stations —their B-17s were powered by Wright engines. Of course, the Lockland story did not tell the entire story of Curtiss-Wright, although the Truman Committee made a point of criticizing (this too was a criticism of Air Force judgment) the performance of the obsolescent P-40 fighter plane. But by this time the more potent P-38, P-47, and P-51 were already operational and would soon completely displace the aging, but deserving of honors, P-40.

A much more pernicious form of corruption afflicted another firm, the Brewster Aeronautical Corporation. The sickness was internal and took the form of a strong union organization under the leadership of one Tom De Lorenzo. The company, its factories dispersed in New Jersey, New York, and Pennsylvania, produced a stubby Navy-Marine fighter, the F2A, which the British nicknamed the Buffalo. Originally designed for the U. S. Navy, the Buffalo was also an export plane which was purchased by the British, the Finns, and the Dutch in the East Indies. The British, wisely, did not employ the plane against the first-rate German aircraft.

Brewster had serious problems at several levels and by April of 1942 the Navy took over, by presidential order, the operations to speed up production. Eventually production genius Henry J. Kaiser came in to serve as Chairman of the Board in the hopes that his methods, so effective in his own company, would work at Brewster. About this same time, in early June of 1942, the Battle of Midway occurred. The performance of the inferior Buffalo in this battle did not enhance the name of Brewster.

Conditions in the plants were as dismal—despite the, or rather because of the powerful union—as the Buffalo in combat. Where any streamlining or reorganization was attempted there was De Lorenzo to limit it or to prevent it entirely. Management found it could not dismiss an inefficient or useless worker—that power remained in the hands of the Union's Trial Board. Favoritism, therefore, placed a few in positions of power and the many in a fearful position of jeopardy. For example, if a loyal worker found a fellow worker sleeping instead of producing and reported him, then, unless he were one of the favored few, the informer—not the sleeper—might very well find himself out of a job.

Strikes were called at the drop of an eyelid. "Our policy," De Lorenzo stated, "is not to win the war at any cost. The policy of the local union is to win the war without sacrificing too many of the rights which we have at the present time . . ." Merely shifting a worker from one department to another might very well spark a strike. From the time of the Battle of Midway until about the Regensburg-Schweinfurt mission Brewster had at least a dozen strikes which denied the men at arms needed aircraft, however inferior (even if only for training).

To this De Lorenzo replied: "If I had brothers at the front who needed the ten or twelve planes that were sacrificed, I'd let them die, if necessary, to preserve our way of life or whatever you want to call it."

This was a shocking revelation to the men who were, in fact, dying to preserve "our way of life or rights." Happily it was also a rare and extreme case, for in general the American unions, John L. Lewis and Tom De Lorenzo notwithstanding, were cooperative and willing to sacrifice for their sons, husbands and brothers. Those caught malingering, turning out shoddy work or sleeping on the job while collecting high wartime (and overtime) wages were treated accordingly.

Besides there was news of "Rosie the Riveter" contributing to the proliferating stock of planes, tanks, guns, and just about every other item of war. Women, it was found, could do much of the work that men did—and could do it better; women could handle certain work with an even greater sense of dedication and responsibility than men. Absenteeism was not so great a problem as with the chronic transient worker (male) who pursued the highest dollar and gave no thought to his brother at the front.

The GI at the front or the airman on a base in East Anglia could keep in touch with the strange currents in his homeland via the home-town paper (rolled tightly and arriving in clusters weeks late) and the same magazines (often in a specially produced digest size on flimsy paper) he had read at home. In *Time* he could read that U.S. women "were . . . more self-reliant. New work in factories and more work at home has given them new responsibilities, and they have met them. But above all, U.S. women are lonely. Some hide it behind cheerfulness or a bright hard face, but the loneliness is there."

Himself homesick and lonely, but stuck with an ugly job, the airman based in England was so occupied with that job that he rarely noted the drastic, almost revolutionary, transitions occurring back home. He took a professional interest in his own special sphere, discussing, for example, the breaching of the Möhne and Eder Dams in the Ruhr by a handful of R.A.F. Lancasters in May; that same month, Deputy Führer Rudolf Hess surprised the world (and most of all his long-time friend, Adolf Hitler) by stealing an Me-110 twin engined fighter and flew off to Britain (and a lifetime of imprisonment) in a mad peace-making attempt. This provided food for thought and speculation among the men fighting the Luftwaffe, though few would have realized that it was an intimation of things to come: the demoralization of a once proud and efficient fighting unit.

Hardly less bizarre was another aerial incident that happened in the first week of June. On a regular flight between Lisbon and London the British Overseas Airways transport was intercepted near the Bay of Biscay by several Luftwaffe fighters. The pilot reported: "I am being followed by strange aircraft. Putting on best speed. We are being attacked. Cannon shells and tracers are going through the fuselage. Wave-hopping and doing my best."

There was no further word and by the following day BOAC announced that the DC-3 was "overdue and presumably lost" with seventeen persons aboard (four were crew); one of the thirteen passengers was popular English actor Leslie Howard. One who was *not* a passenger, though presumed to be by the Luftwaffe, was Winston Churchill. A portly man with a cigar was seen boarding the plane at Lisbon, mistaken for Churchill and the fruitless hunt was on. Churchill had visited the United States to participate in the "Trident" conference in Washington. On his return to England he detoured to North Africa—a visit which was much publicized—and for some reason the Germans suspected that he would return to London via the usual daily airliner from Lisbon. Churchill, instead, returned via Gibralter by warship. Churchill was appalled by the enemy stupidity. "It is difficult to understand how anyone could imagine that with all the resources of Great Britain at my disposal I should have booked passage on a neutral plane from Lisbon and flown home in broad daylight." Someone did, of course, and seventeen people died in a quirk of fate.

But seventeen was but a small fraction of the number of people who had died on that single day; the presence of one famous actor aboard the airliner had rendered the fruitless, though successful, mission very newsworthy. That same June saw the first conquest of an objective, the island of Pantelleria near Sicily, primarily by air power. This was the first step toward the invasion of Italy which would occur in September. By July 19, 1943, however, Allied bombers had begun striking at pinpoint targets in Rome. Late in July the R.A.F. and the Eighth Air Force combined operations against the German city of Hamburg and unleashed a frightfully devastating fire storm. While it was a cooperative effort—with the main thrust furnished by Bomber Command—the objective was ostensibly the submarine yards in Hamburg and not the Luftwaffe.

August of 1943 opened ominously for the American air forces with the Ploesti mission. The full implications of its failure were not bannered in the home-town papers but were fully discussed by the airmen in Britain. They had not flown at all on that August first, nor had they the day before—and would not until the twelfth. For some reason there was feverish activity in the upper echelons and in training, but no missions. They had earned a rest, but while resting there was plenty of time for speculation. What was up?

TWO

The high bomber toll of those missions flown by the Eighth Air Force into Germany in latter July was sufficient proof of the wisdom of concentrating on the elimination of the Luftwaffe before serious thought could be given to the Allied invasion of France and the ultimate defeat of Germany.

That toll curtailed operations out of England in early August. But there was no lull in activity in the various headquarters concerned with the many phases of planning a complex mission. The decision for what would be Mission 84 filtered down to those who would put theory into life-and-death practice: from the Committee of Operations Analysts (U.S.) through, with variations, the Ministry of Economic Warfare (British) and then to the Combined Operational Planning Committee. This last was composed of members from bomber and fighter commands of both the Eighth Air Force and the R.A.F. Its function, a concession to the Combined Bomber Offensive, was to co-ordinate British and American combined (hopefully) operations. Since Harris regarded striking at what he viewed as "panacea targets" with a jaundiced eye, the Combined Operational Planning Committee in fact was primarily a kind of advisory committee on tactical planning to the Eighth Air Force; if Harris and Bomber Command could be brought into certain combined operations, so much the better.

Meanwhile, too, there were some changes in the command structure, if not the bombing policy, of the Eighth Air Force.

General Spaatz had left Britain for North Africa to command Eisenhower's air forces for the Torch invasions. Eaker was moved up to the command of the Eighth Air Force and his position as head of VIII Bomber Command was assumed by Brigadier General Frederick L. Anderson. A veteran bombardment specialist (in 1940 he served as Director of Bombardment Instruction at the Air Corps Tactical School), Anderson's views would have pretty much coincided with those of Spaatz and Eaker. According to the Tactical Mission Report prepared by Anderson after Mission 84, Bomber Command had indeed planned to strike at Schweinfurt at night after the American attack, but after August 17 "the moon was full, causing the nights to be light enough to the point that the R.A.F. Bomber Command could not afford an attack on this target." Although Harris was being pressed into such an attack, especially by one of the British members of the committee that had helped produce the C.B.O. plan and Director of Bomber Operations, Air Commodore Bufton, he remained obdurate.

The full moon served as reason enough to eliminate Bomber Command from striking Schweinfurt. As for the "target experts" whom Harris believed were so enchanted with panaceas, "They paid no attention to the fact that Schweinfurt was too small and distant a town for us to be able to find and hit in 1943." Despite Bufton's persistence, Harris managed to hold off the "panacea mongers" so far as Schweinfurt was concerned until February 1944.

Meanwhile the shaping of the mission continued at Eighth Air Force Headquarters, the concept having filtered down another step. From there it was dispatched to Headquarters VIII Bomber Command APO 634 (High Wycomb, England). It then devolved upon General Anderson and his staff to put Mission 84 in motion. By the first week in August word had begun coming down to the combat groups, via the bomb divisions.

As visualized by Anderson (in a post mission report to Eaker) Mission 84 was to have proceeded along these lines:

a. It was planned to dispatch eight(8) forces, four(4) from the 1st Bomb Division, and four(4) from the 3rd Bomb Division.

b. The four(4) forces from the 1st Bomb Division were assigned the three(3) Ball Bearing Works at Schweinfurt.

c. The four(4) forces from the 3rd Bomb Division were assigned the Messerschmitt Factory at Regensburg.

d. The 1st Bomb Division forces assigned to Schweinfurt were to penetrate enemy territory approximately 10 minutes after the 3rd Bomb Division forces assigned to Schweinfurt [*sic*]. This was planned because the 3rd Bomb Division forces were slightly slower than the 1st Bomb Division forces due to long-range tanks, and also because of the necessity for the 3rd Bomb Division forces leaving the Schweinfurt area before the 1st Bomb Division forces arrived there.

e. It was believed that the 3rd Bomb Division, by preceding the 1st Bomb Division into enemy territory, would receive the preponderance of the enemy fighter opposition and was therefore assigned the majority of fighter escort.

f. It was planned that after attacking the target at Regensburg, the forces of the 3rd Bomb Division would then proceed to advanced airdromes in North Africa. The 1st Bomb Division forces, due to their limited range, were obliged to withdraw over the reciprocal of their route in to the target at Schweinfurt. [*The full text of this document, as well as others, may be found in the Appendix.*]

In addition, in other headquarters, plans were being drawn up for fighter support by U.S. P-47s and British Spitfires as well as several diversionary missions by medium bombers (also with escort) to strike at airfields and marshaling yards in France and Holland, to throw German air defenses off and to draw some of the Luftwaffe away from the Fortresses on their way to Regensburg and Schweinfurt. The complexity was all but overwhelming: sixteen groups of B-17s (numbering roughly 375), four groups of P-47s (about 175 aircraft) and eight squadrons of Spitfires (96 aircraft) to provide "penetration support" for the 1st Bomb Division and two P-47 groups (93 fighters) and eight squadrons of Spitfires (85 aircraft) for "withdrawal support."

But that would not be the only air traffic on the day of the mission, all of which contributed to the necessity for some very intricate and careful planning as to whom would be where at what time.

At around the same time that the bombers were to be taking off, assembling and heading for Germany the several diversions and attacks were to take place. U. S. Air Force Marauders, escorted by Spitfires, were assigned the Bryas-Sud airfield in France; R.A.F. Mitchells, with Spitfire escort, were to strike at the Calais marshaling yards and other Mitchells (of No. 2 Group also), with Spitfire protection, were to bomb the Dunkirk marshaling yards; these were the diversions. In addition attacks were to be made by Hawker Typhoons in dual roles, fighters and bombers. About half the forces assigned to three targets were fighters and the rest bombers. They would hit airfields at Poix, Lille-Vendeville, and Woensdrecht. Some of these lay under the path of the outgoing bombers and, the hope was, that the attacks and diversions might pull the weight of the Luftwaffe away from the heavies (the official designation for this was Ramrod 206).

That was the basic plan: two large forces of B-17s, escorted by P-47s and Spitfire IXs (to the fullest extent of their range, aided by belly tanks in the case of the P-47s), would invade the skies of Germany. The first to enter these skies, the 3rd Bomb Division, commanded by Colonel Curtis E. LeMay, heading for Regensburg would immediately attract the Luftwaffe based in France, the Low Countries and, eventually, in Germany. Thus, for the penetration phase the 3rd Division would be assigned a large number of fighters for its support. Meanwhile, of course, it was supposed that some of the German fighters would be trying to deal with the various diversions.

Instead of turning around, after bombing Regensburg, the 3rd Division would continue southward, cross the Alps, pass over Italy and the Mediterranean to land in Allied bases in North

Africa. This tactic, too, it was assumed, would cause some confusion in the enemy camp. It was, also, historic—the first shuttle mission for the Eighth Air Force.

The second large force of Fortresses, the theory went, would cross the enemy coast about ten minutes after the Regensburg force. This would be the 1st Bomb Division under the command of Brigadier General Robert B. Williams whose experience, like LeMay's, dated back to the very first days of the B-17 (he was, in fact, a passenger aboard No. 80, navigated by LeMay, in 1938 during a good-will flight to South America). Williams had also some firsthand experience with war; he had lost an eye during the London Blitz while serving in England as an observer for the U. S. Air Force. Williams's division, it was hoped, would serve to confute the Luftwaffe, many of whose planes, having already contended with the Regensburg-bound planes, would be short of ammunition and fuel. Those that were not would have to deal with the escorting Thunderbolts and Spitfires (again to the limit of their fuel supply). The Schweinfurt force would then proceed to their target, bomb and turn around for the return flight. By this time their escort would have returned to England, refueled and rearmed themselves, and returned to meet the Fortresses to escort them back to their bases in England.

In all sixteen B-17s groups would participate in the mission; nine from what was then officially called the 1st Bombardment Wing (this was the Schweinfurt force) and seven from the 4th Bombardment Wing (Regensburg to Africa). Since certain organizational changes were under way at the time and would become official by mid-September they were already generally referred to at the time of the double strike as the 1st Bombardment Division and the 3rd Bombardment Division, respectively, and will be so designated in this account. These divisions were subdivided into wings (usually consisting of three groups each) to form the protective combat boxes and, of course, for administrative and planning purposes.

LeMay's units were the 94th, 95th, 96th, 100th, 385th, 388th, and the 390th Bombardment Groups; Williams would lead the 91st, 92nd, 303rd, 306th, 351st, 379th, 381st, and 384th Bombardment Groups.

The special training for the mission got under way when, late in July, a stellar crew from each group was selected for sessions at Bomber Command Headquarters. These crews were "stood down" from missions, isolated from their squadron mates and forbidden to leave their bases. Each crew was provided with a new aircraft, the instruments of which were carefully calibrated and generally put in top condition. Ground crews, however, were affronted because their crews' regular aircraft over which they had so assiduously worked were not used in operations.

A crushing weight of secrecy fell over the mission and the special crews, ordered not to speak even to their squadron commanders about their training, were picked up in vehicles driven by Military Police and driven to their respective division headquarters. In the case of the 3rd Bomb Division, it was to the palace-like headquarters at Eleveden Hall in East Anglia (roughly 25 miles northeast of London).

Because of distances involved and the critical problem of fuel, navigation would be an especially important factor to the success—and safety—of this phase of the mission. The 3rd Division Fortresses were fitted with wing tanks to carry the extra fuel required for the long flight. None of the crews that assembled at Eleveden Hall were informed of their targets or their ultimate destination.

The 100th Bomb Group, which had flown its first missions late in June, had selected the crew of Everett Blakely to attend the very secret meetings at Eleveden Hall. Blakely, "undoubtedly one of the best B-17 pilots ever," in the estimation of one of the men who flew with him often, was to fly the lead plane in the 100th's formation. His co-pilot was Charles Via, his bombardier, James R. Douglass, and the navigator, Harry Crosby. This was a top crew; Crosby, in fact, had only recently earned his third Distinguished Flying Cross for his navigation to distant targets in Norway on July 24.

A tall, lean Iowan, Crosby was youthfully avid to "Get on with the War" and attended the sessions at Eleveden Hall with expectant zeal. No sooner had they gathered at Divisional Headquarters than the traditional "Attention!" rang out and an S-2 colonel purposefully strode into the room.

"He looked more like a minister than a full colonel," Crosby remembers. "A bland kind of fellow, he gave a sloppy-slick salute to Colonel LeMay and then turned to us. His eyes were moist and he immediately proceeded to read a letter from his wife. Believe me, it was really sentimental, it was maudlin: about how the children were doing this and the children were doing that and 'dearest John, a phase in our life is passing and you'll never see the baby while it's a baby'—it was really corny. And about the time we were about to throw up, the colonel stopped and said, 'Gentlemen, I'm going to tell you about something today that will make it possible for us to be home with our families by Christmas'—or something like that."

While this may sound extravagantly put, looking backward through a glass darkly, the view is supported by LeMay himself who later commented upon the mission laconically by writing: "This operation was the outgrowth of a search by those intellectual souls in Plans and Intelligence to find an easy way of winning the war in Europe. That's just about like searching for the Fountain of Youth—there *is* no such thing; never was. But they were trying to find it, and they hit on bearings. The idea was that if we could knock out ball-bearings production, that would automatically cut industry out of the future picture. The German war machine would grind to a halt."

LeMay, only recently placed in command of the 3rd Division, was hardly in a position to contradict the maudlin colonel's promise of a speedy end to the war. He was still feeling his way around in his new job and little given over to theorizing. Besides, the contribution of his division to the day's work was striking at the

Messerschmitt factory and to an airman, that made a lot of sense. An earlier plan to bomb two Messerschmitt complexes, the one at Regensburg (by the Eighth Air Force) and the one at Wiener Neustadt (by the Northwest African Air Forces, later Ninth Air Force) simultaneously was spoiled by English weather. It was one of the factors responsible for LeMay to get his 3rd Division groups working on bad weather practice.

The briefing colonel, having finished with reading the letter from home, then got down to the business of reading from more official papers. From these, though in much less emotional prose, the assembled pilots, co-pilots, bombardiers and navigators were informed that certain highly critical targets would be struck and that, indeed, these were so important that their destruction, as the colonel had stated before, could expedite the war's end.

They were not dissembling; they believed it—it even made sense. Wipe out the Luftwaffe and you could get to the targets and destroy them; destroy the ball-bearing production centers and in time there would be no bearings for trucks, ships, tanks, aircraft, and just about everything connected with the war. Even Arthur Harris would agree with the premise—he only doubted its feasibility.

Not so that briefing room full of airmen. The colonel concluded his remarks and the time came for the real work. Pilot Everett Blakely recalls that "approximately six weeks of target folder study and practice missions" followed. For his bombardier, James Douglass, it meant the scrutiny of some sort of factory somewhere in Germany. His counterparts at 1st Division headquarters studied similar target maps with various indications on them to point out the many important factory buildings which appeared to sprawl to the north of some river (it was the Main and the factory was at Schweinfurt although none of the bombardiers in either division knew precisely what and where the targets were).

All the 3rd Division navigators were told was that it was to be a mission covering great distances and that their time till then should be spent in practicing long distance navigation, although there was no hint given to the 3rd Division men that their flight would carry them, those who made it, across Europe and to Africa. Enlisted men were told even less and spent a good deal of time speculating and griping.

A well-functioning crew was an important factor of survival. It was essential that each man was certain that when he was doing his job that all others were doing the same; teamwork of crews was always stressed in training. You need not love your pilot, for example, but you had to know how he'd perform under stress. These delicate interrelationships often meant the difference between life and death.

Crosby described why such a pilot as Blakely was ideal in the left-hand seat of *Just A Snappin'*. He was "a navigator's dream. He sat in the cockpit, hunched in, head down, eyes all squinty and looking at his instruments. We didn't want any Hairbreadth Harry, hundred-mission crush, types, we wanted beady-eyed guys just absolutely holding the course, sweating and working hard to keep the subtle settings right in."

Blakely "was really eager," Crosby concluded, "he was the eagerest guy I ever knew. He would fly everything by the book and do everything on time and dot the i's and cross the t's. He could fly a B-17 like no person I've ever known."

For some reason all the men expected the mission to come up soon and in his eagerness Blakely, as remembered by Crosby, believed that "when we found out what we had to do, we had to do it tomorrow. We were up at three in the morning and flying practice missions. We'd go to a place where there was a straight railroad track and we'd calibrate our compasses and our drift-meters and whereas, I think, normally we might have got the job done in about two weeks, we had it done in three days. We dropped practice bombs all over the place and simulated the mission: we just worked our tails off. But wouldn't you know, it was 'hurry up and wait.' We had dropped all our practice bombs and calibrated all of our equipment and then the time stretched out and out and out. Having used up our bombs, we really had nothing to do except to go up and fly around. So we went up and we flew around.

"We took guided tours of all of Britain. I'd get out the maps and we'd go to Edinburgh, we'd go to Stornoway, we'd go to Glasgow, we'd go to Coventry and saw the bomb damage. We saw everything! We were the world's greatest authorities on how England looked from the air—and still no mission.

"The enlisted men particularly were getting fed up—they had very little idea of what we were doing. Just getting up and flying around, not telling them what was going on was really very hard on them, and we were practically about to have a mutiny because they wanted to go on pass and they couldn't, so we very democratically decided—all ten of us—that we were going to do some ground work on our practice missions.

"I'm sure we went through some kind of specious reasoning about how we had to do some practice landing on special fields because we didn't know exactly what we were going to do—and it was kind of exciting for the men to land in a B-17 on grass. We found that there was a beautiful resort down in Bournemouth on the south coast. It was a real seacoast town and had a very tiny postage-stamp-sized R.A.F. field. As I've said, Ev Blakely could do anything with an airplane so we headed for Bournemouth and landed on that tiny, tiny grass field.

"The wind was in the wrong direction for the runway and also the runway was too short so Ev came in diagonally across the square postage stamp and screeched grass stains all over the wheels trying to get the plane stopped, but he got it stopped practically sitting on the fence. Then we borrowed an R.A.F. weapons carrier, if I remember, went into town and looked around—and, boy, we found a place! We found two Red Cross Clubs, both very beautiful, one for the enlisted men and one for officers. For about the next two weeks every single day we went down to Bournemouth—we shopped, I remember I bought a tea service for Jean [his wife] and some beautiful linens; we were invited to parties, we were asked to teas. At one tea I met Mrs. John Buchan—he was Baron Tweedsmuir and the author of *39 Steps*. At one tea someone asked me if I wished to meet T. S. Eliot—I had never heard of him—and now wished I had met him. We had just a wonderful time during those weeks there—we even went swimming, which was a frigid kind of thing to do."

While the crew of *Just A Snappin'* enjoyed a brief interval of fun and games another member of the 100th Bomb Group, its youthful (age twenty-four), very capable S-3 (Operations Officer), Major John B. Kidd, worked constantly preparing material for the double strike mission among others. An exceptional pilot, Kidd had proved early—even while the 100th was still training in the United States—that he was an outstanding air commander and administrator.

As Operations Officer of the Group, Kidd was not supposed to fly the mission but spent long hours preparing the materials for the men who would: the various maps, routes, bomb loadings, orders, counterorders that came down from VIII Bomber Command to the Wing and then to the Group, Squadron and ultimately each individual plane. The 100th Group was to contribute twenty-one B-17s to the 402nd Combat Wing—which consisted also of the 95th Group (twenty-one bombers also). It was the fate of the 100th Group on that day to be last group in the formation, placing it in the most vulnerable spot in the train of seven groups that would constitute LeMay's 3rd Air Division. Crewmen generally referred to this position as "Coffin Corner."

By early August the anxious time of waiting had set in. But the planning for other missions went on: Operation Juggler was devised to strike against the German aircraft industry. On August 7 the Eighth Air Force from Britain was to attack the Regensburg Messerschmitt factories while the B-24s (some of them survivors of the Ploesti mission) of the Ninth Air Force in North Africa, were to bomb the Messerschmitt complex at Wiener Neustadt. Weather over Europe canceled out the Eighth Air Force's part of the mission. The B-24s, however, did fly their part of the mission, with success and little loss, on August 13.

Scrubbing missions was bad on morale. It complicated the work of the group Operations officers and contributed to the subsequent depression among crews (a strange mingling of relief and disappointment). Another mission was "laid on" for August 10—this one the big secret one that everyone was fussing over: the double strike. For Kidd of the 100th this meant another long session of complex work and by the evening of the tenth he was writing his wife Jane: *This last night was one of the worst. I finally got to bed at 10:30 this morning and managed to sleep in spurts and starts all day.*

What he did not tell his wife was that the mission on which he had worked so hard was canceled also. English weather had begun to play its capricious role.

It did afford Kidd a brief period in which he could write to Jane in a lighter vein: *If Elaine* [a good friend] *comes down from Maine for a week before Bill does, you two can have fun shopping in N.Y. That would give you a swell chance to get your fur coat.* Jane Kidd's fur coat, too, would be woven into the fabric of the 100th's folklore.

But the tranquillity did not last; the next day, the twelfth, the 100th was back at work with other elements of the Eighth Air Force attacking various industrial targets in the industrial, and heavily defended, Ruhr at a rather excessive cost of twenty-five Fortresses (none, however, from the 100th). On August 15 the tempo picked up and Kidd was again on a grueling schedule: that day the 100th flew a diversion over the North Sea while other groups struck at several German airfields in Holland and France; the next day, further destructive attention was given to other German installations in France, including historic Le Bourget. Again the 100th suffered no losses.

This was good reason for Kidd to rejoice; besides, word had come from Kiska, in the Aleutians, that Canadian and American forces had scrambled ashore only to find that the Japanese that had held it since June of the previous year (taken during the disastrous Battle of Midway) had slipped away in the northern fog. That was good news, too, for it was the closest the Japanese had come to the American mainland. There was word, too, that the war was moving forward, for Churchill and Roosevelt had met on the fourteenth at Quebec for what would be the ten days of the Quadrant conference during which the date of the invasion of the Continent would be set (May 1, 1944), in addition to certain decisions in connection with the Pacific.

Kidd was nearly too exhausted to notice; on the sixteenth he wrote Jane again revealing something of the weariness the week's work wrought: *Sure have kept me busy for the past few days,* he wrote. *They must think I'm Superman. Am afraid my mind will be over full of junk with the million and one things that pass through it every day. I just want to relax.* But, as things turned out, that was not to be.

Meanwhile, simultaneously with the training of the 3rd Division lead crews, their counterparts of the 1st were also being picked up at their scattered bases and taken to division headquarters at Brampton Grange. The same air of secrecy and urgency pervaded the activity there as at Eleveden Hall, although the crews appear to have been spared briefings overlarded with sentimentality about wife and home. Instead, as recalled by Joseph W. Baggs, lead bombardier of the 384th Group, General Williams informed them simply of the importance of the mission and the need to destroy the target. "The mission was Top Secret and after briefing by them [General Williams and Colonel Julius K. Lacey, who would lead the 103rd Combat Wing to which the 384th belonged] we were taken to a special room, which was under guard and were permitted to study the target and general data. We visited this Headquarters and this special room several times prior to the mission. We were alerted several times for the mission, but it was scrubbed . . ."

The tension engendered by the aura of the impending Big Mission, the delays, the unanswered questions, spread small flickers of apprehension through the two divisions.

And, some wondered, what the hell was the Luftwaffe up to all this time?

THREE

The respect for the Luftwaffe in the Allied camp was not misconceived. Although the German Air Force was abused, misused, and dissipated by its own High Command and by some of the twists the fortunes of war had taken, thanks primarily to Hitler who fancied himself as a great military thinker, it was still a formidable adversary. But its airmen fought under severe handicaps, some of them dating from the Luftwaffe's inception, but most was attributable to the inner decay of its top leadership.

The Luftwaffe had won the battle of Poland for Hitler and contributed substantially to the outcome of the battle of France. But time and past battles—notably the Battle of Britain—took their toll. So did strategic deficiencies: to begin with the German Air Force was generally regarded as a kind of flying artillery and was umbilically tied to the ground forces. But of an even greater import was that the German High Command had simply not considered the possibility of a long war, one in which Germany would one day have to fall back on the defensive. Thus there was little to draw upon in the form of long-range plans and reserves. As for the defense of the Reich—any mention of that was considered a sign of defeatism.

Hitler, by the summer of 1943, was deeply preoccupied with his massive strategic blunder in Russia and bemused by the crumbling fortunes of the Axis in the Mediterranean; only then might he give some thought to the West and what that could mean to Germany. Even after Bomber Command began its campaign of burning out German war industries in German cities Hitler refused to listen to pleas on the need for home defense. Revenge was his primary desire—to even things with the British for burning his cities. Thus he demanded bombers to attack to the neglect of fighters to defend.

In this baleful delusion he was sustained by his Luftwaffe Commander in Chief, Reich Marshal Hermann Goering, and Chief of Staff, Colonel-General Hans Jeschonnek. Those astute enough, and who had the experience of real war to draw upon, disagreed with this and made themselves unpopular with the High Command. Such were Lieutenant-General Adolf Galland, the Air Ministry's Fighter Inspector, and General Josef Kammhuber, whose specialty was night fighting and a system of advance warning devices as protection against British night bombers. Both these men realized what the introduction of American day bombers, with their initial tentative probings into the Reich, portended. Galland's and Kammhuber's warnings and arguments were greeted disdainfully by the High Command and with contempt by Hitler. He liked men about him who told him what he wished to hear; Goering and Jeschonnek, among others highly placed, were happy to oblige. And, further, by late 1942 there was more than enough bad news from Stalingrad and El Alamein to go around. Hitler found it almost impossible to reconcile reality with aspiration.

But there were realists in the Reich who could also read the portents and who were in position to do something about it even if it meant working around Goering and Hitler. These were Field Marshal Erhard Milch, a former airline official who knew aviation, and Albert Speer, a young architect. Coincidentally, both men came into power upon the death of others and their rise would affect the future of the Luftwaffe. This, in turn, would have a dire effect upon the Allied heavy bombardment plans.

In November of 1941 Milch assumed the duties of Ernst Udet, who had shot himself. Goering had placed his old First

World War friend at the head of the German aircraft industry as it related to the Luftwaffe. It was a job for which Udet was totally unsuited (ironically he had been moved in by Goering to displace Milch who had originally held that position. Goering believed that his own position would be threatened by a man of Milch's ability and ambition). Udet found the work, rife with personal intrigue, plus Goering's incompetence, too much for him. When it became obvious that his department had broken down he committed suicide. With the re-entry of the tougher, able Milch Germany's aircraft industry underwent a reorganization with a resultant increase in efficiency evidenced eventually in a dramatic increase in production.

Albert Speer was one of the few people with whom Hitler could relax (they discussed architecture and a postwar Berlin worthy of a World Conqueror); and for a time Speer was one of the few Hitler also felt could be trusted. Speer was with Hitler the day that word came that Dr. Fritz Todt, Minister of Armaments and Munitions, had died in a plane crash. Whereupon Hitler appointed Speer to Todt's job. This was undoubtedly one of the few of Hitler's unexpected, capricious decisions that worked.

Speer brought a neat mind to the sprawling problem of German war production and eventually was named Minister of Armaments and War Production. Within six months the output of war materials increased by nearly 60 per cent. Speer's concern was all of German industry (he assigned aircraft production to an assistant, Karl Sauer). Milch, on the other hand, was interested in aircraft, but both soon realized that in the coming battle of Germany aircraft would play a large role. Speer and Milch formed a kind of alliance based on mutual respect and apparently not marred, as were most high-level German confederations, by intrigue and general back stabbings. This would have a favorable effect upon the Luftwaffe.

So it was that even as the Allies prepared for the aerial invasion of the Reich, plans were being laid to meet it thanks to Speer and Milch and despite Hitler and Goering.

The production of fighters, primarily the Messerschmitt 109 and the Focke-Wulf 190 (which had made its debut over Europe in the autumn of 1941) increased so that by the spring of 1943 the newly concentrated factories were turning out about a thousand a month. While this concentration, as proposed by Speer and Milch, resulted in higher efficiency and thus greater numbers of single-engine fighters, it did have a drawback. This was especially true once the American heavy bombers began appearing over Germany in daylight. The bulk of Messerschmitt production was centered at Wiener Neustadt and Regensburg and Focke-Wulf production at Bremen, for a time, and later Kassel and Marienburg. The cost of efficiency was vulnerability to air attack (which eventually led to the abandonment of Bremen by Focke-Wulf).

However, until the day bombers (which according to Speer the Germans feared most) could appear in sufficient numbers the factories producing single-engine fighters continued turning them out at full capacity (Hitler permitting, of course). This was the root of the paradox that confronted the Allies later in the war: the more they bombed the aircraft industries, the more the fighters seemed to appear out of nowhere. Under Udet aircraft production was never what it might have been had he been the administrator that Milch was. The potential had been there all the time, but the recognition had come a little late. Even so, it would be painful to the Allied air forces.

The necessity for a buffered home defense eventually began filtering upward into the Luftwaffe High Command. As early as July (1943) two gruppen of Jagdgeschwader 3 were withdrawn from the Russian front, a rather drastic move considering Hitler's fixation with that theater of war. JG 3, joined by its other gruppe, would be situated in the beleaguered Rhine Valley. Other shiftings drew JG 26 away from the English Channel into Holland, convenient to the customary path of the American heavy bombers en route to Germany. Other fighter wings (geschwader) were taken from the Mediterranean to join veteran units, as well as a few newly activated, to form a spiky ring around the heartland of the Reich. The tactical deployment of these various units was the responsibility of Air Commander Central entrusted with the aerial defense of Germany, a veteran flak expert Colonel-General Hubert Weise.

Besides the flak batteries, several of which had also been pulled in from the fighting fronts, Weise could summon nearly 500 fighters based in France, the Lowlands, and in Germany itself. Most of these were the single-engine Me-109F and Gs and the FW-190, plus a few (i.e. less than a hundred) twin-engine Me-110s. The most formidable adversary of the bombers was the single-engine fighter, and the Me-109s and the FW-190s were roughly evenly distributed throughout the Luftwaffe on the eve of the double strike mission. This was not planned to meet this specific attack, it just happened when, belatedly, the German High Command began to heed the warnings of Galland, Kammhuber, Milch, and Speer. The war that, in the past, had been waged on foreign soil was inevitably coming home to Germany.

Nothing drove this truth home so forcefully as the combined British and American attacks on the city of Hamburg, beginning on the night of July 24–25, 1943 (when German home defense was confused by the first use of "window"—strips of metal foil—to jam electronic detecting devices). The last attack occurred on the night of August 2–3 (in between American bombers struck during the day) with the result that a devastating fire storm wiped out nearly half of the city and more than 30,000 lives. Hitler's immediate reaction was for sweet revenge (he also castigated the Luftwaffe for falling down on the job)—the thought of protecting Germans could hardly take precedence over killing English. But the incineration of Hamburg had a sobering effect upon Goering and Jeschonnek, who fell in with their prescient but unpopular subordinates at long last and realized that the Luftwaffe must be developed as means of defense.

The planners of Mission 84 at VIII Bomber Command did not belittle the potential of the Luftwaffe in the defense of targets in Germany; thus the carefully arranged diversions by U.S. and R.A.F. medium bombers and fighter escort, as far as that would go. There would be four U.S. fighter groups with the Republic P-47 Thunderbolt and eight squadrons of the R.A.F. with Spitfires. Because of their restricted range at the time, neither the Thunderbolt nor the Spitfire was capable of escorting the bombers to the target and back. The Thunderbolts, some of them equipped with belly tanks, could remain with the Fortresses as far as, roughly, the town of Eupen, Belgium, just short of the German border. From that point on the B-17s would have to depend on their own mutual defense: formation into combat boxes and heavy guns.

The crews flying the mission were informed the morning of the mission that "There are a large number of both single- and twin-engine fighters based along the fighter belt which includes northwest France, Belgium and Holland inland from the coast for 150–175 miles [these units included JG 1, JG 2, JG 3, and JG 26; other fighters were based in Germany proper and along the route of the Regensburg attackers in Italy]." The briefing also pointed out that "Further inland and in the vicinity of the target [Regensburg] twin-engine night fighters [Nachtjagdgeschwader 101] should be the only opposition encountered."

The final word on the expected fighter reaction within the area of the "belt" was that "Under normal conditions the number of fighters to be encountered would be very large, but due to numerous diversions which are to be run in this area a very minimum of fighter opposition is expected."

The briefing officers who spoke these confident words to their crews before dawn would have them return to haunt them by dusk.

II

REGENSBURG

FOUR

Fog.

Damp, swirling murk enveloped East Anglia where the bulk of the Eighth Air Force was stationed (to the north and east of London); and it had not crept in "on little cat feet," but had lumbered in with a depressingly elephantine tread on the morning of August 17th.

Socked in. Curtis LeMay peered out of his quarters at Eleveden Hall; he did not smile—in fact, these days he rarely did. But this was scowling weather, sullen and glowering, unfit for airplanes with men and bombs in them. His own word was "stinking." The word *scrub* irritated LeMay's mind. The fate of the mission now had been affected by Factor X. The very whisper of yet another postponement was not good for the disposition. What now?

There was certainly no point in attempting to drive through the vaporous early morning to Snetterton Heath, home base of Colonel Archie J. Old, Jr.'s 96th Bomb Group which had been selected to be the lead group that day. LeMay elected to remain at Eleveden Hall with a baleful eye on the weather and his ear on the bell of Bomber Command's phone.

At Snetterton Heath, less than five miles distant, Mission 84 began, as it had at fifteen other bases, in the early evening of the previous day, a Monday. The 96th Group Narrative Report, in the customary objective language of such documents, put it thus:

1. The bomb loading for this operation was received from Headquarters, 4th Bombardment Wing [*not yet called 3rd Bomb Division*], by telephone at 1815, 16 August 1943. The order called for 24 aircraft to be loaded with 10×500 bombs each, with 1/10 seconds nose fuse and 1/100 seconds tail fuse.
2. The attack order was received from Headquarters, 4th Bomb Wing, by teletype.
3. Flight plans and details of the mission were completed, briefing being set for 0200 and takeoff time at 0700.

This is, in fact, what happened, but not what was supposed to happen. The succinct language oversimplifies, omits the involutions and consequently the heartbreak that soon followed upon 0700. The complexity of the paper work alone was almost overwhelming. That began with the "Advance Information on Field Order No. 181" (from Bomber Command) alerting the Schweinfurt forces as to takeoff time ("about 0600 17 August 1943") and including information on the composition of the two Air Task Forces selected to attack Schweinfurt, in what order and what the bomb loadings would be. This was soon followed by Field Order No. 181, which also included information pertaining to the Regensburg and the Schweinfurt force with information about the disposition of fighter support, diversions, friendly activities: 4TH AIR DIVISION WILL PRECEDE 1ST AIR DIVISION [not yet officially called the Third or First Bomb Divisions respectively] FORCES BY 9 MINUTES FLYING A ROUTE WHICH IS APPROXIMATELY THE SAME AND ON TO TARGET GY-4828 [Regensburg] THEN ON TO A SECRET DESTINATION [North Africa].

Reams, literally, of teletype paper must have been consumed to inform all the bases of the targets and MPI's (Main Point of Impact of the bombs) as well as secondary and tertiary targets, routes and approximate time schedules of the lead aircraft of the various Air Task Forces as well as communications, call signs, transmission and receiving channels, Special Instructions (explaining that the time and composition of the forces were planned in order to afford a maximum of protection) and so on with "Zero Hour and Date: 0830 BST [British Standard Time] 17 August 1943." Zero hour was that moment when all the aircraft were assembled into their respective Air Task Forces and ready to go. The various times were computed from that moment, i.e. the Regensburg forces were scheduled to appear over the target at "Zero plus 103 min."

Field Order No. 213 eventually followed No. 181 with a repetition of the same information, though a bit more thorough; another came after that, even more detailed, from the 4th Bomb Wing—LeMay's headquarters—with only that information that applied to his seven groups, including the information that "Maximum fuel load (full Tokyo—[i.e. extra wing]—tanks) will be carried." Once the Field Orders were out, more or less complete, they were followed by the Annexes and Supplements with the changes and additions that came down from Bomber Command. These then had to be digested and sent to the groups from the two wings, on down to the squadrons. Likewise the fighter groups and medium bombers participating in the escort and diversions had to be informed of any changes. The work that may have begun in earnest in the operations rooms at "1815 [6:15 P.M.] on Monday became frenetic by midnight and the early hours of Tuesday. Some of the urgency was revealed even by the impersonal, clattering, teletype. When the second annex (that is, change in the original plan) came through the teletypist alerted all with the message: STAND BY FOR URGENT B/CAST. The next line contained one intelligible word, BUST, followed by a series of letters that made no sense at all, then: AND DAMN THE GUY THAT BROKE IN ON THIS URGENT.

Meanwhile, throughout East Anglia, the bases also clattered and reverberated, to the sound of preparations as ground crews—unsung, but not unappreciated, heroes—checked, loaded, and otherwise readied 376 Flying Fortresses for the special mission.

All of this, the weeks of planning, practice, the early morning activity in the operations rooms, on the hardstands where the ground crews toiled—all this now appeared to be so much sound and fury, signifying nothing, all because of some common condensed water vapor that had moved in from the Channel. And inexorably it moved for, having obfuscated the bases where LeMay's forces strained toward Zero Hour, the dense fog slithered inland and westward to smudge Brigadier General Robert B. Williams's 1st Bombardment Wing also and with them, as a matter of course, all other bases: fighters and mediums.

LeMay was disgruntled but he was not dismayed. He had never expected co-operation from the cursed English weather; and it was too much, he had decided long before, to hope for perfect flying conditions over both, England *and* the target area in Germany. And the word was, for the moment at least, that the weather promised to be fine over Regensburg (the word was pretty much the same for Schweinfurt). But it was obvious the mission was in jeopardy, though as far as LeMay was concerned he could find some small consolation in his having insisted, over the previous month, on bad weather practice. "They trained hard on this. When ceiling and horizontal visibility were O.K. then I'd make our pilots take off on instruments—get the seat down, and take off completely on instruments." But just for assurance, and insurance, "Over in the right-hand seat the co-pilot would be ready to operate visually. If something went wrong, he could take over, and that would save the airplane and the crew. But in the meantime, our pilot was training for an instrument takeoff in case he had to do that when the big day came."

The big day had come and, if they were ever to get off, that was what the pilots of 160 of the bombers in his command would have to do.

At Eighth Air Force Headquarters, High Wycomb—about ten miles west and slightly north of London—Brigadier General Frederick L. Anderson, head of VIII Bomber Command, was afflicted with his own soul-searching. The ultimate decision devolved upon him: Would they go this time or not? The weather outlook over England was hopeless, but there was always the possibility of some break. But for the moment, after consultation with his staff, he could only advance the Zero Hour one hour, with the option perhaps of an additional hour if necessary. LeMay had phoned and suggested the hour postponement and Anderson concurred. The teletypes then began their clamorous annexing.

While Anderson, LeMay, and Williams suffered internally, striving to balance professional conviction with personal doubts, the business on the bases continued "as planned," as if there were no fog. There were those who took comfort from the wispy blanket, for it could mean that once the Top Brass got smart they could all go back to bed.

After breakfast they gathered for briefings in a "smoke-wreathed hall," in the words of the late British novelist R. F. Delderfield, "jammed tight" . . . "earnest young men straining every nerve to appear jovial, carefree and hard-boiled." Operations Officers went through the usual routine: routes—the Regensburg and then on to North Africa mission was cause for a strong vocal reception—flak centers along the route, the expected fighter reception ("very minimum") and all the other last minute details coming in via teletype. Before the crews broke up into occupational units for the special briefing of pilots, navigators and bombardiers, the senior S-2 of each group in LeMay's 3rd Division was instructed to inform the crews that "This is the most important target to be attacked by any aircraft to date. The production is estimated at 200 aircraft per month or approximately 25 to 30 per cent of entire single engine [fighter] production. There has been a remarkable increase in production within the last year of this particular fighter aircraft [Me-109]. There has been an increase of 120 per cent as compared to 2 per cent for the other type of single-engine fighter [FW-190].

"This plant is the second largest of its kind in Europe, the largest being at Wiener Neustadt which was attacked by [the] Ninth Air Force on 14 August. It is estimated that 72 per cent of [the] increase which has occurred in the operational strength on the Western Front has been derived from this plant alone.

"The plant is almost self-sufficient in the entire assembly of all parts and components except engines, as well as complete aircraft are assembled here [*sic*]."

The conclusion had a heartening ring: "It is estimated that the complete destruction of the plant will entail a 9 months delay in production and that immediate results will be felt in operational strength within 1½ to 2 months."

But even more heartening for some—and alarming for others—was the murky swirl that enveloped them, briefings over, as they boarded their trucks and jeeps for the ride to the hardstands where their planes waited. To those who were certain that the weather would scrub the mission again there was cause for jollity, boisterous horseplay and general high spirits. It was heartening, indeed, for they would go out to the hardstands, loll about, talk, and leave the "sweating out" to their commanders and then go back to the barracks, another day of the war gone by. To the silent others, not so sure of the fog's impact, it meant a long wait of stomach-churning anxiety: What if they went in spite of the fog? Climbing through the soup was as hazardous as a mission itself what with its high potential of collision. Once at the hardstands they would all have to wait, the loud-heartened ones and the reticently alarmed, "sweating it out," literally, in their heavy flight suits and various shadings of anxiety and dread.

For Major John Kidd of the 100th Group the morning of August 17 meant neither of these: he was too tired. After having written his wife ("I *just want to relax*"), he literally fell into his cot after days of long-houred, detailed planning, hoping to be awakened later in the day to hear how the Messerschmitt plant had been clobbered (a current term) and the 100th safely in North Africa. But in the interim between his grateful bedding down and the misty enfolding of East Anglia it had become obvious that the 100th's Air Executive, Robert Flesher, who was to have led the Group in the mission had taken ill, and was unable to go. Colonel Neil B. Harding, Group commander, decided he would have to burden young Jack Kidd, exhausted as he was, with one more responsibility.

Kidd blinked unbelievingly when, as it seemed, he was awakened in the darkness only a moment after falling into bed, to be informed that he would fly the mission to Regensburg.

In the briefing room at around four in the dark early morning, he joined the rest of the 100th to hear Harding announce the importance of the mission and the group's S-2, Major Marvin Bowman, succinctly supply all the general information they would require. Kidd, of course, was familiar with all of it; he had gone through it enough over the past few weeks. Alert, but still bleary-eyed he joined his bright-eyed crew of *Just A Snappin'* fresh and ready to go after many trips to Bournemouth.

The 100th had the distinction, if that is the word, of being last in the attack force—"Tail-end Charlie"—regarded by crews as the most vulnerable position in the formation. First over the target would be the 403rd Combat Wing composed of three groups, the 96th (with LeMay in the lead plane) leading, followed by the 390th Group (in the high position) and the 388th in low. Roughly, the 96th would come in in the vanguard at an altitude of about 18,000 feet, then the 390th at around 19,000 and finally the 388th at 17,000 feet. Within the group formations themselves, the aircraft of the various squadrons were stacked in defensive boxes, miniature reproductions of the Wing, with a lead (center), high and low squadron. Three minutes after the 403rd Combat Wing passed over the target (theoretically), it would be followed by the 401st Combat Wing, with the 94th Group leading (at ca. 17,000 feet) and the 385th trailing at around 16,000 feet. After which came the 402nd Combat Wing, led by the 95th Group (ca. 18,000 feet), with the 100th in tow, roughly at 17,000 feet. Crouched in the nose of *Just A Snappin'*, Harry Crosby would later ponder why he had spent so much time boning up on the navigation when all they had to do was follow the six groups ahead.

There was still another distinction for the 100th. Colonel Beirne Lay, Jr., airman-writer (*I Wanted Wings* and, after the war, *Twelve O'Clock High*) would fly along with the 100th in *Picca-*

dilly Lily, piloted by Lieutenant Thomas E. Murphy, as a guest-observer from Eighth Air Force headquarters. Lay was being groomed to take over his own group and wished to accompany the 100th "in order to educate himself," in the words of a subsequent minutes of a Group Commander's meeting. This was to be his fifth such combat mission.

By taxi-time, around 5:30 A.M., the briefed 100th crews, carrying such unusual items as mess kits, canteens, and blankets, were ready in their B-17s awaiting word for the takeoff. But then word came through that they would be "stood down" for a while to see if the soup would thin out.

LeMay had conceded to a delay of an hour then an additional half—Anderson had agreed to an hour and then would have granted another, but LeMay pointed out that too long a delay would mean arriving in Africa and its completely strange fields after dark. They compromised on the hour and a half, although no definite word was given for takeoff. This was Anderson's lonely, unenvied, province. The word from the weathermen had not been good at all and if the East Anglian bases were bad, the problem inland was even worse. He had to consider LeMay's forces, waiting and the complication of a night landing in North Africa. He had to juggle the whole concept of the double strike and how its intricate planning would confuse the Luftwaffe. But even more critically he would have to consider the importance of the two targets, even if it did upset the complex time table.

They would go.

Anderson later rationalized his decision in these words: "One additional factor affecting the decision to carry out the plan . . . was the fact that weather conditions over the entire route and at the target areas were the best which had been forecast for a period of over two weeks. Inasmuch as the importance of these targets increased almost daily, the risk involved in dispatching the two Bomb Divisions individually was felt to be commensurate with the results which the destruction of these targets would achieve."

The word was flashed immediately to LeMay, as he reported it,

"26 minutes before the take off . . . [expecting to hear the mission had been canceled] I was still at Headquarters and the plane I was to ride in was on the runway waiting, so when I arrived at the 96th, I was thrown in the back door of the plane with my belongings on top of me, and away we went."

If his entrance into the B-17 was not especially decorous, LeMay's presence aboard the aircraft had prompted the 338th Squadron to furnish him with an elite crew. Captain T. F. Kenny was pilot, Major J. E. Hayes, co-pilot, First Lieutenant Dunstan T. Abel was navigator (with Captain R. Hodson aboard as assistant navigator), Captain J. L. Latham was bombardier. In the tail, doubling as gunner and observer of all that was to ensue in their wake, was Lieutenant E. B. Baxter. The enlisted crew consisted of Technical Sergeant O. B. Haslop (radio operator), Technical Sergeant H. I. Hayford (crew chief, top turret), Staff Sergeant A. G. Livengood (ball turret), Staff Sergeant A. Korolchuk (right waist gun) and in the left waist gun position, Staff Sergeant E. B. Baxter. LeMay was in good company.

"The air was like dark gray jellied madrilene," he was to recall later of that morning, "if there could be any such thing. It was so foggy that we had to lead the airplanes out with flashlights and lanterns, in order to get them onto the runway."

Engines sputtered, coughed, sputtered, coughed, then caught and roared throughout the East Anglian bases. Englishmen still abed were awakened by the reverberating din of more than six hundred Wright Cyclone engines. Obviously the Yanks were up to something big, but to those countrymen who had already been abroad tending to their cattle, a question arose in even the least inquiring mind: what about that fog?

Well, what about it? would have been LeMay's retort, had anyone asked. After the weeks of heavy weather practice they were certainly ready for it. What he wasn't ready for was the misunderstanding about the delay and the moving forward of the Zero Hour by an hour and a half. For some reason, in LeMay's words, "There was a little confusion on the part of the 96th Group as the navigator was under the impression that the zero hour was only moved up one and one-quarter hours, allowing only 15 minutes for assembly due to weather. The 401st Combat Wing Headquarters may have been responsible for this confusion."

Kenny trundled the big plane along the runway (it was loaded with ten 500-lb. bombs), moved into position. There was only a slight wind—15 mph. roughly SSW—he noted as he and Hayes completed the pre-flight check list routine: the tail wheel was locked in place, the gyro was set and the generators on. All three trim tabs were set at "0"; throttles were advanced to 1500 rpm's for engine check—no roughness. They were ready for takeoff.

What little he could see of the runway was unobstructed and the tower cleared them for takeoff; Kenny began gradually "walking the throttles" forward as Hayes kept his eye on the various instruments. LeMay stood behind the two seats, as was his practice at the time. Slowly the Fortress increased speed as they accelerated into a wispy nothingness. When the airspeed reached about 110 mph. and then a fraction more, Kenny gently pulled back on the control column and the bomber lifted off the fog enshrouded field. Once they had climbed through that surface soup, they found that between 2,000 and 3,000 feet there was a layer of strato-cumulus cloud. This meant climbing blind and praying. At around four thousand feet they broke through only to find that above them was still another layer, this of alto-cumulus. This broke at around 14,000 feet. So far, so good.

It was a matter now of waiting for the rest of the 96th's twenty-one B-17s to follow. As they circled Snetterton Heath for assembly the rest—all in fact—of the group's Fortresses singly, and at times in chilling pairs, surfaced above the second cloud layer. Here, too, a little confusion ensued. There were twenty-one big bombers milling around in the sky, their pilots hopefully seeking out a leader to follow.

"We used smoke signals for the first time," LeMay recounted, "which did not work too well but were better than nothing and helped in the assembly" which, he admitted, "was not good but it was miraculous under the conditions [under which] we had to operate." The unspoken dread was, of course, of midair collision and the miracle was that none occurred.

So it was, without untoward incident, that the vanguard of LeMay's Third Air Division formed for the strike on Regensburg. The 96th Group, as the lead was sandwiched in between the 390th, as high, and the 388th, as low, groups. The seventy-one aircraft were stacked by groups in the standard defensive formation, in units of threes (with about fifty feet of clearance between wingtips and noses and tails), the so-called group strength "combat box." Bitter experience had taught that this staggered, yet tightly knit, formation afforded the most efficient mutual protection, leaving the widest possible field of fire for top and belly turret gunners. The B-17G had not yet appeared, with its twin fifties in the "chin" turret and so the combat box formation provided some additional fire power, from top and belly, for the bomber which was most vulnerable frontally.

Even under the best of conditions it was a tricky problem to assemble so great a number of bomb-laden monstrous aircraft, but on that day they had to contend with 9-10 to 10-10 cloud. And all of it concentrated over England. Colonel William B. David, of the 388th (low) Group, which began taking off at 6:45 A.M. and completed that operation as its 24th B-17 lifted into the mist at 7:02, matter-of-factly described the takeoff, with just an intimation of the problems: "We took off and assembled between layers of overcast. These layers were 1200 feet apart and we climbed through to altitude. Saw two other groups [the 96th and 390th, no doubt] climbing together and went over to see who they were.

"We looked for the letter on the tail which looked like a 'C' to us, which would be the 96th Group. The other group shot two red flares and we thought we were all set and stuck with them till we got our altitude. We ran into a bit of overcast at Splasher No. 5 and had difficulty telling where we were. Could not see Splasher No. 6 until fairly close to it. We were in very good position before reaching the coast and the 390th on top were also in good position." The "Splashers," it should be noted, were navigational aids which sent a pulsating radio signal (a different pulse for each Splasher) on which navigators could zero. They were important particularly during assembly—and, of course, in getting back to base when the weather turned sour.

Colonel Edgar Wittan, of the 390th, was not so certain. "With the last minute change," he said, "we got off earlier than we should have and arrived at the Combat Wing Assembly line about 40 minutes early. We cruised around there and everybody [there were twenty Fortresses] in the back spread out. We waited another 15 minutes and when no one showed up, we flew from Splasher No. 4 to No. 5, where we saw six groups milling around. The 96th went to Splasher No. 6 and then headed toward Lowestoft [on the east coast of England] so we got over on top of them." And so it proceeded from about seven until roughly 9:30 A.M., when the rest of the Division was assembled and ready to leave the English Coast: the 401st Combat Wing, with the 94th leading and the 385th following in the low spot of the box and then the 402nd Combat Wing, 95th leading and the 100th in the low position. The various formation commanders reported very little trouble in assembling with the Division.

The various fill-ins, at least those not required to replace aborts, were sent back to their respective bases. The 388th, for example, had gotten twenty-four aircraft off the ground, three of them fill-ins (legal aborts). One of the latter was piloted by Second Lieutenant James A. Roe of the 563rd Squadron, and it was a bitter disappointment to him when over the Channel he had to drop out of the group's formation and head back for Knettishall since none of the 388th's planes aborted. To Roe, the entire concept of the mission was "exciting and I really wanted to go in the worst way." He almost did, for during some moments over the Channel he toyed with the idea of disobeying orders and continuing on to Regensburg. He thought better of that, gracefully winged out of the formation and headed for home.

It was, incidentally, during the massive assembly phase of the

Third Air Division that the first fable that grew out of the mission was born. While it could not have possibly occurred it was readily believed and became part of the folklore of the Eighth Air Force. The 100th's Harry Crosby "very vividly" recalls the myth that was to serve as the explanation for what happened during the double strike mission. The incident, the story went, happened just about at that moment in the morning when the Third Air Division, completely assembled, was about to move over the Channel toward Germany. Suddenly out of the mist a B-17 materialized and, obviously, because it was marked with a triangle on the rudder and right wing, it was a stray from the First Air Division. Then someone, so the tale continues, concerned over the fact that the First Division's aircraft were not equipped with extra fuel tanks—but obviously not giving a single thought to the radio silence restrictions—picked up his microphone and said, in the clear, "Hey, First Division B-17, you're in the wrong formation. You can't go with us, we're going to Africa!"

There were no First Air Division aircraft in the air at 9:30 in the morning; they were all fogged in in the Midlands. But the legend persisted. Frank Kegel, of the 452nd Group, which did not begin operations until the following year, recalls hearing this same story and that thus the Germans had been "tipped off and had a reception committee waiting" for LeMay and his striking force.

It was on this same mission that the famed, and equally "true," "Legend of the Bloody Hundredth" came into being; but as the great air armada surged toward the European coast Crosby was unconcerned with mythmaking. He wasn't even bothering with navigation, he didn't have to, for the 100th trailed all the other groups. Besides, he was too preoccupied throwing-up into the No. 10 brown paper bags (he had brought a locker full from the States) which he always carried with him on every mission. The 100th's lead navigator was heavily susceptible to air sickness and had little to look forward to for the next several hours.

While all this activity ensued, and the air over East Anglia reverberated to the massing of LeMay's division, all was quiet at the fogged-in stations at Williams's Schweinfurt forces. The crews clustered around their Fortresses at the hardstands, as usual, waiting.

LeMay, standing behind Kenny and Hayes, his various forces assembled, was ready to head for the enemy coast. They crossed the English coast, at Lowestoft, at 9:35.

It was, finally, Zero Hour.

FIVE

The Germans, across the Channel from East Anglia, did not need the blundering of a mythical blabber-mouth GI to inform them that something big was impending across the hated Ditch.

"We never did fool these people very much," LeMay has observed. "We did fool the Japanese once in a while, but you couldn't fool the Germans. All of our diversions, and stuff like that, didn't help very much."

While the Third Division was assembling above the clouds, a dozen Spitfires took off and headed for Brittany; these were the forward support fighters dispatched to attack an airfield. Five minutes after they had taken off, a larger formation, forty-two Spitfires as escort, and a dozen Westland "Whirlwind" fighter-bombers (in this instance, bombers) made a successful rendezvous and followed the forward support unit toward Brittany. The weather was miserable over the Channel and it was becoming obvious that it would be some time before the Fortresses would be on their way, thus canceling out the purpose of the diversion. About five miles from the French coast the aircraft were ordered to return to their bases and that portion of the mission was abandoned.

But to Jafu 2 (Jagdfuehrer 2-Fighter Leader 2) which controlled the fighters based in Northern France and the Pas de Calais area, something was definitely brewing. The Brittany diversion could be readily recognized for what it was and generally ignored. Then when it became apparent that these had been called back, intuition had proved correct and full attention could be given to the activity over East Anglia.

By 9:23 all of LeMay's Fortresses were airborne, as were thirty-seven Thunderbolts of the 353rd Fighter Group; and, within a minute of that, fifty Thunderbolts of the 56th Figher Group. German radar, all the while, was picking all of this up and word began flashing to the various fighter units throughout France, the Lowlands, and Germany. By 9:52 the first units of Jagdgeschwader 26 were up and waiting. At 9:55 German control reported that there were "Allied aircraft 47 miles southeast of Lowestoft," off the coast of England and over the Channel.

Visibility over the Channel was remarkably good considering the situation over England. The clouds began breaking almost immediately after the English coast was passed and continued so over the continent—and at Regensburg it was absolutely clear, with visibility extending over 25 miles. It was over the Channel that the gunners tested their guns, a few rounds to make certain the weapons were in good working order. The big planes shuddered under the vibrations of the testing and the good clean air filled with traceries of blue smoke and the characteristic smell of cordite.

The fill-in Fortresses, the "legal aborts," which had come along to serve as replacements for those aircraft suffering the various malfunctions that were revealed en route, either moved into the holes in the formations or turned around and headed back for England. As the mission proceeded, twelve B-17s were forced to turn back with some mechanical trouble or other; six Fortresses from the 95th, two from the 96th, one from the 100th, and three from the 385th. Some were replaced before the fill-ins left, but those that left the formation over the continent left also little chinks in the protective armor of LeMay's combat boxes.

Jafu 2's radar screens soon began cluttering up with the Allied air traffic, coming and going. Annex No. 1 to Field Order 181 had warned of some R.A.F. activity from the night before, "Watch for

Sterling bombers returning from a mission between bases and Channel."

Meanwhile the various diversions were under preparation: Diversion "A" was to be a strike on the Bryas-Sud airfield by thirty-six Martin Marauders of the 386th and 387th Bomb Groups with no less than eight squadrons of R.A.F. Spitfires as Forward Target Support, Cover and Escort; Diversion "B" provided for a half dozen Mitchells of No. 2 Group, R.A.F., and three squadrons of Spitfires to hit the Calais marshaling yards and Diversion "C," also with six Mitchells from No. 2 Group and three Spitfire squadrons, was to have bombed the Dunkirk marshaling yards (this last did not come off, for the bombers, for some reason unable to attain bombing altitude, aborted halfway across the Channel and returned to base).

Added to these three Diversions were three Attacks upon German airfields at Poix, Lille-Vendeville, and Woensdrecht by R.A.F. Hawker Typhoons in the dual role of bomber-fighter (the former being called "Bombphoons"). Ten squadrons participated in this phase of the operations. The Diversions and Attacks were generally uneventful (though one Spitfire, Sergeant Poirer of 341 Squadron, and one Typhoon, Flight Lieutenant Walter H. Bewg of 182 Squadron were lost). But, what with the weather and the delays, and some confusion, these actions occurred too late—between 10:30 and 11:17 in the morning—to assist LeMay's Third Division (for the German fighters from these fields were already too busy with the Fortresses to be properly diverted) and too early to be of any aid to Williams's First Division still "sweating it out" in the Midlands.

The crews in the mediums did not realize they were participating in the double strike mission; they were merely dispatched with an unusually heavy Spitfire escort to deal with a German airfield near the town of Saint Pol in France. Nineteen-year-old Sergeant Leroy D. McFarland, B-26 tail gunner of the 386th Bomb Group (M) was aboard the aircraft piloted by First Lieutenant Anvil B. Mullins. McFarland, the youngest member of the crew was nicknamed "Pee Wee"; radio operator Staff Sergeant Len Fasol, at thirty-two the oldest in the crew, was, of course, nicknamed "Pop"; needless to say, the pilot's nickname was "Moon."

That day's mission was McFarland's first so that the details remained vivid: "I was sitting in the back of the room [during briefing] on a table swinging my feet. I was apprehensive and nervous, but I don't particularly remember being scared.

"They took our personal effects at the door and issued us escape kits. I was wearing an OD shirt and khaki pants with coveralls over that. I also had a summer flying jacket. The briefing room was hot and I remember wondering if I had enough clothes for the altitude [this would have been around 12,000 feet for McFarland's plane was in the low box]. We did not have to wear as much as the 'heavy boys,' but we still had our cold days.

"I don't remember being scared at any time during the mission, I always attributed that to 'The First Mission' and not knowing what to expect—I suppose being a greenhorn to war, I was too stupid to be scared. I can assure you I learned what fear was before I finished my tour.

"It was a clear day and target visibility was good, but bombing accuracy was not so good. We were new in the ETO and had a long way to go . . . I do not recall any flak or fighters being present that day."

Had he realized what was actually occurring young Pee Wee McFarland might have begun his education in fear right from the beginning. For as they were approaching the target they were bounced by, according to R.A.F. count, twenty-six Me-109s. The high cover escort, Spitfires of 341 and 485 Squadrons, the prime victims of the attack fought back, accounting for one Messerschmitt destroyed and one probable; soon after more than a dozen FW-190s came upon the scene, one of which was destroyed, although the No. 341 Squadron lost one Spitfire. These actions occurred too high above Sergeant McFarland and he did not see them; his view from the tail of the B-26 was limited. Nor did he see the flak, "which was weak over target," and damaged two of the Marauders, though not seriously. The Spitfires of Nos. 65 and 122 Squadrons—the forward support units—reported sighting about forty German fighters, but that the Wing "returned to base without incident." The Me-109s and FW-190s were after bigger game; the "Little Brothers" were secondary.

Despite the weather improvement over the Channel, which would make good tight formations possible, LeMay was not happy. The confusion over the length of delay time, and then the tedious assembly above the overcast had thrown them off schedule. This would make them five minutes late for rendezvous with the fighters.

"Hit the enemy coast a little late," he recalled, "missing the fighter support. I saw four fighters coming out of Belgium on their way home as we were going in, but that was all the fighter support I saw." As he led his fifteen-mile-long division on, the first bursts of flak came up once they crossed the Dutch coast; it was meager and inaccurate and presented no problems. The Luftwaffe fighters would be another story.

Though LeMay, in the vanguard, saw just the two fighters (which may well have been German), there were, in fact, thirty-two Thunderbolts (originally thirty-seven; five had aborted) of the 353rd Fighter Group led by Major Loren G. McCollom overhead. They had made the rendezvous with the B-17s, "as planned," in the vicinity of Haamstede (on Schouwen Island, the Netherlands).

The Third Division had flown a generally westward line, as if heading directly toward Germany; over Holland a sudden jog pointed the forces southward, toward Belgium and France. It was at this point that McCollom's Thunderbolts began climbing to get above the bombers, ranging from around 17,000 feet (the low, and last, 100th Group) to 20,000 (the high 390th in the lead wing). At 26,000 feet word came that "bandits" had been spotted at 30,000 to the north and racing for the Fortresses. When the 353rd reached 27,000 feet McCollom saw them, twelve FW-

190s high and in front of the bombers. But it was too late, the P-47s could not get to the FWs before they dived into the bomber formation.

They came in out of the sun—roughly in the vicinity of Antwerp at 10:16—ignoring, momentarily, the high 390th and the lead 96th—and struck the low 388th. As McCollom observed, he saw one of the FW-190s, trailing black smoke and falling, apparently hit by Fortress gunners.

It was the job of the 353rd that day to escort the bombers as far as Diest, roughly 80 miles southwest of Haamstede. The 56th Fighter Group, led by Colonel Hubert Zempke, was detailed to pick up the bombers about 60 miles inland, at Herentals, and escort them to the absolute limit of the P-47's range, as far as Eupen, near the Belgium-German border and about 120 miles inland from Haamstede. Zempke had forty Thunderbolts (seven had developed various troubles and with three to serve as escort, were sent home).

The presence of the Thunderbolts was noted and carefully tracked by both German radar and reconnaissance aircraft trailing the bomber formations. Allied intelligence intercepted a radio message from German control at 1028: "Look out for Thunderbolts"; at the same time another intercept from Jafu 2 ordered German aircraft to "fly above clouds and stay away from hostiles."

Both McCollom and Zempke noted a disinclination on the part of the German fighters to mix with the Thunderbolts; few victory claims were made for the penetration support by American fighters. About five miles from Diest—at 10:25—McCollom decided it was time to turn for home; three minutes later they practically ran into a formation of Messerschmitt 109s. McCollom moved in behind the last one in the formation of twelve, fired a few bursts into what must have been an unsuspecting aircraft which burst into flame and plunged downward out of control. By now the Thunderbolts were low on fuel and had to head for their base at Metfield where all landed by 11:23.

The 56th Group Thunderbolts, which was to take over from the 353rd, dropped their belly tanks "in the estuary off Woensdrecht." Thus trimmer and lighter, the group climbed to 26,000 feet and began overtaking the bombers about ten miles north of Antwerp. The fighters passed the 100th and the 95th and soon caught up to LeMay's wing in the vicinity of Bilsen, still well above the B-17s. Zempke estimated seeing about 15 to 20 enemy fighters along their escort route. "Red flight [61 Squadron] and Yellow 3 and 4 [63 Squadron] had inconclusive engagement in vicinity Hasselt [about halfway along the 56th's escort route to Eupen], but make no claims [i.e. for enemy aircraft destroyed]. E/A appeared unwilling to mix it and either stayed below the bombers or well out to the side."

Lieutenant J. Brown of the 63rd claimed damaging an Me-109; so did Captain Gerald Johnson of the 61st Squadron. "I was leading Keyworth Red flight in the first section of our squadron," Johnson reported. "We were flying on the right side of the bombers and about 3,000 feet above. As we passed the first box of bombers I saw one Me-109 starting a head-on attack. We immediately started down on him but before we could close within firing range he broke off his attack (about 1,000 yards from the bombers) and went straight down. We pulled back to about 23,000 feet and continued on toward the leading box of bombers. We passed over the second box without incident. As we approached the rear of the leading box near Hasselt I saw one Me-109 starting an astern attack. We started down on him but couldn't get to him before he completed his pass. However, he only closed to about 500 yards on the bombers then turned right and went down slightly. By this time we were closing very fast and I am sure he didn't see us coming. I opened fire at about 150 yards at about 20° and observed strikes on his right wing. He immediately flipped on his back and started down. My number two man, Lieutenant Grosvenor, and number three, Lieutenant Conger, fired on him as he broke but observed no strikes. We then pulled back up to about 20,000 feet and started toward the coast. We crossed the coast at about 15,000 feet and proceeded home without further incident.

"I claim one Me-109 damaged."

If the German fighters refused, as much as was possible, to "mix it" with the P-47s, they were certainly pecking away at the bomber boxes. Johnson's attack on the Me-109 occurred at 10:40 (the 56th was running low on fuel and about to turn for home); at 10:25, Zempke noted, an unidentified B-17 detonated over Diest with no parachutes reported. Five minutes later he saw another B-17 "going down over Maastricht . . . six chutes appearing." Incidentally, the earliest mention of a parachute was a German intercept and may have been that of a German fighter pilot, one of the first to attack the bombers as reported by Major McCollom.

For it was around this time, and it would continue for nearly two hours, that the most hapless element of LeMay's force, the 402nd Combat Wing—the Tail-end Charlies—the 95th and 100th Groups began suffering and bleeding. The first intimation came with the appearance of two specks in the distance and slightly to the right of the direction of flight. "For a moment I hoped," Lieutenant Colonel Beirne Lay, Jr., guest-observer with the 100th later wrote of the mission, "they were P-47 Thunderbolts from the fighter escort that was supposed to be in our vicinity, but I didn't hope long. The two FW-190s turned and whizzed through the formation ahead of us [the 95th Group] in a frontal attack, nicking two B-17s in the wings and breaking away in half rolls right over our group . . ." Soon after one of the 95th's Fortress began smoking and dropped down out of the formation. A second (AC#0274, pilot Baker) vanished in a flash of brilliant red. In yet a third plane (AC#0283, pilot Mason) the drama was extended over a few moments of time. As squadron mates watched, eight parachutes were seen to drop out of the plane—everyone was out but pilot and co-pilot apparently. "Several minutes" later a ninth chute blossomed under the B-17 as the Fortress began dropping behind the formation.

Still Mason remained with the plane; he feathered the propeller of No. 4 engine and attempted to regain his place in the formation. "Then, five minutes after the ninth parachute had been noted, the tenth left the ship. Shortly thereafter it blew up." The 95th would lose one more plane (the fourth) that day, after Regensburg was bombed—making the group third highest in the day's losses; second highest was the 390th, high group in the lead wing, with six.

But the day's heaviest losses—nine B-17s—belonged to the 100th bringing up the division's rear. This was the group's twenty-first official combat mission and one on which it would symbolically come of age and literally bloodied.

John Kidd, seated to the right of Everett Blakely in the 100th's lead plane, quickly realized they were in for a hard day. "I saw ships from other groups ahead going down; one, afire from cockpit to tail, pancaked over with fire coming out of three gas tanks. Something happened every way I turned my head . . ." He was still limited in so far as keeping up visually with the fate of his planes and would check in from time to time with the officer in the tail-gun position for a report; all too soon he would receive a running commentary on disaster.

"From my position as Group Lead," Blakely has written, "I saw little of the action behind, being concerned with holding a steady lead to permit good formation and fire protection. One graphic incident is engraved in my mind; a black ball about twelve inches in diameter sailed over our left wing from behind and exploded about fifty feet in front. At the time it was most puzzling because flak was vertical while this moved horizontally. (I learned during the critique upon reaching Africa that there was a Ju-88 out of range to the rear lobbing rockets into the formation—a German first for the war)."

This innovation was startling, and because it was new, unnerving. But even more so—and more effective—were the persistent head-on attacks by the German fighters, alone, in pairs and various groupings. But that was not all, for there were attacks coming in from every possible angle in what would become a maelstrom of desperate confusion.

Earlier Kidd had looked up with some pride at the B-17s of Major William Veal's 349th Squadron. "The high squadron, the only one I could see, was tucked in tight." So was the 418th, Kidd's own squadron, but he could not see Major Dale Cleven's 351st bringing up the rear of the Third Division. Soon Kidd was too preoccupied with calling out the various clock positions of incoming Messerschmitts and Focke-Wulfs . . . "At Antwerp [we] got our first fighter attack, which lasted about two hours. I estimate," he later told LeMay, "we had intense fighter attacks of 150 to 200 individual attacks."

They came in like vengeful flocks of hawks, from all sides and, once within range, would slash through the larger formations with wing gunports flashing. Lieutenant Colonel Lay watched with near-morbid absorption as "two whole squadrons, twelve Me-109s and eleven FW-190s, climbing parallel to us as though they were on a steep escalator," an illusion resulting from the speeds of the converging aircraft. The fighters then would race ahead of the bombers, turn, to come charging at the Fortresses, often two at a time.

This was disquieting because of the high probability of even a skilled pilot to misjudge the closing speeds and a fraction of a moment could readily mean the difference between life and death, even if the pilot's marksmanship were poor. Then, too, there was the possibility of the pilot—or plane, or both—being hit by the B-17 gunners. Out of control the little plane might smash into the big bomber. Colonel Budd Peaslee, in his book *Heritage of Valor,* describes such an incident—watching a lone FW swing around to charge into a bomber formation, then boring in as massive Fortress firepower concentrated on it. Undaunted, the German kept coming until it was obvious, in a fleeting moment, that something was wrong. While there was no sign that the plane has been hit by the Fortress gunners, it was clear that the fighter would not break away in time and would ram one of the bombers.

"The tiny fighter and the massive bomber come together. The impact is only a few yards away from our bomber yet no sound is audible. It is as though the bomber opened its mouth and swallowed the fighter in a single gulp. Where the nose of the bomber had been, including the bombardier-navigator compartment and pilot–co-pilot cockpit, there yawns an empty void. Small pieces seem to drip from the chin of the bomber as it appears to stop in midair . . ."

For a lifetime (of the crew of the stricken bomber and the German pilot), although for only a fraction of a moment, the B-17 remained poised, its propellers churning, its forward section a torn and twisted metallic wound. As Peaslee watched, he saw a single object drop out of the tail. It was the Focke-Wulf's engine, torn loose by the force of impact, and hurtling through the length of the bomber—literally eviscerating it: men and machine; it presented "the illusion of slow motion as it drops away toward the rear." The lifetime (rather: eleven lifetimes) over, the mutilated B-17 dropped earthward in a vertical dive.

There was plenty of fear for all as the great flocks of German fighters came up to engage the Fortresses in the unpredictable hazards of three dimensional warfare. They began working over the hapless 100th Bomb Group, with special attention given to the last squadron, Cleven's 351st. In the first assault, just south of Antwerp, all three B-17s in his second element were shot out of the air.

Crosby, in the 100th's lead plane, was too busy to cater to his airsickness, or navigate; he was thoroughly occupied with manning the nose guns of *Just A Snappin'*. The details of the mission have remained a great blur to him: "One long day of people shooting at us—the voices [of gunners shouting on the intercom]—the smell of fear reeking out of our sheepskin flight jackets."

The air was cluttered with all imaginable debris, pieces of aircraft, men with and without chutes, unrecognizable burning fragments, numerous parachutes, both white (U.S.) and dull yellow (German) bloomed like innocent mushrooms below the carnage above. Sixty of these blooms in the air simultaneously was not uncommon; even then individual incidents were forever inscribed on the memory in spite of the multi-confusion.

A friend of LeMay's wrote later of "that one airman going down, doubled up, just turning over and over. He went right through the formation, and nobody seemed to hit him, and he didn't seem to collide with any of the airplanes. He just fell fast and furious, over and over, no chute, no nothing. I wondered who he was . . ."

All the while the 100th was being torn to ribbons, and fighting wildly. Bombardier Blanton Barnes, firing from the nose of *Blackjack,* caught an approaching FW-109 square in a vital spot; the German fighter exploded in the air. As Barnes turned to another corner of the churning sky, Paul Pascal, the navigator, observed the sequel: "I saw that German guy thrown out, his chute caught fire, and he clawed at the shrouds while it shriveled up."

They saw their own men burn, too. Curtis Biddick's ship had taken a large shell—probably 20-mm.—in the fuselage, just below the co-pilot's position, obviously ripping out oxygen lines and causing other damages which began a blazing fire. "There seemed to be fire all over the inside of the ship—everywhere you could see in the nose, cockpit and turret there were flames," recalled Major Veal, leader of the high squadron. Flame poured out of the gash, as navigator John Dennis and bombardier Dan B. McKay, leaped through the flames and parachuted to safety (not before, however, the latter suffered burns). Co-pilot Richard Snyder was seen to emerge from the fiery opening; for a moment he remained poised on the wing, and appeared to be reaching back inside the fuselage (some thought for his parachute; to others he appeared to be attempting to beat out the flames with his hands). Suddenly he lost his grip and footing and was whipped back into the slipstream, struck the tail and fell.

Biddick remained in the burning cockpit to enable some to escape the doomed aircraft; except for the chutes of Dennis and McKay, and the death of Snyder, no other exits were observed by the men in the 100th Group. The blazing ship lifted its nose upward and vanished in a great burst of flame, smoke, and torn swirling metal.

All elements of the 100th were taking punishment; a German fighter rose up from the rear of the 418th Squadron pouring fire into the B-17 piloted by Captain Robert Knox. Hot metal smashed across the wing, slashing away the skin, snapping wiring, shattering tubing, rending and perforating the B-17. The hydraulic system went out immediately and so did No. 1 engine; soon after No. 4 went. With so much power gone the plane began dropping behind the rest of the group—and out of Kidd's lead element, leaving yet another hole in the formation.

In the cockpit Knox and co-pilot John Whitaker decided it was pointless to try to keep up with the formation; the only real question (since they were roughly south of Cologne) was whether to break for neutral Switzerland or to head for home. A quick canvass of the crew via interphone (which was still working, despite the great amount of damage to the plane) decided upon attempting the trip back to Thorpe Abbotts, East Anglia. Knox carefully banked the plane and turned away from the rest of the group, still plodding and still fighting its way toward Regensburg.

"After flying for approximately five to ten minutes at approximately 15,000 feet," Ernest E. Warsaw, the navigator on the plane, recalls, "a group of Messerschmitts and Focke-Wulf fighters (approximately fifteen) were approaching from 5 o'clock and surprisingly gave no indication of attacking—it was as if they didn't see us. When they came within range, I, as fire control officer, gave the order to fire, which we did."

Within minutes the apparently unsuspecting German fighters were decimated; according to bombardier Edwin Tobin, no less than nine: "Our top turret man, Glover Barney, got one, Joe

LaSpada [tail gunner], got three, Frank Tychewicz [waist gunner], two, Warsaw, one, and myself two . . ."

Warsaw continues: "In the ensuing confusion of battle, the following occurred. Our intercom was shot up and didn't function. I shot down three of the attackers and as I followed one going down, I saw that our wheels were down . . ."

When had that happened?, Warsaw wondered. It was probable that one of the attacks had severed the electrical system, or destroyed the fuse panel on No. 6 bulkhead (mid-fuselage), causing some malfunction or a short actuating the landing gear mechanism which lowered the wheels. (This possibility has been confirmed by Edward C. Wells, chief designer of the B-17.) No one heard Knox say anything about putting down the wheels—the signal for aerial surrender.

But that also meant that they had undoubtedly been down when the German formation had approached them, explaining why, as Warsaw had noticed, the fighters seemed disinclined to attack the Fortress. But once the bomber gunners opened up hitting some of their number the Germans, confronted with what appeared to them "a flagrant violation of the Code of the Air," attacked with violent fury.

The 109s and 190s came in with a vengeance, recklessly and savagely, all possible firepower lacerating the Fortress. "Two or three cannon bursts hit the ship and . . . someone rang the bailout bell," Warsaw continues. "I immediately put on my chute (a paratrooper safety type) and bailed out. Bailout practice habits remained, since, instead of releasing the bailout door, I opened it, fell out, and it closed after me. The bombardier [Edwin Tobin] turned to follow me, but saw the door in place and presumed I [had gone] to the pilot's compartment."

Tobin reached the cockpit with difficulty, for the plane was in a flaming dive, and saw Knox and Whitaker getting into their parachutes. Then nothing: an explosion (probably detonating oxygen bottles) blew him out of the plane and into an oblivion that lasted for days. At the same moment (in which Knox and

Whitaker perished) radio operator Walter Paulsen was also ejected from the plane by the explosion—and like Tobin unconscious and with an unopened chute. After he was captured Warsaw was asked by his captors, the Gestapo, to identify two sheet-covered bodies. They were Tobin and Paulsen, presumed dead by the Germans and by Warsaw; however, both, apparently had recovered from their explosive exits from the plane in time to open their chutes, though perhaps much too close to the ground. They struck with such force that all life appeared to have been knocked out of them. Eventually some signs of life were observed and the two shattered men were taken to a hospital where German doctors worked on them and they would remain hospitalized a long time. One legend had it that bombardier Tobin was unconscious for six months; actually he awakened in the hospital two days after the mission. About nine months later Warsaw and Tobin were reunited in prison camp, much to the former's surprise; he learned as well that Paulsen also presumed dead had survived, too. Top turret gunner Glover Barney, also blown out of the plane managed to open his chute somewhat sooner than his crewmates Tobin and Paulsen, although the delay resulted in a hard landing, which broke both legs, and captivity. These four, Tobin, Paulsen, Barney, and Warsaw were the only survivors from Knox's plane.

Having jumped, Warsaw floated downward, keeping an eye on their plane. The fighters swarmed around it while it burned and small explosions racked it. The heavily damaged Fortress, carrying its dead, fell out of control until it smashed to earth near Aachen. Out of its crushed, flaming ruins was born the myth of the Bloody Hundredth and its equally mythical—and equally false—Luftwaffe grudge which supposedly dogged the group from that day on.

A week after the raid Warsaw was awaiting transfer to a prisoner-of-war camp in the airport at Cologne. A German pilot, a captain, approached him and they talked for a while. It soon became evident, although Warsaw's understanding of German "was not good enough to understand all the nuances of his complaint," that the pilot had been one of those they had shot down while their Fortress had its wheels down. "As I recall," Warsaw said, "the attitude of the German captain was somewhat disturbed and he was somewhat high on schnapps and therefore it would be difficult to tell whether or not he was hostile or drunk. He kept referring to the fellow who shot him down as a 'Luftgangster' . . ."

There was sufficient torment afflicting the 100th that very day without the added burden of the myth (often subsequently demoralizing for replacements). Some time after Knox and crew had been forced to drop out of the lead squadron, Cleven's tail-end Charlie's, the 351st, came under attack as if the myth were already in force. Cleven's Fortress, named with a mild scatological touch "Phartzac" (a name that was to cause some State-side flurry when an innocent newsman used it in a Boston paper), seemed to attract hot metal like a magnet ever since Antwerp. He tightened up the formation with his three survivors to fill in the void left by the destroyed three B-17s of the second element to provide what protection he had left for the underside of the 100th's now tattered formation. They were still about a half hour's flying time from Regensburg when "Phartzac" suffered the full attentions of the Luftwaffe. In his recommendation for a Medal of Honor for Cleven, the group's commanding officer, Neil Harding, set down the ordeal of the Fortress—and its crew—in the objective language of such official statements:

> About thirty minutes before reaching the target, the airplane received the following battle damage:
>
> A 20-mm. cannon shell penetrated the right side of the plane, exploded under the pilot, damaging the electrical system and radio compartment, killing the radio operator [*Norman Smith*], who bled to death after both legs were cut off just above the knees.
>
> Another 20-mm. shell entered the left side of the nose, tearing out a section of the Plexiglas about two feet square; it also tore away the left gun installation [*Cleven's plane was a B-17F, as were most that participated in the double strike*] and injured the bombardier in the head and shoulder.

A third 20-mm. shell penetrated the right wing, went on into the fuselage and shattered the hydraulic system, releasing the fluid in a flood into the cockpit.

A fourth 20-mm. shell crashed through the cabin roof, and cut the cables to one side of the rudder.

A fifth 20-mm. shell hit Number 3 engine, destroying all engine controls. The engine caught fire and lost its power—luckily, the fire later died out.

Confronted with this structural damage, partial loss of controls, fire in one engine, and serious injuries to personnel, and faced with fresh waves of fighters still rising to the attack, Major Cleven had every justification for ordering his crew to abandon ship. And his crew, many of them inexperienced youngsters, were already preparing to bail out; no other alternative seemed possible.

Cleven, one of the 100th's most capable pilots, knew his aircraft and although he had become in just a few chaotic moments the proprietor of a flying junk heap, was certain they could make it. He concentrated on the various dials and switches in the cockpit, shot a look at No. 3 engine, which smoldered but seemed to have burned itself out. Then back into the cockpit where he noticed that his co-pilot, like the rest of the crew, was preparing to get out. Cleven, however, was not ready to leave and ordered the co-pilot back into his seat. The distraught airman found it difficult to understand the point of that: they were doomed unless they got out of that wrecked airplane.

He pleaded with Cleven, who, with icy control, kept the rattling B-17 on its way to Regensburg. Over the intercom the rest of the crew was arrested in its preparations to abandon ship to listen to the drama in the cockpit (most regarded the co-pilot as their spokesman).

Cleven's one concession to the Wild Blue Yonder mystique was the pistol he carried strapped to his side (he was a native of Odessa, Texas). He drew the pistol and pointed it at the co-pilot's head and said, "You sit there and take it, you son-of-a-bitch, or I'll blow your brains out!"

That did it; it shook up the co-pilot who suddenly realized they were indeed still flying and not burning, that the fighters had begun concentrating on another hapless grouping in the formation —and that he was still alive. He slumped into the right seat and throughout the rest of the ship the living members of the crew settled down also and turned to the business of the day: they too, torn up as they were, would bomb Regensburg.

At about the same tense moment, Allied intercept heard the voice of a lone German fighter pilot asking, "Where are the rest?"

SIX

Where *were* the rest?

Was this lone anonymous airman seeking his brother pilots or more enemy bombers? Only moments before he had probably winged through a tumultuous sky, filled with darting fighters, heaving bombers, smoke, tracers, bits and pieces of metal and the inevitable thistle-thick parachute cluster. Then inexplicably he was all alone in a frightening vastness, cleansed of all traces of battle.

LeMay, however, was not alone. But as the Third Division passed the IP (Initial Point, the reference point just before the target where the bombing run began), they were minus twelve B-17s (more than half of them from the 100th Group), courtesy of a determined Luftwaffe. In just about an hour of violent action the effectiveness of the carefully planned mission had been diminished —the Luftwaffe had substracted some of the potential impact.

As LeMay later told his group commanders: "We came into the IP and the maneuver there was excellent, and performed as briefed. The 390th was probably a little too far back for a normal mission, but for this one it was all right and we had all the distance necessary for a good bombing run. We were briefed that the opposition at the target would be negligible, and on the strength of this we came in to the target at a lower altitude than normal, although we expected opposition from flak. I saw only two bursts. However, we were hit by ten to fifteen fighters coming down from above, but the bombing of the first [i.e. 403rd] Combat Wing was good, with everybody getting their bombs off on the first run."

LeMay had complimented Lieutenant Dunstan T. Abel, the Wing's lead navigator, on his work in getting them to the target. Navigator Abel had little to add to LeMay's comments. "We used DR [Dead Reckoning—navigation according to route as planned and indicated on their maps and computed en route] on the way across the continent," Abel said, "and had no trouble staying on course. We picked up the target after turning at the IP and I had no trouble locating it for the bombardier [Captain Latham]."

Flak all along the route was no deterrent, it was the fighter planes that took the toll. Although the attacks eased up between the IP and Regensburg, they had never actually stopped altogether since the first attack over the Belgian coast. It was as if the Luftwaffe rose up in relays; when one unit finished with them another arrived to take up the battle where the previous one had left off. The Fortress crews wondered where all the German planes—literally hundreds—had come from. They noted too that as they penetrated deeper inside Germany the number of twin-engine fighters, mostly Me-110s and Ju-88s, increased. A number of these had been recruited from Nachtjagdgeschwader 101, a night fighter training unit which had been formed to contend with the R.A.F. attacks and based around Ingostadt, about 35 miles southwest of Regensburg.

Once Abel had brought the Third Division armada within sighting distance of Regensburg—and they could see it from 25 miles away—his work for that phase of the mission was finished. The next belonged to Latham once the 96th made the turn at the IP. Latham began zeroing in on the Aiming Point—"Building No. 8," marked 04252/7 on the target map. Once this had been done and the B-17 began its run, there would be no evasive action, no sudden maneuver to throw off the fighters or flak. Kenny turned over the aircraft to Latham, who kept it precisely moving on a given heading after compensating for various factors: *altitude* (affecting the length of time the bombs would travel before striking; the *atmospheric conditions; deflection,* depending on the wind's direction and velocity); *true airspeed,* affecting the thrust of the bomb and its point of impact relative to the aircraft; *ballistics* (the size, shape and weight of the bomb, which affect its trajectory). These and other factors would have to be taken into consideration, computed and all synchronized into the bombsight.

Latham controlled the Fortress for the three minutes of the bomb run with the Automatic Flight Control Equipment (AFCE), straight, level and true, a very long three minutes until "Bombs Away!" The instant this occurred control of the aircraft reverted to Kenny and the navigation to Abel; at almost the same moment. As the bombs came tumbling out of the open belly of the Fortress, the rest of the aircraft of the 96th, bomb-bay doors gaping, released their loads also—a total for the group of 95,000 pounds of high explosives from nineteen B-17s. It was 11:43 A.M. Tuesday, 17 August, 1943, when the bombs began falling toward the Messerschmitt factory at Regensburg. Two minutes later the 388th and the 100th decidedly ahead of schedule, on different compass headings, passed over Regensburg adding their cargo to the tonnage, the initial portion of which, the 96th's, was by then hurtling directly for the target. The 100th's fourteen survivors (with Cleven's plane flying on three engines) dropped more than two hundred 250-pound incendiaries. And so it continued for over twenty minutes as the Third Division passed over Regensburg—there would have been less time spent over the target, but when the turn came for the 401st Wing (the 94th leading the 385th) the first bombs had already struck and a thick wall of smoke billowed up to obscure the target. As the 94th made a great sweeping turn to the left in order to attempt a second run, the 385th continued on, sighted the target, dropped their bombs and turned also to accompany the 94th during its second try. "Fifteen bi-motored Me-110s and Ju-88s hit us and we were under constant attack to the targets . . . On the second approach . . . we found the smoke still there, but studied the area closely and got our bombs on the target." It was then 12:07 P.M.

During the twenty-four minutes of the Regensburg attack, although fighter attacks slackened and flak was meager and sporadic, the Germans had not stopped fighting back. The few flak bursts LeMay had noted were not totally ineffective.

IZA Angel, piloted by Henry Nagorka of the 388th Group, which followed the 96th during the mission, suffered certain problems over Regensburg, the least of which was a hung up 500-pound bomb that did not fall at "bombs away." Another 388th Fortress flown by Charles Bliss left Regensburg with two such hang-ups, which were jettisoned not long after. But the flak was more pernicious than mechanical failure and the fighters even more deadly. Nagorka in *IZA Angel* kept a wary eye on what appeared to be a Ju-88 which remained on the outer edges of the formation and ordered his ball turret gunner to check the hung-up bomb. They had barely left Regensburg when the German plane as Nagorka remembered it, "pulled up into a climb and fired off something which exploded far short of the group. It was a curious looking eggshaped batch of sparkling metal. We could not understand what he was throwing at us. The crew kept a good watch—expecting everything and anything—remembering some of the air-to-air bombings the Germans had done on other occasions . . ."

Thus preoccupied with the mysterious Ju-88 and the bomb, *IZA Angel* and crew suffered a sudden surprise. "Almost without warning . . . an enemy fighter made a run from about seven or eight o'clock slightly above us. His first batch of shells hit us. He raked across the ship with one projectile coming through the side next to me and just touching a knuckle on my left hand as it passed, completely severing all my indicator cables and the instruments went dead. The shell continued forward and down into the nose and struck [Francis] Tierney's hand as he was holding a machine gun in firing position, almost cutting off his hand at the wrist, continued on down to ricochet off the armor plating on the nose floor and struck the boot of the bombardier [John Leverone] completely spent, bruising his instep—lying there unexploded.

"What a moment before had almost seemed a milk run had suddenly become a fearfully hurt aircraft and crew—fighting for control and trying to save itself.

" 'Oh, God! My hand!' came over the intercom.

" 'Who is it? What position?' I asked quickly.

"I had trouble pinning down the hurt crew member. The ship was giving me trouble—I was trying to stay steady—leading an element—and I sent the co-pilot Gilbert Parker to help Tee [the nickname of Tierney, the navigator]. I checked the rest of the ship for injuries and damage, but there seemed to be no more. Park helped Tee into the passage between the pilot seats, lay him down and administered a shot of pain killer [morphine] out of the first-aid packet, tried to stanch the bleeding and make him comfortable.

"I signaled the wing men that I would break out of formation and go forward in order to get help for Tee. I broke radio silence and got an OK from the leader—Roy Forrest, if I remember—and proceeded to make a shallow descent, picking up speed and very slowly passing under the formation. Turning the ship over to Park, I stepped down to comfort Tee. He had taken out his rosary—and was white as a sheet—praying and going into shock. We covered him with extra blankets. I told him we would be there soon—hold on—we were taking special action to get help as quickly as possible.

"In the meantime the boys had gone back to releasing the hung-up bomb and, as we were passing over the Alps just over the Italian border, the bomb fell. I looked out to follow its drop and it looked as if it were going into a beautiful small town on a lake. My God—I thought to myself—into that unsuspecting town full of people . . .

"By now we were ahead of our formation but behind the lead group [the 96th carrying LeMay]. Our altitude was about 10,000 and dropping. It made matters a bit easier to get rid of the oxygen masks. Park had done all his helping with the aid of an oxygen bottle. Now it was simply a matter of stretching that descent as far as possible to make sure we had gas enough to get to Africa. If we went into the drink Tee was a goner.

"We trimmed the ship for the most efficient flight, throttled back slightly and maintained our gradual descent.

"As we passed by Corsica and Sardinia it occurred to me that we had not figured whether delay would put us into a night landing. This led me to add a little coal and speed up the approach to Africa."

LeMay observed this maneuver and, disapproved of what he regarded a dangerous break from formation. But before he was to note this strange behavior of *IZA Angel,* other events occurred over and near Regensburg.

The high group in LeMay's Wing (the 390th) was suffering vicious attacks from fighters, losing two B-17s during the run from the IP. And then, within a moment of the bombing, the group report noted "A/C 313 observed going down just after Regensburg was reached at about 1150 hours. No chutes seen. Two A/C high squadron 390th group left formation after leaving Regensburg." (One more 390th B-17 fell out of the formation, ditched in the Mediterranean and was later found by Air-Sea Rescue boats and the entire crew rescued.) All four planes had succeeded in dropping bombs on Regensburg. The three first mentioned crews were, of course, lost, along with their planes. The young 390th (which had flown its first combat mission only five days before) lost six aircraft.

The group which spent the most time over the target area was the 385th, companion to the 94th which made two runs. One of the most harrowing experiences of the day could be attributed neither to fighter nor flak. This occurred in the B-17 piloted by Lieutenant Irving H. Frank named *Raunchy Wolf,* the victim being ball turret gunner Staff Sergeant Aubrey Bartholomew.

The 385th was tooling around at about 16,500 feet contending with fighters while waiting for the 95th to complete its bombing. Bartholomew traversed his fifties in the turret, keeping an eye on the fighters that had slashed through the formation. Then, he fell backwards out of his turret—the catch holding the door had flipped open and out he tumbled.

His intercom and oxygen lines snapped, and he had no chute, there being no room in a ball turret for both gunner and a parachute. But as he slipped out head first, Bartholomew's feet caught in some part of the mechanism of his guns. But merely dangling there about three miles over Regensburg, with the rush of the B-17's slipstream bent on finishing the job that the faulty lock had begun, was no solution. Struggling as he was in the rarefied air meant he might pass out very soon, if he wasn't blown out. Since he could not call for help, Bartholomew fought his own private war with fate—and won.

After it was all over, and that must have been within minutes, Bartholomew could not recall how he managed to crawl back into the turret; the details simply evaporated with the danger. He was back inside his little domain, plugged into the life-sustaining systems of the Fortress, and headed for Africa, rather dazed but miraculously alive (when Bartholomew returned to England the next week he learned that during his absence, and near demise, he had become an American citizen; Canadian-born Bartholomew had earned it).

As the last of the 401st Combat Wing's Fortresses winged over Regensburg, a tall, roiling, column of smoke began surging upward. A total of 127 aircraft dropped bombs on the target (with one additional plane from the 390th dropping on a target of opportunity, "believed to be over Heilsbron"). Even the laconic LeMay would admit that the bombing had been excellent—"one of the finest examples of high altitude precision bombing yet produced by the Third Air Division."

In the target area they had placed 971 500-pound high-explosive bombs and 448 250-pound incendiary bombs, the bulk falling generally around the selected Main Point of Impact, striking factories, shops and the airfield associated with the factory causing damage, ranging from complete to minor, to various buildings and to parked aircraft. None of this was visible to the crews because of the rising dust and smoke. Having dropped their bombs on the

Messerschmitt factory their next concern was getting away from there.

After striking Regensburg they proceeded almost directly southward to a Rally Point where LeMay's 403rd Wing was to circle to enable the planes to form up for the flight across the rest of southern Germany, Austria, and Italy. As his Wing circled, they were joined by the 402nd Wing (the 95th and 100th Groups). The trailing 401st Wing, late because of the two runs made by the 94th Group, would have to catch up with the other two Wings at a second Rally Point LeMay had selected on the other side of the Alps. He had to consider the ever-encrouching problem of dwindling fuel and did not want to spend more time circling than necessary. So the five groups, the 96th, 388th, and 390th (of the 403rd Combat Wing) and the 95th and 100th of the 402nd Wing, formed up into their respective wing combat boxes. Beyond Regensburg the fighter activity picked up again and the Luftwaffe attacks nearly equaled the ferocity of the attacks on the way in. Although the decision to go on to Africa and not to return on the accustomed reciprocal course may have confused the Luftwaffe they had already encountered, the home-based fighters of Jagdgeschwader 27 and JG 51, as well as the night fighters were there to challenge their safe withdrawal from German skies.

And the irony of the deception was that, although they had properly fooled the fighters awaiting their return to England, these fighters would instead be fully armed and fueled and ready for the First Division when it was finally on its way to Schweinfurt.

Still LeMay had to concern himself with the fighters they would encounter on their southward passage—and soon he knew they would have to face one other inexorable, unconditional, enemy. "We turned toward the rally point and fell into formation quite well," he recalled. "We had another rally point picked north of the Alps where we had to make two big circles to pick up the next Combat Wing. We used the flak at the north end of the Brenner Pass for our locator as it shot straight up in the air. By this time we were beginning to run short of gas . . ."

Nor did the bombing of Regensburg end the battle. The Luftwaffe continued charging in as if vengeance bound. Cripples especially were "smothered by enemy fighters," some of them stragglers that had fallen behind and beyond the help of the formation defense. A dozen B-17s had been knocked out of the Third Air Division before the target; two had fallen over Regensburg and from there until the Fortresses reached the Alps German fighter attacks were nearly as intense as those they had endured on the way to Regensburg. At 12:07, the moment of the 94th Bomb Group's "Bombs Away," the last group to drop their loads, a German controller was overheard informing his aircraft of the presence of "hostiles to the south of Regensburg" and that "they were proceeding toward Italy."

For nearly an hour the American formation was again under attack from fighters—and this would add an additional ten bombers to the cost of the day's mission: one from the 388th, four from the 390th, one each from the 94th, the 385th, the 95th and two from the 100th. Half of these losses ended up in ditchings and subsequent rescue or captivity for the crews. The strain on the engines in crossing the Alps was too much for several of the battle damaged Fortresses. The two post-Regensburg 100th Group losses were not typical. Pilot Ronald Hollenbeck, for example, managed to get away from Regensburg despite the loss of two engines, but the climb over the Alps overtaxed the two operational engines and it became obvious that they simply were not going to make it. Before they lost control he rang the bailout bell and they all left the Fortress. They could not have selected a worse position: both Hollenbeck and his co-pilot, E. Reed, floated down directly into a prisoner of war camp. One of the gunners, Glen M. Kiersey, managed some time later to escape to U.S. lines after the Allies invaded Italy.

Glen Van Noy, also of the 100th, found himself in poor shape. Like Hollenbeck's, his plane was short two engines, and he decided they might make a try for Switzerland. The Luftwaffe had other plans for his B-17 and continued chopping away at it until they were nearly at the Swiss border, when the fighters turned back. This problem having cleared up, Van Noy decided again for the southward flight and passed low through the Brenner Pass, attempted to bomb an enemy airfield in northern Italy (although the single perverse bomb they carried away from Regensburg still refused to drop), crossed over between two warships in Genoa Bay—neither of which fired at them. The crew had thrown out most of their equipment not nailed down, including the waist guns; besides, only the top-turret gun still had ammunition. When a couple of enemy seaplanes came to investigate, this sole gun discouraged them.

But Van Noy had reason for dejection; they remained precariously aloft practically on one engine and with the Mediterranean in sight (they were about 40 miles off the coast of Sicily), Van Noy set the plane down in the water and the crew took to their dinghies. (The next morning an enemy seaplane, with a single Me-109 as escort, came and plucked them out of the sea.)

By one in the afternoon the German fighter threat had ended, as the aircraft of Luftflotte 2 were ordered back to their bases by Fighter Control. One fighter pilot was overheard questioning the order and was duly informed by Control that the quarry was, by then, "out of range." LeMay's concern was with keeping his formation, including the cripples, intact in the event of further attacks when they passed over Italy and the Mediterranean.

"The weather was clear over the mountains so we didn't wait on the other [401st] Combat Wing, but went to the second rally point on the other side of the Alps. Had to wait fifteen minutes to get the Division in good formation going across the Mediterranean near Sardinia . . .

"One plane left the formation while abreast of Sardinia and headed off to the right," he interjected. "Where he was going, I don't know. [This was undoubtedly Nagorka's *IZA Angel* rushing Tierney to Africa]. He got ahead of us and I lost him. If I found out who he was, he would no longer be a plane commander. One ship fell back, in sight of the formation, apparently trying to save gas."

He continued the narrative of the flight across the Mediterranean ". . . near Sardinia, as we might be hit by fighters. We got some flak out of Italy at the south end of Lake Garda, but had no fighters after leaving the Alps. There were fighters on the ground at Verona but they did not come up. After leaving the coast of Italy, everybody seemed to relax a bit and the formation was not as good as I should have liked it.

"The closer we got to Africa with a worry of gasoline shortage, the poorer the formation became, although we were fairly well together."

One Fortress, *Pregnant Portia,* was in a delicate, if harrowing condition, indeed. At one point in the battle one of the life rafts flipped out of its compartment, was blown out of one of the waist windows and inflated caught in the tail section. As described in *Target: Germany,* "In vain, members of the crew tried to shoot it off; one gunner from Texas even tried to rope it. [Sic!] Enemy fighters, seeing that the Fortress was in trouble, gave it their best attention."

The plane was within sight of the Alps, but the crew had some doubts, what with the drag caused by the useless life raft; there was even some fear that because of it the tail section of the B-17 would "flop off any minute."

But *Pregnant Portia* managed the Alps, having eluded the Luftwaffe, but halfway across the Mediterranean, with the red lights flashing on the instrument panel it became all too evident that ditching was inevitable. When the fourth light came on the pilot eased the plane into the water. All went well and the ten-man crew reluctantly abandoned the plane—but with a single five man life raft, the other still being furled around the tail. *Pregnant Portia* soon sank into the Mediterranean taking half of their emergency equipment with it. They were all alone at sea.

"I never want to spend another night like that," one of the crew later told an interrogator. "Five of us sat in the dinghy and five hung on outside. Don't let anyone tell you about the warm Mediterranean seas. It ain't so. The night got blacker and we got gloomier.

"When trails of daylight finally came up we were all half dead. With the sun though, our spirits rose again and we took stock of ourselves. During the night everything we had—even the stuff in our pockets—had floated away. At eleven o'clock the little automatic radio transmitter we had went out and that is when we started praying in earnest. (Incidentally, the following Sunday we attended church en masse!) Anyway, as the afternoon came on a B-26 sighted us and stayed right over us until one of those British Air-Sea Rescue launches came out and picked us up.

"We thought we were hard as nails; after all, we were a combat crew. But right then we felt like ninety-year-old men."

As the bedraggled formation of B-17s approached Africa, some carrying dead and wounded, some having to give up the struggle to splash into the sea, LeMay took small comfort in the thought: *Telergma is your field . . . There you'll have supplies . . . everything you need . . . That's the place to land. You can get well serviced there . . .* These were the words of assurance tendered him the previous month, during his reconnaissance visit to North African bases in preparation for the shuttle mission, by Colonel Lauris Norstad, who was by then the A-3 (Operations and Training) Officer in Major General James H. Doolittle's Northwest African Strategic Air Forces. When he and LeMay had conferred, Norstad was Chief of Staff to General Spaatz, who was in charge of forming an air force in Africa.

But there had been one little contingency they had simply not considered: the war in North Africa had moved onward—and eastward—in the interim, virtually making LeMay and his flock orphans of war. The comfort he anticipated was cold comfort indeed. "Let me show you how things are apt to happen in wartime," he has written. "They had to move their damn depot because of the change in the North African war condition. Norstad and that bunch down there had promptly forgotten that I ever existed. The war moved on, and they moved with it."

Chaos: "We hit the African coast about 18 miles east of where we intended, but as soon as we pin-pointed ourselves, we made a turn over the field at Bône so those planes short of gas could land. Forty-four ships landed, with four landing in wheat fields and dry lake beds. The remainder of the planes went down to Telergma and Berteaux and landed at the fields they were supposed to. The project officer from N.W. Africa [Northwest African Air Forces], who was assigned to help us out, was not on the job and the enlisted man in the tower gave some instructions he wouldn't have given if an officer had been there. He gave instructions to fly straight west and land at another field. The pilots of the first Combat Wing thought the plans had been changed and [that] they were supposed to land at the other field. Some tried to do it but couldn't find the other field, so some came back and landed anyway.

"Everyone got down very rapidly. There were always four planes on the runway. One plane landed at Bône with a flat tire and ran off the edge of the runway. Another ran partially off the runway which didn't leave much room to get through, but the rest landed all right.

"From then on the trouble started. We planned on using Telergma because it was a B-17 parts depot and should have had all the parts necessary plus 500 mechanics.

"We found no parts and no mechanics . . .

"In Africa, deluxe accommodations were a cot and blanket. Normal accommodations were slit trenches."

The hard military fact was that the war in North Africa was virtually over and the Allies were seeking other conquests. On May 12, over two months before, the wily "Desert Fox," Erwin Rommel, had skulked out of Africa by air, leaving the remnants of his vaunted Afrika Korps to surrender Tunisia to the Allies—and consequently saving his own face. With a toehold in Sicily, which surrendered that day, the invasion of Italy appeared attractively imminent to the Allies. But with the military center of gravity having shifted westward, LeMay's orphans found their African reception and accommodations austere.

While the original planning of the mission had taken into consideration the critical problem of fuel, there had been no possibility to predict the ferocity and persistence of the German fighter attacks. That too would serve to consume fuel; so would the various stages of battle damage that the aircraft suffered in the attacks. So it was that after nearly eleven hours aloft, the surviving Fortresses were forced to contend with yet another hazard just as they were on the approach to sanctuary, however minimal.

The 100th's Harry Crosby recalled the blueness of the Mediterranean, "it was incredibly blue," but then "the planes began running out of gas and hitting the blue. And as we approached landfall at Bône—where we were to turn west, fly along the coast till we came to a harbor and then turn south to follow a railroad to Telergma, our base—I really began to worry about our gas supply. None of us had any desert navigation, but I also questioned the possibility of making the base 'as briefed.' I decided to fly a short cut across the desert, directly from Bône, and Major Kidd agreed. Of course, if I were wrong we would fly off into the desert and run out of gas there. We made it—I recall in company with only two other planes, Charlie Cruikshank's and John Brady's—with nothing to spare."

Bône, directly on the coast, became the haven for the B-17s in real trouble. Getting to Telergma meant an additional flying time inland and westward of about a hundred miles. Nagorka, in his frantic dash away from the formation to get medical attention for Tierney, brought *IZA Angel* in close to Bône, made a gentle turn and headed for Telergma. He had radioed about having a wounded man aboard and thus arranged for an ambulance to meet them. He brought the Fortress into a landing pattern and shot off flares announcing wounded aboard, then brought the plane down.

"It was not the best of landings after the tense long flight, but we were in a hurry. I wheeled the *IZA Angel* around to a parking position, cut the engines, and looked for an ambulance. None in sight!

"I got on the radio again. Then jumped out onto the tarmac to run to the tower to give 'em hell. Then an ambulance came along. We pulled Tee out into it (the damned medics were so chicken about blood that I got livid at their dragging, and we did it ourselves). I jumped into the ambulance and rode to the hospital with Tee, my hand on his shoulder, talking to him. The ride was much too rough—bad road and bad springs—and much too long—about twenty miles from the way it felt.

"After Tee was unloaded I talked to the doctor. 'Please do what you can to save his hand,' I pleaded. 'Two of his fingers are warm—can't you stitch it up even if it isn't done, just on the chance that it will work?'

" 'We'll do what we can,' he answered without emotion.

"When I called on Tee the next day his hand was gone."

Tierney, who recovered and returned to England, was one of the seven seriously wounded among those who managed to arrive in Africa. There were four dead, two men slightly wounded and, in the twenty-four planes that were lost, some 240 missing, many of them dead and seriously wounded also.

With his division dispersed over several miles of North Africa LeMay, who liked precision, had little idea of just where he stood statistically. Planes from the same group frequently scattered and landed at three different places—Bône, Telergma, and Berteaux—so that even the group commanders had little idea of their survivors. One of the first things he attended to was to get Air-Sea Rescue out to the positions where the ditched planes had been noted. (Four of the five were picked up by Air-Sea Rescue and the crew of the 100th was taken captive by the Germans.)

But the problem at hand was a bit more difficult. Somewhere out there he had roughly 120 aircraft and as many exhausted, emotionally drained crews. To have arrived after the intense battles through which they had fought and then find that no one had expected them was a bit above and beyond. LeMay's caustic comment, dismissing the battle and referring to their arrival, summed up the attitudes of many of the crews: "From then on the trouble started." Harry Crosby was even more succinct: "Everything was wrong."

Henry Nagorka, disturbed over Tierney's serious injury and what followed, was in an unusual state of mind. "The anguish and bitterness I experienced could easily have led me to murder," he recalls. "It had been building up all during the flight and during the emergency and then was compounded by the casual treatment we got on the ground in Africa. I wanted to get drunk—or to kill . . ."

LeMay, who never wore his heart on his sleeve, did neither, but he did move around, unsmiling, cigar clamped in teeth, moving and shaking, acquiring whatever services he could from "N.W. Africa." That failing, he zeroed in on the crews themselves to attend to their own needs. This may appear to have been rather callous, but it gave them something to do besides meditate on their losses, gripe ("bitch" was the correct term) and generally feel miserable.

It took about two days for nerves to settle down and for the situation (SNAFU) to straighten out. The losses and damages were assessed and where possible the aircraft were patched up and rendered operational, excepting thirty or so. In time LeMay would have eighty-five B-17s ready for another mission.

John Kidd soon learned that of the twenty-one 100th planes that had set out for Africa, nine were lost and that, once accounted for, twelve were scattered here and there. But of these eight were actually flyable and of these only six were capable of operations. It was three days before he had the time to write to Janie Kidd:

> Surprise! [*he wrote from Telergma on August 20, 1943*]. Didn't ever expect to be writing from here. Can't tell you exactly where we are, but you can imagine from reading the papers. About all I can say is that it's hot . . . This is quite a rugged life—have slept underneath the airplane for the last three nights and have

gotten plenty of exercise that was badly needed. Am even getting tan.

There having been no arrangements for billeting, the crews slept under or in their planes. The "rugged life" to which Kidd refers was the chore of refueling their planes with hand pumps—two hundred gallons per aircraft. As LeMay put it, "It took four days to gas forty planes . . . It took the same amount of time to get the others ready as it did those at Telergma . . . The first day we ate emergency rations, but after they saw we would be there a few days, they got in enough supplies so we had fairly decent meals." John S. Durakov of the 385th Group recalls that their plane landed at Bône with the fuel tanks of three engines empty, and then upon joining the rest of the group at Telergma, eating off a garbage can lid.

With only six planes operational, Kidd found time to write again on August 23:

> I might as well be there with you because I'm not doing a thing outside of griping. Have had lots of time in the last few days to think about you—that's just about all I've done. [*He would learn that on August 17, as per his own suggestion, Jane Kidd had gone out and bought a fur coat. The concurrent purchase of the coat and the battle of Regensburg became a kind of group legend.*] Still sleeping under the stars and dreaming of you. The nights are fine—nice and cool and clear—have had three blankets for the past six nights. The days, though are hot and dusty—and I thought Kelly Field was dusty! If you hear from Ann [*Oakes, wife of pilot Donald Oakes who had landed in Switzerland*], tell her Don has a darned good chance!

Most of the crews, once the trauma of the mission had worn off and the work of refueling, rearming and repair was attended to, revealed themselves as the typical American tourist, Kidd among them. He found the Arabs and the Italian prisoners of war interesting. "The latter are very hard workers, they need no guard—they're the waiters in the officer's club. All very courteous and they all want to go to New York after the war. They seem to like Americans!"

Arab life, however fascinating, was not too attractive:

> Yesterday I went into a nearby Arab village & bought two dozen eggs. They're about the only things you can be sure are clean. The meat market was simply a chunk of goat strung up on a tripod, flies buzzing all over it. Am sure it would turn your stomach. Don't know how these Arabs manage to survive . . . The little kids are fairly bright, though. One, ten years old, asked me for a light for his cigarette and said, "You're a major, aren't you?" They go around picking watermelon rinds out of the dirt and eating them. Our food in the mess is quite good, considering. Have had the first white bread in three months, and all they have is goat butter, which is just about like cheese. It's enlightening to see how the rest of the world lives—am resolved there's no place like the U.S. One of the funniest things is to watch a big Arab riding down the road on a jackass which is only about three feet high . . .

These little beasts charmed several of the visitors, who once their chores were over and had time on their hands, wandered here and there sightseeing and souvenir hunting. Before long certain members of the crews strutted around wearing red fezzes instead of GI issue. Some also sported some rather deadly Arabian knives; but the more adventurous acquired the diminutive donkeys as pets.

Just how many of these little animals were smuggled back to Britain is not known (LeMay even heard that one crew had brought back an Arab boy—but that was never substantiated). But one of the donkeys was definitely brought in under LeMay's quick eye in *Miracle Tribe,* a plane of the 96th Group with which LeMay traveled. This was "Lady Moe," who became a favorite around the base but who wandered out one day onto a railroad track and was hit by a train. The other known donkey was the 100th's "Mohammed," whose arrival at Thorpe Abbots inspired pixy pilot Owen "Cowboy" Roan's immortal, "I'm coming in with a frozen ass!" The ambulance met the plane only to witness one of the crew emerge from the Fortress with tiny "Moe" slung over his shoulders. This donkey eventually succumbed to the rigors of English weather.

Another pastime was swimming in the Mediterranean for those who remained at Bône or who could manage to get there. Constantine, just north of Telergma, provided those crews who could "liberate" a Jeep for a while, a view of what Harry Crosby described as "classy French society," characterized by handsome spit-and-polish French officers and their even more handsome, elegant ladies. The lovely, lush city appeared to have been untouched by the war, as did even its fashionably attired warriors.

LeMay's strongest impression of the African stay was the weather, although, like his men, he managed to find something pleasant under adversity. "It was hot as hell down there," he recalled, "but the brewery was operating. We all got some American-type beer, served in earthenware cups—cold, American-type beer which we hadn't had since we left home."

Henry Nagorka, meanwhile, kept an eye on the progress of Tee Tierney and the patching up of *IZA Angel.* A ground crew was found that could cover the hole in the side of the plane which marked the entry of the projectile that had caused so much anguish and rehook the various wires and instruments. Another patch was placed over a rent in the right wing (not until they had returned to England did Nagorka learn that the shell that had caused it had remained, alive and unexploded, inside a fuel tank).

Once *IZA Angel* was pronounced operational, Nagorka laid on a strictly personal mission: "I called the tower and told them I wanted clearance to flight-test the craft. They OK'd the flight. I tipped off some of the crew and off we went."

His objective was Bizerte, on the North African coast in Tunisia, a flight of about 200 miles. Just before taking off for Regensburg, Nagorka had learned that his fiancée, Izabella Helhoski, served in an American hospital near Bizerte. Nagorka's B-17 had been named in her honor—the three first letters of her name and the fact that she was an "angel of mercy," had produced the name of the Fortress. His reasoning was: "Now here I am . . . She must be somewhere nearby. After a bit of asking, I found that the hospital was not too far." At least not as the B-17 flies, besides Nagorka had not seen Nurse Helhoski in a year and a half.

"As we approached Bizerte I saw a rather small fighter strip—hard-packed mud—and decided this was the place. We came in, crosswind, and crabbed the ship about thirty degrees until almost the moment the wheels touched. Then I gave it a violent correction and set it down. The meat wagon, fire trucks, and local personnel all came chasing us down the runway until I waved them off.

"When I checked on the location of the hospital they told me I landed on the wrong side of town.

"OK. We took off as we landed—the ship making hopping jigs in the crosswind. We came down in the other field with less drama, but not until we had approached the hospital, which was situated on the side of a hill, and buzzed it at window level, looking in at the faces and running attendants.

"I walked into the dining hall with my hot-pilot hat back on my head and my forty-five dangling on my belt. Izabella was sitting at a table. She almost fell off her bench. We drove out to the field and I introduced them to each other." This was when *IZA Angel* met her namesake—in a most unmilitary fashion.

Thus did those who endured the terrors of Regensburg and the frustrations that followed the aftermath bounce back. Visiting exotic places, collecting souvenirs, even making unauthorized "test flights"—it all helped; youthful resilience did the rest—and the determination to keep going. LeMay was certainly determined; by August 23, the day John Kidd wrote his last African letter, LeMay had scraped together eighty-five Fortresses (of the 122 he had led into Africa), saw that they were fueled, armed, and bombed up and ready to go again the next day.

POSTSCRIPT

The Regensburg phase of the double strike mission came full circle on August 24 when, as LeMay put it, "General Eaker decided, on a request from General Arnold, to run a problem on the way back." The target on the return mission was the Bordeaux-Mérignac airfield and repair plant believed to be the home base of Focke-Wulf 200s, the airliner turned reconnaissance-bomber. These were the aircraft of Kampfgeschwader 40 engaged around that time in attacks (not very effective) on Allied shipping.

While other units of the Eighth Air Force flew diversions and bombed various industrial/aviation targets in France, LeMay's Third Division moved in from the south to attack Bordeaux. They left Africa around six in the morning, roughly six hours later the bombs began raining upon the Focke-Wulf base (the bombing was rated "good to excellent") and, in another five hours, the first planes, those that made it, began landing at their home bases (or at any base they could find), a week to the day since that had taken off for Regensburg.

The Stars and Stripes quoted an anonymous pilot as saying, "The trip to Regensburg was undiluted hell, the trip back was a milk run." This was true, in a sense, if the absence of hostile fighters is taken into consideration, as well as the fact that the flak was described as "meager" and "inaccurate." But the Regensburg battle's impress, and the stay in Africa, had taken their toll. LeMay managed to get off with eighty-five planes—"We left the trash there"—but by the time they had arrived over the target, the number capable of bombing had been reversed: 58. Planes developed all kinds of malfunctions, causing them to turn back over the Mediterranean, to head for Spain, or any haven. Kidd's 100th, for example, got six planes up for the mission and one turned back for Africa. The 96th, again the lead for the mission, took off with fifteen, but also had one turn back for Africa. The fine African sand that had worked its way into the engines and other delicate parts of the Fortresses was more destructive that day than the Luftwaffe. Only four B-17s were lost during the day's missions, one from the diversionary sweep and airfield raids that had been set up by the Eighth Air Force from England, and 3 from LeMay's Regensburg returnees. To complicate the ending of another long mission for the African strays, the weather turned bad after the bombing of Bordeaux and the tired crews experienced a sequel to their African arrivals—fuel shortage—in addition to the strain of setting down at bases through the murk.

When the 55 Fortresses fluttered into their various bases in East Anglia, their arrival was hailed in the press, both military and civilian. Soon word leaked out of the great numbers of enemy aircraft the crews had claimed in exchange for their heavy losses —no less than 157 by LeMay's Third Division alone. These were, of course, excessive. So was the wishful thinking that issued forth even officially as to the consequence of Regensburg and what it portended for the Germans. Major General Harold L. George, commander of Air Transport Command visiting Britain on an inspection tour at the time, was quoted in *The Stars and Stripes* predicting, prematurely it would prove, that the "economic structure of Germany is going to fall by the end of the year," and he further estimated that it would take Germany six months to restore the factory at Regensburg which, he honestly believed, was "literally wiped off the map." The Luftwaffe, he was certain, would be deprived of from 1,500 to 2,000 fighters—and that did not bode well for the enemy.

"If I were on the other end of the Regensburg and Schweinfurt raids," George concluded, "it seems to me I would have a feeling of helplessness followed by hopelessness. It is a loss of hope as much as loss of lives that makes the enemy give in."

As genuine was George's belief in what he said, time proved him off on each of his predictions. He had not, of course, been on either end of the Regensburg and Schweinfurt raids. The Germans were neither beaten into general hopelessness, nor would the Messerschmitt factory be out of operation for six months.

The crews that had flown those missions might have agreed with General George; they fervently wanted to believe him, but they could not come forth with long-range predictions, nor grand sweeping statements. They survived from day to day and few who had made those missions did not intimately know helplessness and hopelessness themselves. But survival was a great healer and for most the dread and fear they had known over Germany on August 17 evaporated in the knowledge that they had been granted one more day.

They were practical men, not prognosticators or dreamers, so that instead of voicing sanguinary prophecies, they were content to make simpler and, to them, more pragmatic, statements at post-mission interrogations. Typical of these were a few of the suggestions volunteered by crews of the 390th Group; some were complaints about food (it was ever thus), about the long time spent in forming up over England and the accommodations—or rather, lack—in Africa. No one, for example, had had the foresight to arrange for a supply of medications for such local maladies as dysentery and malaria.

And there were cogent, succinct, recommendations for the future:

Stop giving medals for enemy aircraft knocked down.
More ammunition in waist.
Bring mess kits, toilet paper . . .

III

SCHWEINFURT

SEVEN

At the moment Curtis E. LeMay was leading his Third Division over Regensburg, the fogbound First Division's aircraft were finally poised on the runways, ready to go. It was around 11:30—they had been sitting there for hours—many of the crews had been up as early as two that morning. They had been ready for a long time and not in a good mood generally: tired, tense, and bitchy. The enlisted men of one B-17 crew in the 351st Group complained that they "couldn't get enything to eat at [the] Mess Hall from 0200 to 1100, so [the] Red Cross fed us." They may have been fortunate; the gunners of another crew, same group, reported that "Breakfast this morning was bad—eggs were rotten and made some men sick."

It may have been the long wait, as much as the eggs, that had made them sick. It happened to many as the time dragged on. The day had begun early, developed staggeringly boring irritations and frustrations and then erupted in a prolonged violence that few had ever experienced before—and for some, ever again.

For many August 17 began in a manner not unlike that in the films that Hollywood was grinding out about the war: pre-dawn setting, youthful crewmen briefed by their elders in an almost formal, formula-like speech. Bombardier Lieutenant Edward P. Winslow, Jr., remembered attending the 91st Group meeting. It was "so early that it was not yet daylight outside." The Group Intelligence Office [Major John J. McNaboe] strode in, pulled back a curtain "revealing a gigantic map of Europe with our mission indicated by colored strings."

" 'Our target today, gentlemen,' said the major, 'is the ballbearing factory at Schweinfurt. If we are successful in putting this plant out of operation we shall, no doubt, shorten the war by a considerable length of time.' "

Winslow found it difficult to follow the major's words for his attention was focused upon the map with its colorful strings stretched across it and wondered how would it be possible to go that far, bomb and get back considering the fuel capacity of their Fortresses at the time.

"The briefing continued," Winslow wrote in his diary not long after the mission, "with instructions from another Intelligence Officer who told us the number of German fighters we could expect, pointed out flak areas and projected pictures of our target on a screen. The Group Operations Officer [First Lieutenant Frederick W. Dibble] was next, giving us formation positions and telling the pilots that they must fly with the mixture controls at 'automatic-lean' in order to conserve enough gasoline to get us home again. The briefing ended with a synchronizing of watches and a reminder that any of the Catholic officers who were to fly could receive Communion in the little chapel at the rear of the room.

"After the briefing came the usual hurried, tasteless, breakfast and a rush to get into our flying clothes and down to the line. Oxygen masks, parachutes, 'Mae Wests' [life-jackets that were rather generous at the chest], throat-mikes and other pieces of equipment were piled on a truck with us and taken out to the ships.

"At dawn we were at our stations and ready to go. The powerful engines were started but soon shut off again. The pilot [Lieutenant Jack Hargis] called down that take-off had been postponed. We climbed out of the ship and relaxed nearby. Our squadron commander drove up in a Jeep and said that we must wait a few hours until the weather cleared. He had good news for our ball-turret gunner [Sergeant Star Tucker]. His Staff Sergeant's rating had just come through so he could sew on another stripe when he got back."

The bearer of good tidings glanced at the nose of the Fortress where the name *Dame Satan* had been lettered. (The crew's regular plane, *Frisco Jinny,* had been under repair when the mission was mounted and the crew was assigned a different aircraft. *Frisco Jinny,* in fact, was readied in time for the mission to Schweinfurt and made it there and back with another crew.)

"One good thing about *Dame Satan,*" the squadron commander observed, "she always comes back."

A small icy sensation ran through Winslow. *I wish he hadn't said that,* he thought. The Jeep drove off and they resumed their waiting.

For Brigadier General Robert B. Williams the frustrations and tensions had begun, as they had for LeMay, very early in the morning with that blanket of fog. According to planning he was to fly in a 91st Bomb Group aircraft from the 324th Squadron piloted by Captain Richard Weitzenfeld. It was a veteran group, having been operational since November of 1942, and had suffered through the early period of the strategic daylight bombardment controversy. It was among the first of the American units to strike at Germany proper with a fine reputation for perseverance and dependability. Williams had chosen to fly with the lead group although not in the lead plane: that was occupied by Colonel William M. Gross and crew, with Group Commander Colonel Clemens K. Wurzbach serving as pilot. They would lead what was called the 2nd Air Task Force (according to the initial plan LeMay's was called the 1st Air Task Force). The remainder of Williams's First Division was designated the 3rd Air Task Force, led by Colonel Howard M. Turner who would fly with the 306th Bomb Group formation in the B-17 piloted by Major William S. Raper.

The composition of these two Task Forces was rather complex. To enable Gross and Turner, and in turn Williams, to control the large numbers of aircraft (over two hundred) that were to bomb Schweinfurt that day a great deal of paper work was suffered.

The two Air Task Forces were subdivided into Combat Wings, two to each Task Force. Gross's 2nd Air Task Force was made up of the 101st Combat Wing, with the 91st Bomb Group in the lead, and the 381st as low group; high group of the wing was a "Composite Group" consisting of seven B-17s from the 351st and six each from the 91st and 381st Groups. The 101st Combat Wing was supposed to put up a total of fifty-seven Fortresses for the mission.

A "Composite Combat Wing" rounded out the 2nd Air Task Force and was made up of twenty-one bombers of the 351st Group and eighteen from the 384th Group. To round out the Wing, in turn, a "306th Composite Group" was formed of twenty aircraft from the 306th, 305th, and 92nd Groups. Thus the total of the bombers that comprised the 2nd Air Task Force added up to 116 heavily loaded Flying Fortresses.

Turner's 3rd Air Task Force was to be led by the 102nd Combat Wing: 306th Group (twenty-one Fortresses), 305th Group (twenty), and the 92nd Group with twenty B-17s. This would be followed by the 103rd Provisional Combat Wing with the 379th in the lead (eighteen planes), the 303rd Group (eighteen also) in the low position and a Composite Group (six planes from the 379th and eleven from the 303rd) in the high position. The 3rd Air Task Force, then, mustered 114 bombers. Williams's total force for the mission added up to 230 aircraft.

As Williams would later observe in a report to his chief, General Anderson, "Assembly of all these heterogeneous units was a tedious task to which considerable planning was devoted." The reason for this at times cumbrous heterogeneity was to provide two nearly equal bomber forces capable of attacking the target at Schweinfurt with an evenly distributed, heavy and cumulative and intense bomb pattern—the effect of which hopefully might very well be terminal as far as Schweinfurt was concerned.

The general view was expressed at the early morning briefing of the 384th Bomb Group when the message from Group Commander Colonel Julius K. Lacey was read to the assembled crews: "Congratulations on your excellent performance and bombing on your last two missions. Let's do as well today on our most important target to date." It was to be the Eighth Air Force's first, though not last, mission to Schweinfurt.

Soon after Lacey's morale-raising message, however, the dispiriting impediments began to function. Field Order No. 181 had set the Zero Hour for 0830; by Annex No. 3 it had been set back to 1000. The crews in the 91st Bomb Group had been ready to start engines at 0550.

The deadly wait had begun.

The delay was not confined to the various bomber units, but also to the fighter groups detailed to penetration and withdrawal support. The final Zero Hour was flashed to both R.A.F. and U.S. fighter stations in an emergency message, Amendment No. 4 to Field Order 106:

> Second and third task forces have been unable to take off on schedule due to weather conditions at their bases. They will take off later with the Zero Hr. for this force only as indicated below. Their routes to the target and upon withdrawal will be as indicated in the original F.O. The two forces will be flying in four boxes of approximately sixty B-17s each with 3–5 min. intervals between leaders each box. The two forces will be given penetration support from the enemy coast line as far as Antwerp by 8 squadrons of Spitfires. Spitfire units will withdraw to the south of bomber course.
>
> • • •
>
> Zero Hr and date for Second and Third Task Forces only: 1330 Hrs. 17 August 43.

The five-hour delay meant apprehensive tedium for the waiting crews and frantic activity for the upper echelons flashing the changes to the crews. The juxtaposition was anomalous: near ennui for the one, aggravation and near frenzy for the other. Twenty-two-year-old Lieutenant David M. Williams sat in the lead aircraft, *Oklahoma Oakie,* keeping up with the changes as they came in recalculating "all the times with the new winds each hour as the mission was postponed. Timing was critical and forming under low visibility conditions required split-second timing. I carried two watches for the occasion. My log began to wear thin with all the erasures and many of us felt the mission would be scrubbed." Williams (no relative of General Williams) had been selected to be lead navigator for the mission to Schweinfurt.

Williams, like all the lead navigators for the mission, had been taken off operations several weeks before and with the lead bombardier (in his case, Lieutenant Sam M. Slayton), was whisked off to Brampton Grange, First Bomb Wing Headquarters. "All was very secret and our Group C.O. did not even know what it was all about," Williams recalls. "We were simply grounded and some suspected we had contracted V.D.!

"We went to Bomber Command to study a sand mockup of the target area. I will never forget that area—and during the mission it appeared exactly as the photos and mockups we had studied. I can't recall, but I am sure we knew the target as I vividly recall studying the route from the IP at Würzburg to the target above the [Main] river.

"We only flew one practice mission and it was not a large-scale mission—only lead crews participated—over England largely to simulate altitudes, timing, and fuel consumption, and to practice form-up procedures."

The penetration and withdrawal routes were carefully plotted in order to skirt the known, and infamous, flak concentrations such as those in the vicinity of Aachen, Koblenz, and the Ruhr. A special point was made at the morning's briefing: "The target is a heavily defended area with fifty-six guns reported." This was roughly accurate as it applied to the light antiaircraft guns, but did not take into account the presence of more than forty heavy guns. But, though they were troublesome—sometimes fatally—the flak guns were not to be as effective as the Luftwaffe's fighters.

Ever since the morning encounters with LeMay's Fortresses the various German fighter units had been preparing for the return trip; then by the time they were informed of the Third Division's ruse, the First Division's activities became apparent—and the Luftwaffe was ready and waiting. And they were waiting in even greater numbers than those that had struck the Third Division so violently.

For example, to swell those numbers because "heavy attacks by American formations [were] anticipated on central Germany," units were ordered in from as distant as Jever, near Wilhelmshaven practically on the North Sea. Early in the morning Jagdgeschwader 11 had been ordered south to Rheine, remained there for an hour and a half and then was ordered to the west, to Gilze, in Holland, practically adjacent to the projected bomber route. The fighters had settled in there shortly after eleven o'clock—the Regensburg battle by then had moved considerably eastward. There was nothing for the pilots to do but wait for refueling, rearming, ogle the pretty Dutch girls who served them lunch at their Messerschmitts and—wait some more. As it eventuated, it would be the rocket-bearing Messerschmitts of V-JG 11 that would first challenge the progress of Williams's First Division toward Schweinfurt.

Even that challenge might have never occurred had the expected cancellation come, but of course it did not. But the "importance of the targets" at Schweinfurt was decisive and the Orders of the Day proceeded, initially as scheduled but ultimately went much awry. Mission Record forms contained these Orders of the Day which, following arousal of the crews, neatly timed Breakfast, Briefing, Stations (the time crews were to be assembled at their planes), then Start Engines followed by Taxi and finally Takeoff. The Record also noted the Estimated Time over Target (ETT) and ETR (Estimated Time of Return at home station).

David M. Williams, as lead navigator for the mission, kept a careful log of its evolution. "Station time for crews [for the lead 91st Group] was originally set at about 5:40," he has written, "start engines at 5:50, taxi for lead at 6:05—with takeoff scheduled for 6:20 A.M. Our actual takeoff was at 11:20 . . ."

Williams, as did other lead navigators, spent the long wait readjusting computations to the changing situation. Even the bomb run required a switch. The original early morning plan had taken into consideration the position of the sun and the wind direction at the time they were to have arrived over the target. The run was neatly geared into the unchanging pattern of the Main River and the rail lines that ran through the target area. The river and railroad would still be there, but the sun would not. A change in the axis of attack would be necessary.

The hours ground away and then, at last, word came that the mission was on. Colonel Clemens Wurzbach, the 91st's commander, climbed into the left seat of *Oklahoma Oakie,* the mission's lead aircraft. General Williams boarded Weitzenfeld's *Lady Luck,* leading the group's second element. Williams was carried on the squadron's loading list simply as "Observer."

The 91st Group, as noted earlier, provided two dozen Fortresses for the mission, eighteen in the 2nd Air Task Force lead box and six for the "Composite Group." The first aircraft, in fact, to leave the ground, even before *Oklahoma Oakie,* was William Wheeler's *Our Gang,* lead plane of the composite squadron which was scheduled to join up with the aircraft of the composite group. Wheeler pulled *Our Gang* off the runway at 11:18 and was followed a minute later by yet another famed 91st Group plane, Elwood Arp's *Bomb Boogie.*

The 91st Group Operations Officer, Major David G. Alford, prepared a mission narrative which objectively and laconically summarized it on less than a single page. His description of how the group took off, assembled and headed for Schweinfurt is a model of the unwasted word: "This group took off twenty-four airplanes in the order composite squadron first then the group of eighteen airplanes. Assembly was uneventful. After assembly the group plus composite squadron headed in the general direction of Ridgewell and picked up the 381st and their composite squadron [thus adding twenty-six to the 91st's twenty-four, twenty for the main force and six for the Composite Group]. At Bury St. Edmonds the 351st composite squadron joined us [another seven planes]. The combat wing was in formation after the turn at Brandon. The second combat wing [i. e. the Composite Combat Wing] joined at Splasher 7 with the help of a couple of 'S' turns. Climb was started at Chelmsford, 350-400 feet per minute and 150 M.P.H. Shortly after climb was started the groups started getting strung out so air speed was reduced to 145 for remainder of climb. Altitude was reached at Dutch Coast and cruise started at 160 M.P.H."

Colonel Gross's description is no less succinct while providing greater detail and an occasional personal view. "The plan for assembling the 1st Task Force was fairly simple," he said. "Assembled the 1st Combat Wing in the area east of Cambridge, and the 2nd Combat Wing in the area west of Cambridge, and converged the two Combat Wings on Splasher No. 7. Began climbing a little south and left the coast at Orfordness, one-half minute late at 15,000 feet. Climbed to altitude going over the Channel. Assembly was exactly as planned, with the exception that the high group of the 2nd Combat Wing was a little late. However, all were together and on time at Splasher No. 7. We were able to change the formation and notify the 2nd Combat Wing leader, Colonel [William] Hatcher of the turns coming up so he could maneuver into the best possible position.

"At the end of the climb we were a little closer to the enemy coast than planned because of increase in wind, so we used VHF and closed the formation. Notified them that the lead group [the 91st] would S until formation was closed. Went over the enemy coast at 21,000 feet. The 2nd Combat Wing was echeloned to the right and stacked up slightly. Felt it would be better to have them closer than the five minute interval on crossing the enemy coast and it worked out pretty well."

Colonel Howard M. Turner, leading the 3rd Air Task Force of two wings also, reported pretty much the same about the formation of his units. "Our assembly was without difficulty," he said.

But shaping these two task forces of 230 Fortresses, took time while the Luftwaffe waited. The 91st Group crossed the English coast at Orfordness at 1314, according to the log of Lieutenant David Williams in the nose of *Oklahoma Oakie*. The first German radio intercept was noted at 1342—"Many Allied aircraft eight miles east of Haamstede."

The Messerschmitts of V-JG 11 had been alerted earlier, in fact via radar one minute after the 91st had reached the English Channel, and took off immediately to intercept the formation. Leading the staffel was Heinz Knoke, whose aircraft was fitted with a long tube under each wing—which the pilots call "stovepipes"—from which he could fire rockets into the bomber formation. Noting that the Fortresses were escorted by Spitfires Knoke did not attempt to lead an attack—an air battle encumbered with the stovepipes would have been pointless. Knoke knew that the Spitfires would have to turn back eventually. So he trailed the bombers from the vicinity of Antwerp until Aachen, when his moment came.

He raced into the bomber stream ready to release his rockets when, before he could, found himself in deep trouble. Heavy gunfire from the Fortresses pummeled his Messerschmitt, blowing away one of the stovepipes and puncturing the left wing. He had trouble keeping the plane under control and sensed anxiety about the state of his wing—perhaps the main spar had been damaged, which could lead to the loss of the wing. Gingerly Knoke righted the fighter, turned with caution and released his remaining rocket which passed "through the middle of the formation without hitting anything."

This was the story with most of the rocket-bearing planes; Knoke was certain, however, that two of his men had scored direct hits, but most of the rockets merely shot through the combat boxes without effect.

With an ugly, and disconcerting, hole in his wing Knoke realized there was scant wisdom in remaining airborne—if indeed he could—any longer; he began scanning the ground below for a haven and perhaps a repair depot. As gently as possible he turned away from the battle.

Meanwhile the attack on the bomber formations continued; there seemed to be no break in groups and streams of Messerschmitts and Focke-Wulfs with their red, their orange, their red and yellow noses and spinners—the air churned with the rush of their black-crossed wings. They had a discouraging tendency to come into the bomber stream from directly ahead: "Many attacks," a narrative report of the 91st Group stated, "were made by whole squadrons in line astern, at times as many as twenty to twenty-five coming in one after the other, attacking from the front and at about level."

But that was not the whole story for many "other attacks were made by groups of two to five from the 3, 9, and 11 o'clock positions, from both level and below. Repeated nose attacks by from seven to fifteen enemy aircraft in javelin-up formation made evasive action extremely difficult. A few attacks were made by three and four aircraft coming in abreast and attacking simultaneously."

But there were additional surprises: the air to air bombings and the rockets, such as Knoke's staffel carried. These were, in fact, more psychologically disturbing to the bomber crews—primarily because they were innovations—than tactically effective. The rockets especially could be daunting, for their firing was characterized by a great flash of fire, which all but obscured the enemy fighter, and then this was followed by bursts of black smoke within the bomber boxes nearly double the size of a flak burst. To the inexperienced (and that took in nearly everyone) this new diabolical weapon from the "wily Hun" was impressive and apparently formidable.

Knoke estimated a force of about 250 Fortresses that day, but by the time he tried to knock one out of the sky, it was considerably less. The total had been 230, but that number began decreasing practically over the Channel. The various and often inexplicable mechanical malfunctions began to plague the formations forcing the pilot to abort and leaving gaps in the formations. These were filled as the Fortresses closed up. But the elimination of each plane also subtracted eleven heavy machine guns from the armament of the forces heading for Schweinfurt.

Two of the early returnees came from the lead 91st Group. Lieutenant Robert E. Wine, in the unenviable Tail-end Charlie spot, found it difficult to stay in formation properly because of roughness and loss of power in No. 2 engine. But then more trouble materialized. "Shortly after crossing the European coastline," recalls the plane's navigator, William G. Ryan, "the bombardier, Lieutenant Leonard S. Salleng, passed out from lack of oxygen . . . This, added to the difficulties of staying in formation, prompted Lieutenant Wine to decide to abort the mission. Had he not decided to do this, undoubtedly, we would have been shot down, killed or captured.

"On our way back to base we discovered that Lieutenant Salleng's oxygen line had been merely pinched by a piece of equipment . . ." By this time, of course, it would have been impossible to turn around to catch up with the formation, especially since only three engines were functioning with any efficiency. Wine put himself on the spot for his crew and continued on back to Bassingbourn after unloading his bombs in the Wash. He eventually would have to justify his decision to the Abort Board, which he did, since engineering (which generally was blamed for aborted missions) questioned his evaluation of the trouble.

Another 91st plane which dropped its bombs into the Wash was the much photographed, famed *Bomb Boogie*. (Its fame rested on the fact that its controls had been so shot up on its first mission so that the pilot, a Flight Officer Pitts, landed the plane by using the automatic pilot alone. Pitts had found one member of the crew, the engineer, panicking and refusing to parachute out of the plane. Pitts chose to remain with the plane and brought it in for a remarkable, if bouncy, landing at an R.A.F. field. The other eight members of *Bomb Boogie*'s crew jumped to safety over England. This would lend the plane another distinction—for it may well have been the one plane in the Eighth Air Force from which its crew baled out twice; this would occur in September when the plane was knocked down on the way to Stuttgart).

But on August 17 *Bomb Boogie* developed oxygen trouble. Tail gunner Don Hayes recalls that as a rather memorable, but for his crew relatively uneventful, mission. "We got almost to the German border (over France) when we had to abort. As I recall one engine was acting up, the ball turret was acting up and one of the crew members (waist, I believe) couldn't get oxygen." What had occurred was that the oxygen system simply went bad and would not function in the cockpit at all and was low in the ball turret position; pilot Elwood Arp had no alternative but to swing around, descend to a breathable altitude and head back home. Then, as Hayes would recall, "we landed back at Bassingbourn and waited . . . and waited for the others to return." Arp had set their Fortress down at 1423 (after unloading the bomb load in the Wash); they would have a long wait before the others returned—those that would.

Once the bomber force had left the Channel behind the weather cleared beautifully. Lieutenant David Williams, perched in the Plexiglas nose of the B-17F leading the boxes of Fortresses—by about then the number was reduced to 219, eleven from the various units having been forced back—"had a grandstand view of the entire (scary) mission . . ."

A sizable escort of Spitfires (ninety-six from Nos. 129, 222, 303, 316, 331, 332, 404, and 421 Squadrons, R.A.F.) joined the bombers shortly after 1:30 at a point north of Walcheren (a fact Lieutenant Williams noted in his log—an interesting point, for General Williams, flying alongside, did not spot a friendly fighter during the course of the entire mission). This time it soon became obvious that the German fighters would not be quite so hesitant to attack Allied fighters as they had the Regensburg escort forces. The idea was to keep from tangling with the enemy fighters as much as possible, but at the same time to stop the enemy bombers. The Spitfires, which left the bombers a few miles short of Antwerp, engaged several Me-109s and FW-190s, claiming four of each and losing none of their own.

Following the withdrawal of the Spitfires, forty-one Thunderbolts of the 4th Fighter Group led by Colonel Donald Blakeslee took over the escort job. They spotted what appeared to be the two trailing Combat Wings to their north. The 4th was then east of Antwerp. Upon arriving at the rendezvous point Blakeslee saw no bombers at all; he led the P-47s onward and, in the vicinity of Duren, "caught leading box of bombers, then being attacked from astern and underneath by 8/10 E/A which broke away on approach of our group. Starboard turn made and group returned along the same route [as they had come in on], passing over two more boxes of bombers. First of these boxes being shadowed by nine E/A but group unable to close and E/A evaded . . ." Blakeslee reported seeing, close up, one Me-109 "camouflaged blue under the wings and bore a black cross in a white square on the fuselage." Also in the vicinity of Hasselt "a large aircraft, believed a B-17, seen to go down exploding as it struck the ground. No chutes seen."

It had been rather inconclusive and frustrating. More frustration ensued when the Thunderbolts of the 78th Fighter Group, supposed to take over from the 4th to escort the bombers east of Eupen to the limit of their fuel supply, was eight minutes late for rendezvous. Leading the formation of about forty P-47s (seven had had to abort because of defective belly tanks), Lieutenant Colonel James J. Stone reported "small gaggles of FW-190s and Me-109s scattered at approach of group" and that "no E/A seen attacking bombers. E/A appeared to have just intercepted bombers near Aachen."

In the vicinity of Aachen the 84th Squadron of the 78th Group turned to see a formation of twin engined enemy aircraft approaching the B-17s from astern. They were about 4,000 feet below the Fortresses and climbing. Squadron leader Major Eugene P. Roberts, above the bombers at around 25,000 feet, rolled into a diving turn to the left followed by his wingman, Flight Officer

Top American airmen in the European Theatre at the time of the double-strike mission: Generals Ira C. Eaker (left) and Carl Spaatz (right). The former was head of the Eighth Air Force in August 1943 and Spaatz commanded the Northwest African Air Forces for Operation Torch.

U. S. AIR FORCE

Brigadier General Frederick L. Anderson, who, as leader of the 8th Bomber Command, was forced to make the lonely decision as to whether or not his bombers would strike at Regensburg and Schweinfurt on August 14, 1943, despite poor weather over England.

Brigadier General Robert B. Williams, an old B-17 hand, who headed the First Air Division and flew to Schweinfurt with the 91st Bomb Group.

Colonel Curtis E. LeMay (right), commander of the Third Air Division which attacked Regensburg and flew on to North Africa. LeMay flew in the lead plane of the 96th Bomb Group. To his right is Brigadier General Haywood S. Hansell, Jr., one of the architects of the air planning, beginning with AWPD-1 (Air War Plans Division) and going through the Combined Bomber Offensive.

U. S. AIR FORCE

U. S. AIR FORCE

The curse of aerial operations out of England: English weather.

MARTIN PHOTO

To assist the big bombers, mediums were dispatched to attack German airfields alon the projected pathway of the Fortresses. These Martin B-26s of the 387th Group ar bombing a German airfield in France—although this photo was not taken on Augu 17, 1943.

Left, David Williams, lead navigator, 91st Bomb Group, for the mission to Schweinfurt.

Right, Dunstan T. Abel, 96th Bomb Group, lead navigator to Regensburg and Africa.

U. S. AIR FORCE

Left, Captain T. F. Kenny, pilot of the B-17 that carried mission commander Curtis LeMay to Regensburg and beyond to North Africa.

Right, Richard Weitzenfeld (here a Lt. Col.), who was pilot of the aircraft which carried the Schweinfurt commander, Robert B. Williams, round trip, although not without a brief stop en route.

U. S. AIR FORCE

Left, John B. Kidd, Operations Officer of the 100th Bomb Group, who had spent exhausting days and nights planning the 100th's part in the mission only to be rudely awakened the morning of August 17, 1943.

Right, Gale Cleven, 100th Bomb Group, outstanding pilot and leader, who refused to permit his men to leave their stricken Fortress — and thus brought them safely to Africa.

J. B. KIDD

"Little Friends" on the ground and "Big Friends" in the air. The Republic P-47, w an extra fuel drop tank under the wing and Boeing B-17s overhead.

Bomber crewman's view of fighter escort—above the Fortress formation: Thundert contrails reveal the presence of friendly aircraft.

Contender: Focke-Wulf 190, one of the most formidable German fighter planes.

Contender: Messerschmitt 109; although older than the FW-190 it was still, in the hands of a skilled pilot, a hazard to the bombers. Coming in head on, as in this shot, it was an unnerving adversary.

U. S. AIR FORCE

Prime target of the contenders: a B-17. German fighter pilots were more concerne with stopping the bombers than with mixing with the Thunderbolts. This Fortres belonged to the 390th Bomb Group, which flew in high position on August 17 and los six aircraft. This photo was taken over Germany, although not during the double-strik mission.

J. B. KIDD

Target of the Luftwaffe: greatest losses during the Regensburg phase of double stri were sustained by the 100th Bomb Group, in the last and low position of the bomb formation—almost always the most deadly spot.

AIR FORCE

ɔd formations were essential to the safety of the bombers; vapor trails, such as these, ·ever, revealed the presence of the bombers to fighters making them easy to spot.

D. HAYES

Famous plane that did not get to Schweinfurt. Mechanical problems forced pilot Elw D. Arp to turn back before reaching Germany (he is directly under the nose of plane at far right) and return to England. At left are radio operator John Wenning and tail gunner Don Hayes. Waist gunner Dean Millward is standing in center of photo. Men and plane belonged to 401st Squadron of the 91st Bomb Group.

amous plane that did not get to Regensburg. It was around this aircraft that the legend f the "Bloody 100th" grew. Unknown to the crew the wheels of the plane had lowered uring combat so that when approached by German fighters they continued shooting. his was considered a terrible breach of the Code of the Air and Picklepuss *was merci-ssly attacked and knocked down. Although the men in the back row cannot all be lentified (there being a mixture of ground and air crew), kneeling in the front row are eft to right): Edwin Tobin, Robert Knox, Ernest Warsaw, and Robert Whitaker. First vo men standing in back row (from left) are Frank Tychewicz and Joseph LaSpada; oth were killed that day.*

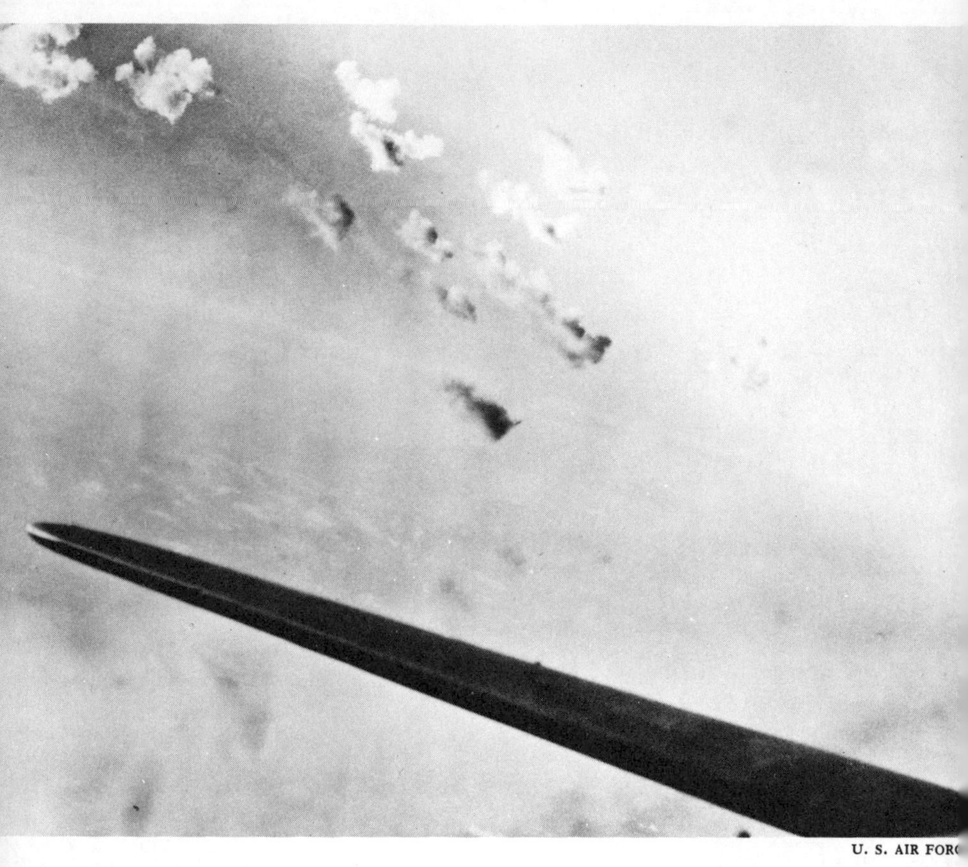

U. S. AIR FORC

Rockets bursting in a bomber formation; these were lobbed into the combat boxes fro German aircraft that flew alongside the bombers, out of range of the bombers' guns. direct hit by rocket could tear off a wing or split a Fortress in two.

U. S. AIR FORCE

Strike photo of the 96th Bomb Group hitting Regensburg, August 17, 1943. Completed Messerschmitt aircraft are parked on airfield just to the left of the bomb-burst concentration.

U. S. AIR FORCE

Regensburg burning. A lone Fortress hovers over the smoke clouds in lower center of

U. S. AIR FORCE

The Third Air Division over the Alps after bombing Regensburg; these are probably Fortresses of the lead 96th Group, there being no others preceding them.

U. S. AIR

Fortresses leaving a burning Schweinfurt. Target area is obscured by smoke, making the job of subsequent groups difficult.

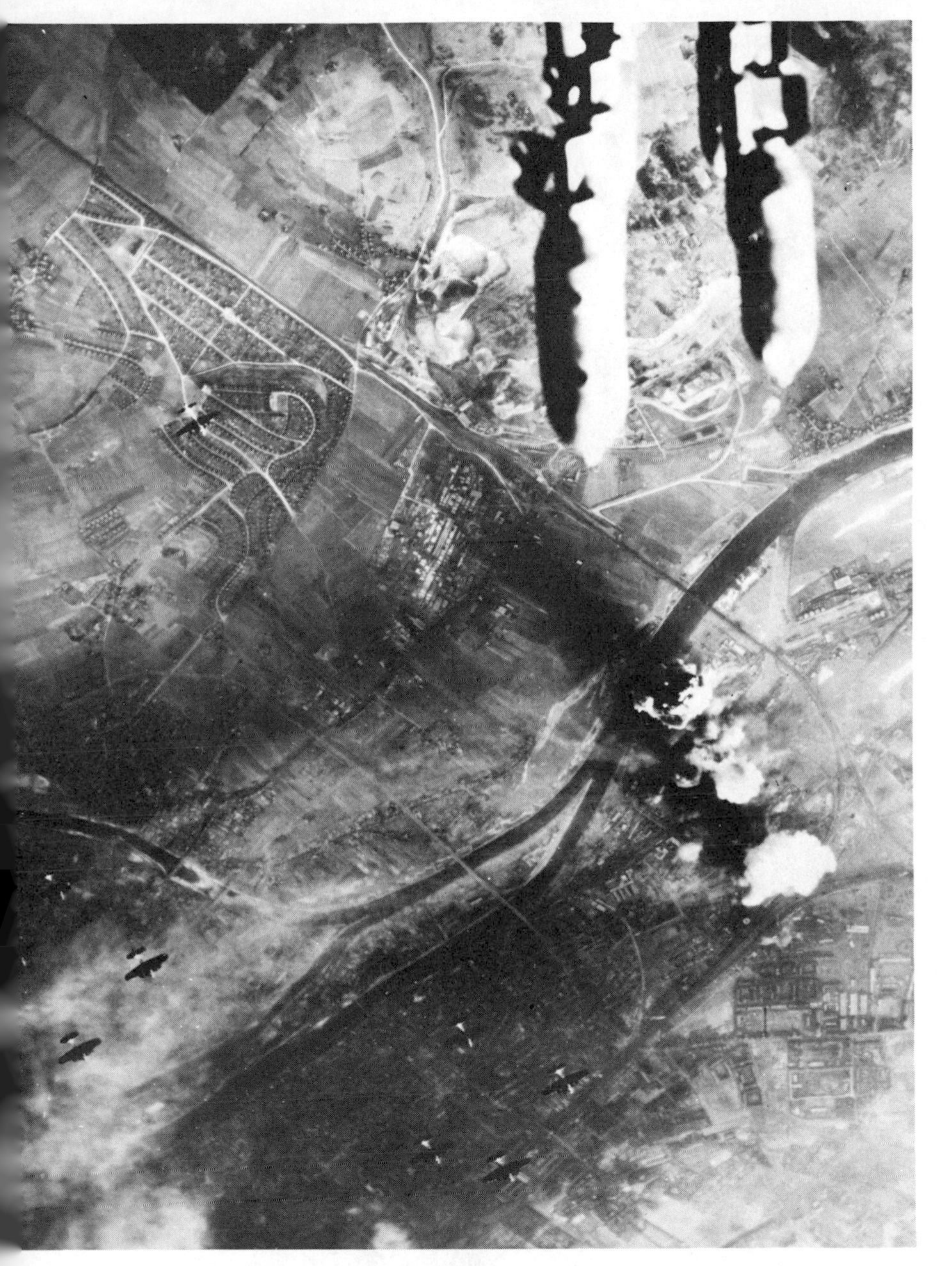

ombs Away, Schweinfurt, August 17, 1943. As bombs from a lower group strike, ombs from a higher group begin to fall toward the target.

J. B. KIDD

North Africa after the bombing of Regensburg. Crews had to do their own maintenar because original plans for them went awry—the war in North Africa having mov westward from their landing areas. Fuel barrels await pumping by hand to refuel Fortress for the return to England.

HARRY CROSBY

Fezzed and helmeted members of the 100th Group make plans for another visit nearby Arab settlement for souvenirs. Navigator Frank D. Murphy (front left) car an Arabian dagger at his waist; Major John Egan wears his insignia jauntily, while Charles Cruickshank helps hold the map. The strain of the battle of Regensburg is apparent. One of the souvenirs brought back by the 100th was a tiny donkey na "Mohammed."

Glenn H. Koontz. At 19,000 feet they came in behind a formation of "about eight enemy aircraft." Roberts selected an Me-110, "which was painted white," and when he had caught up to the plane opened fire at 250 yards. He could see he was hitting the Messerschmitt: ragged punctures opened up along the wing and then a bright flash of flame erupted from the left engine and soon after black smoke began pouring from the right engine also. He then pulled away to make certain that Koontz was covered. The wingman, following, observed the German plane in trouble with "about fifteen or twenty feet of flame trailing" and, as he saw Roberts pull up, fired a burst into the 110 for good measure. At the same moment the aircraft exploded.

Koontz, blinded by the smoke, pulled back on the control stick to get out of the smoke and debris. But so did the Messerschmitt swerve upward because of the explosion and Koontz felt that heart-stopping crunch that accompanies a mid-air collision. Roberts, meanwhile, attempting to get at other enemy aircraft, managed to get one quick glance at the Messerschmitt by then in "a steep dive, engine pouring black smoke and pieces falling." One of the pieces may have been about eighteen inches of Koontz's left stabilizer. Undaunted in the incident, Koontz rejoined the formation for the flight back to base. (He confirmed Major Roberts's claim but made none for himself.)

Flight Officer Peter E. Pompetti, in the second element of Major Roberts's squadron shortly after their dive, pulled up behind a white Me-210 (these white aircraft may have been Russian veterans), only to have it pull away in evasive action. Pompetti then dived after him, got him in sight and practically fishtailed as his shots raked the plane from wingtip to wingtip, from right to left—and across the fuselage. Both engines gushed flames and the last Pompetti saw the burning plane "tumbling down, nose over tail."

Although other German aircraft were seen, there were no further encounters and, low on fuel, the P-47s of the 78th Group returned to Duxford. It was here, after he had landed his Thunderbolt, that Koontz realized the extent of the damage from the collision with the Me-110. The German plane's entire tail section had been sliced off, but only a portion of Pompetti's; he observed that during the flight home he "did not notice any difference in the flying characteristics of the plane."

This spoke well for the Thunderbolt (the 78th at this time was equipped with P-47Cs and Ds), which had only in the previous April been introduced into combat. Early operations revealed some problems. It was, indeed, a tough aircraft, but it required some adjustment and familiarity. Its behavior in an extremely high speed dive could be chilling. This was illustrated by a true folktale that occurred about a month before actually postdating the double strike mission. This occurred over Emden when an overeager, and perhaps not too experienced P-47 pilot, made a steep dive on an FW-190. Having made his pass, he found himself—because of the delay in pulling out—in a power dive. To his dismay he found the controls without effect. He could not pull the big ship out no matter how hard he yanked back on the stick. He prayed, however, as he attempted other possibilities. He rolled the stabilizer trim tab full back; the aircraft shuddered but continued in the plunge and the pilot continued praying.

After 10,000 feet or so of pure terror and prayer, the plane began to come out slowly until—at 5000 feet—it pulled out and the pilot assumed control. His words at this moment: "Thank you, Lord—I'll take over now."

The Thunderbolt proved itself during the fighting on August 17, 1943—provided it could actually meet with the German fighters. The initial, Regensburg, phase had found the Luftwaffe rather careful, waiting for the P-47s and Spitfires to turn back before raking through the bomber boxes. There were complaints from LeMay ("Our fighter escort had black crosses on their wings") and Williams concurred. Others did not agree—it being, to some extent, a matter of positioning in the bomber stream. Colonel Turner, who led Williams's 3rd Task Force, commented that

"The pursuit escort was very effective with us. We didn't get any attacks going in as long as we had our escort."

There was a tendency for the Thunderbolt groups to fly rather high above the bombers, expecting the traditional "Hun in the sun," but when the German fighters came in from under the Fortresses, or swooped in around the flank of the formation and then rammed in headlong, there was little that could be done. But then there was the fuel consideration and the fact that the fighters simply could not cover the route to and from the targets and, generally, that was when the Luftwaffe took its most frightful bite out of the bomber formations.

EIGHT

"We were under severe attack constantly from penetration of enemy territory all the way through to the target and halfway back over the Channel," David M. Williams remembers. As lead navigator for the vanguard 91st Group, he experienced the "scary" mission from delayed beginning to bitter end.

"If my log looks a little unkempt and sparse," he explained, "it was because I was on the twin fifties frequently and we had spent 50-caliber machine-gun cartridges almost up to our knees. Occasionally, the log fell to the floor and became buried. But primarily I busied myself with the task of navigating . . ."

The intense battle made proper navigation difficult. For example, written across a portion of Williams's log is a note: *Tell radio to get off air*. Williams explains this: because of the incessant German fighter attacks, "the gunners would call in the position of the fighters almost constantly. However, in the lead ship it was imperative to keep this to a minimum to allow communications between myself and the pilot.

"We were approaching a mandatory turn in accordance to flight plan and would be subjected to intense flak if we didn't make the turn immediately (don't forget you can't turn a large formation on a dime—it takes time!). The radio man was calling out the directions of a particularly heavy attack and I could not get through to the pilot. So I scrawled the note and showed it to Pete Adams [the backup navigator] and he passed the message along to the top-turret. I found it more effective to communicate directly with the pilot, rather than pass up a series of notes to him."

How Williams managed to attend to his main chore was one of the day's several miracles. *Oklahoma Oakie* was hit often—the Plexiglas nose in which Williams plotted and manned the fifties was shot up. And, as they would learn later, a 20-mm. shell entered the main fuel tank in the left wing and stayed there unexploded. Also, "a bullet came through my gloves and pant legs without touching me—I was skinny at the time!"

On *Oklahoma Oakie*'s left wing flew the B-17 piloted by Lieutenant William Munger, its crew fighting off the same German fighters. Suddenly the plane "was blown completely out of the sky," the explosion was violent enough to tear away a portion of the left wing of *Oklahoma Oakie*.

The battle was especially vicious on the way into Schweinfurt. It was Colonel Turner who would later comment that his task force had no navigational problem. "We were aided by the fact that we could practically follow a line of parachutes and B-17s all the way in."

Eight of those parachutes came out of the B-17 named *Eagle's Wrath,* piloted by Lieutenant Anthony Arcaro in the vicinity of Frankfurt. The two who remained inside the doomed Fortress were not capable of using their chutes nor did they need them. Radio operator Sergeant Delmar E. Kaech of this 91st Group aircraft recalled that mission: "I have no idea of how long we were under attack by fighters, but I think it was from the time we passed over Antwerp and the time we were shot down over Frankfurt.

"There were many targets to shoot at and at one time I caught a fleeting glance of a B-17 diving at us from the front and above and released a short burst before I realized it was a B-17. It must have been out of control as it was still in a dive when it passed by my range of vision. We were all too busy to pass on any information of what was going on . . ."

Several group narratives underscored the quality of the fighter attacks. The 381st Bomb Group's summary described the attacks as "exceptionally determined, persistent and savage . . . E/A frequently closed to spitting distance." Many groups described "pack attacks," as swarms of fighters overwhelmed a single aircraft, or concentrated on a specific squadron, or even group. Such attacks battered Arcaro's Fortress, raking it from nose to tail until all communications were shot out and the plane itself crippled beyond any hope—and two men lay dead inside the plane.

Arcaro remembered the German fighters coming in at him four at a time "from around 11 o'clock and a little high." They would come in disconcertingly close, for he remembered one Me-109 that swept in, fired and then rolled over, passing by the nose of *Eagle's Wrath* so closely that he could see the German pilot as if in a close-up. "He came in right across our nose upside down. His slipstream shook the hell out of us and I damn near ran into him!"

One of these attacks placed 20-mm. shells in the nose section injuring navigator Lieutenant H. K. Warner seriously (although he did parachute from the plane he did not survive the jump). The shells ignited the oxygen system and the whole nose spewed flame. Arcaro knew then it was time to get out of *Eagle's Wrath.*

"We got as far as Frankfurt," Kaech went on. "The ball-turret operator [H. K. Michaud) was killed in action. I was trying to get him out of the ball-turret when the co-pilot [Lieutenant R. Niemczyk] came aft to tell us to bail out. I have no idea what altitude we were at—anyway, when I got to the radio room where I had left my chest pack the plane went into a dive. When the automatic pilot took over I went out the nearest exit, via the radio operator's hatch, and pulled the ripcord immediately on clearing the plane. That's the last I remember until approaching the ground." Kaech, along with pilot Arcaro, co-pilot Niemczyk, navigator Warner (who did not survive), bombardier Lieutenant W. E. Glover and gunners Staff Sergeants E. F. Lindholm, R. E. Dearth, and W. G. Golden managed to get out of *Eagle's Wrath* to spend the rest of the war in prisoner of war camps. The plane then became the flaming coffin for ball-turret gunner Michaud and flight engineer Sergeant W. Jones—who had taken off that morning on what was to have been his last official mission. For both, the quick and the dead, it became the last mission of the war.

This was true also of *Dame Satan,* the plane the 322nd Squadron Commander had assured its crew "always comes back." It neither accomplished that, nor did it even get to Schweinfurt. The 91st's formation suffered battering from the Luftwaffe as soon as the Thunderbolt escort was forced to turn back, *Dame Satan* escaped damage, although one of its wing aircraft dropped out of the formation. As for the German fighters, Winslow noted in his diary, "Most of them were FW-190s and some of their pilots had plenty of nerve—rolling, banking and twisting through our formation with their guns blazing all the time . . .

"The deeper we got into enemy territory, the more we were attacked. As we were nearing the target, a fighter came in from '12 o'clock'—straight on towards the nose and hit the supercharger on our number two engine with its fire. We started to lose speed and altitude so the pilot [Jack Hargis] called down for me to salvo the bombs. I opened the bomb-bay doors and flipped a switch. When the panel lights indicated that the bombs had gone, I closed the doors again; but we were still slipping behind the rest of the formation.

"A few of the fighters took advantage of our vulnerable position and attacked. We fought them off and the tail-gunner [Staff Sergeant Leland Judy] called in that he had hit one and set it on fire! [Hargis] announced that we would have to turn back and asked the navigator [Lieutenant Carl Darling] for a course out. We turned and took a heading toward Belgium. This would take us over the narrowest part of the Channel where we would have to 'ditch' in the water, for we did not have enough gas left to get us all the way back.

"The fighters left us for a while and during the 'breathing

space' I reloaded by gun. Unfortunately though, the only belt of ammunition left was the one with short rounds in it but I had no choice [on the way out, when the machine guns were tested over the Channel, it was discovered that one belt carried several short tracer rounds which jammed the gun]. We flew back over southern Germany, giving all the cities in our path a wide berth for each one would shoot up an umbrella of flak as we approached it."

The crew of *Dame Satan* was in serious trouble; they were all alone in the sky, with a damaged aircraft, low on ammunition and with no escort to protect them from the Luftwaffe once its fighters, as was inevitable, would materialize again.

Somehow they managed to get across Germany without enemy interception, but they were yet to pass over the hornet's nest, Belgium. As they neared Brussels their luck began draining away; the enemy fighters had arrived. The first made the usual head-on pass, just slightly from the left, firing but scored no hits. Then the second approached, head-on also, but slightly from the right. Winslow could see the cannons flashing in the wings and began firing back at the approaching fighter. He succeeded in getting off no more than a couple of rounds when the defective—or tampered with, as the crew believed—ammunition belt jammed the gun.

This fighter did not miss. *Dame Satan* lurched in the air and began to shudder, making it difficult for pilot Hargis and co-pilot Carl Smith to maintain control. Winslow that instant looked up to see the belly of the German fighter pass almost directly over him and over the interphone he heard, "Oh . . . I'm hit!"

"Who's hit?" Hargis asked.

It was radio operator Sergeant Victor Ciganek, who had been wounded in the chest.

"Prepare to bail out," Hargis ordered. "Someone help Vic."

In the nose Winslow and navigator Darling prepared to jump. Winslow tore up some papers and threw them out a window. Then came the word, "Bail out when ready, bail out when ready."

Darling motioned to Winslow to follow, then went to a small exit door just aft of the nose and jumped. Winslow heard Hargis again, "Hurry-up you guys. I can't hold this thing up all day!"

Winslow would recall later: "I took a last deep breath of oxygen and kneeled at the escape hatch. Things below on the ground looked so small. I bent forward and tumbled out head first. Instantly there was a terrific jerk and a sensation of being pulled through space at a tremendous speed. Something was wrong. I couldn't see, but I could still hear the plane's engines roaring. I decided I must be caught on the tail; my chute had opened too quickly! I was terrified by thoughts of what might happen if I was still caught when the plane crashed. Suddenly the parachute twisted and popped open above me like a beautiful white umbrella. The noise of the ship died away."

As he floated down in a great, unreal, silence, Winslow counted six other parachutes. Where were the other three? Probably the wounded Ciganek had been helped out of the plane before anyone else and may have already been close to the ground (he was found and taken to a German hospital). Star Tucker, who had been informed just before the mission began that he had been promoted would not live to sew on the extra stripe. When he was found, it was found that his parachute had not been opened (Winslow later learned from Tucker's father that the gunner had suffered from fainting spells). The other missing chute belonged to pilot Jack Hargis; it apparently ripped upon opening and he plummeted to the ground.

Four of the floating parachutes belonged to co-pilot Smith, engineer Technical Sergeant Jarvis Allen, waist gunner Staff Sergeant Al DiMinno and tail gunner Judy, all of whom eventually, after evading German patrols, and with the help of the Belgian-French underground, made it back to England. Another chute was navigator Darling's, who succeeded in getting as far as Paris before being captured.

Of the others who were taken captive, Ciganek, with his chest wound, was first. Staff Sergeant Gerold Tucker (one of the waist gunners) also suffered an injury the moment his chute opened; the harness had slipped and resulted in a broken right arm. Winslow, descending from above the six parachutes, was having his problems despite having successfully slipped loose of *Dame Satan*'s tail section. "The wind was swinging me so much that at times I thought my parachute would collapse. I could see green fields and woods below with a few farms and buildings scattered about.

"As I neared the ground I heard dogs barking and imagined that the German patrols might be using them to search for us. I noticed that I was drifting sideways with the wind and toward a wagon that had sharp poles sticking up on it. I pulled a shroud-line and slipped sharply to the left. I must have spilled some air from the 'chute in doing this for I hit the ground very hard and felt my right leg snap." (Winslow, as revealed later in an X ray, suffered a compound fracture—his right leg was broken in three places; when Gerold Tucker landed with his broken arm, he succeeded also in breaking a foot. Both Winslow and Tucker, with the aid of the Belgian underground—and the ministrations of a remarkable doctor, Dr. Jean DeGavre—eluded the Germans for some three months after *Dame Satan* went down. They were finally turned over to the Gestapo by a girl posing as an underground escort. They spent the rest of the war in German prison camps. When Winslow was evacuated from Stalag-Luft 1, near Barth, Germany, by Fortresses of the First Air Division, including some carrying the "Triangle A" on their fins—from his own former 91st Group.)

The hardest hit group, the 381st, second in line after the 91st, reported what had occurred in a post-mission Narrative: "Enemy aircraft began their attacks a few minutes after the enemy coast was crossed, although attacks were not numerous either on the route out or the route back while we had fighter support. Combats continued until the enemy coast was reached on the route back, with attacks diminishing in number in the vicinity of the target.

Attacks began at 1340 hours and continued to 1635 hours, a total of 2 hours 55 minutes."

The 381st, the low group of the formation suffered the fate of so many of the low elements that day. Not that the 91st did not bleed also, being sandwiched between the high Composite Group and the 381st. Those German fighters that slashed through the 91st found more targets in the trailing and lower 381st.

Here is a transcription of the report prepared for the group's operations officer (S-3), Major Conway S. Hall (exactly as it appears in the Narrative, somewhat out of chronology) enumerating the 381st's losses:

(A) 42-3227-G went down approximately 51 degrees 10 N—05 degrees 00 E. No. 1 engine feathered and No. 2 engine on fire. Nine chutes seen, one did not open. Time 1415. Another ship also reported 10 chutes seen to leave this a/c and all opened. Still another ship reported this a/c down close to Vogelsand Airport, Germany, all men bailed out.

(B) 42-30245 went down at approximately 49 degrees 50 N—08 degrees 10 E. Appeared hit in cockpit by two e/a. Ten chutes seen. Time 1430. Another ship reported this a/c made a complete slow roll under fighter attack and went into a spin. One chute came out. Time 1435.

(C) 42-29978 went down at 49 degrees 50 N—08 degrees 10 E. No. 4 engine hit, right wing on fire, five chutes seen. Time 1425.

(D) 42-29983 seen with No. 2 engine smoking. Salvoed bombs and began to go down under control between Coblenz and Frankfurt, Germany. Five chutes came out. Time approximately 1445. Another ship reported this a/c salvoed his bombs, peeled off to left and started back with No. 2 engine out. Time 1420.

(E) 42-29731 was hit over target. No. 3 and No. 4 engines out, five chutes seen. Another ship reported this a/c with No. 3 and 4 engines out. Went down in long glide to 17,000 when lost sight of. Another ship reported this a/c hit by flak and 8 chutes seen to come out. Another ship reported this a/c went away below group with No. 3 and 4 engines out right over target. Two bailed out. No fighters around him. Still another ship reported this a/c with No. 3 and 4 engines feathered, one smoking on a 2200 heading, letting down gradually on a straight course. Yet another ship reported this a/c lost two engines over target and pulled out heading for Switzerland which it appeared he could make.

(F) 42-3225 dropped out of formation at 1630 between Bonn and Aachen. Fighters were all around him.

(G) 42-30140 went down under control at 49 degrees 50 N—08 degrees 50 E at 1440. Another ship reported this a/c had No. 2 engine burning fifteen minutes inside coast after first enemy attack. Went into a very steep dive. Three chutes came out, then one moment later entire ship caught fire. Shortly after entire tail assembly from ball turret back snapped off and five more chutes came out. Another ship reported seven chutes came out of this a/c.

(H) 42-3220 went down at 49 degrees 50 N—07 degrees 20 E during a fighter attack. Still under control with one engine feathered. Time 1425. Another ship reported this a/c had a broken windshield before target and that ten minutes before target one chute came out. After target was flying along level when went into a spin.

(I) 42-3092 at 1358. Seven chutes came out of a ship believed to be this one. Two chutes failed to open.

(J) 42-3092 was seen to go down at 1420 near Vogelsand Airport. All men bailed out. Another ship reported 10 men bailed out of this a/c but one did not open. Right wing on fire.

The final loss, reported to S-4 (Supply), had a happy ending: "Our A/C No. 735, Flight Officer G. R. Darrow, pilot, ditched in the Engish Channel at 2330 hours. The R.A.F. Station at Manston reported that the entire crew all O.K. Had been picked up by the Air-Sea Rescue and were being billeted at Manston for the night." The following day a Fortress was dispatched to Manston to pick up Darrow and his uninjured crew and returned them to the 381st's base at Ridgewell.

All groups prepared such narratives after the mission; all are equally concise—and yet contradictory, containing variants of the same incident as seen from different aircraft by men under varying conditions of terror and stress. The bulk of the narratives in so far as losses were concerned concentrated on those of the group itself, but most also reported distressed aircraft from other groups as well. The 91st Narrative, for example, reported "One B-17 seen going down near Treis [about one-third of the way across Germany, but still a long way from Schweinfurt], at 1433 hours, from 20,000 feet, split in half in mid-air and folded up, with one parachute out." Could this be the plane mentioned in the 381st's Paragraph "G"? The times do not agree; the 91st observer saw the split Fortress seven minutes *before* the one reported by the 381st's. Also there is a discrepancy in the number of chutes leaving the aircraft—but that was typical of many of the reports. The battle moved along at about 150 miles an hour and none of the action remained frozen long enough for anyone, no matter how cool under fire, to record it. Besides, there was simply too much going on for anyone to remember: pinpointing a moment in time and a moving particle in space (though to the ten men within each of those particles that moment was eternity and their craft the universe).

Such a universe was *Lucky Thirteen* of the 384th Bomb Group which brought up the rear of 101st Combat Wing. Leading the 384th's eighteen Fortresses was Lieutenant Colonel Thomas Beckett as lead pilot; his co-pilot was John Butler, navigator Edward Knowling and bombardier Joseph W. Baggs. The last plane in the formation was *Lucky Thirteen,* last and low in "Coffin Corner." This aircraft was not the crew's regular plane; that had been *The Battle Wagon* which had been so badly shot up two days before while bombing German airfields in France that it was sent, in the words of waist gunner Staff Sergeant L. Corwin Miller, "to the hanger for an autopsy."

On the mission to Schweinfurt Miller came close to suffering the same fate. "The 384th took off," he recalls, "made our rendezvous and headed across the Channel. The last time I looked at the ground we were still over the inlets of Holland. That's when we met our first attack. I must have been hit by the first pass. A 20-mm. exploded in the radio compartment and three fragments hit me, one passing through my right lung. There was no pain—it just felt like someone slapped me across the back with a board. It knocked me off balance, but I regained my position at my gun where I remained until I lost consciousness from loss of blood. I didn't realize I was hit that bad until I felt myself going out.

"From there on in the attacks were pretty constant. It was five and a half hours before we got back to base and during that time I regained and lost consciousness a number of times. I had no idea where we were, but I was thankful we were still in the air. I would regain consciousness to find Staff Sergeant John F. Schimenek firing first his gun and then mine. I could look out the window and see enemy fighters. I could hear and feel the concussion from the antiaircraft fire. The 'whump' would lift me off the floor and the empty brass would roll in under me. I signaled for more oxygen and Schimenek opened the valve for me.

"Staff Sergeant Frank [Francis] Gerow, our radio operator, would remove my oxygen mask periodically and scrape the frozen blood out so that I could breathe."

Meanwhile the group continued on to bomb Schweinfurt, losing five of its planes, and once the bombs dropped the turn was made and pilot First Lieutenant Philip M. Algar and navigator First Lieutenant Frank A. Celantano brought the *Lucky Thirteen* back home as quickly as possible. Algar descended as much as was safely possible and Celantano rapidly calculated the shortest distance, skirting flak centers, back to England. Thus was the oxygen preserved for the gravely wounded Miller as they raced with the Grim Reaper. At the same time the gunners were faced with the German fighters that swarmed to attack the stray.

Miller's perceptions came and went; loss of blood removed him into another world of foggy unreality as faces and things came into focus and then faded away into a peaceful blackness. "The last time I regained consciousness while still in the ship was just as we were landing at Grafton Underwood. I could feel the ship touch down and the ground never felt so good to me as it did then."

He was, of course, in a serious condition—and considering the long five or more hours of suffering from a critical wound, his survival was a miracle. "I was taken to our base hospital where Dr. Stroud did the initial work that saved my life. The next day I regained consciousness at the 160 Station Hospital. I can't say enough in praise of the doctors and nurses who attended me. They made me feel like I was the only patient they had and I'm sure that the rest of the airmen felt the same way. Lieutenant Catherine Ventre of Altoona, Pennsylvania, went out of her way and got me some chicken (something unheard of outside the black market). This was the first food I was able to eat." The war ended for L. Corwin Miller over bloody Schweinfurt.

Although the 384th flew in the unenviable low and rear position in formation of the Composite Wing, its losses (five) amounted to less than half of those of the 381st which flew the same spot in the preceding 101st Combat Wing. The Luftwaffe seemed determined to get the lead wing—or so it appeared to tail gunner Staff Sergeant Tom Murphy manning the twin guns in the aft section of *The Joker,* Captain William Baultrisitus's Fortress (532nd Squadron, 381st Group).

Murphy had suffered his first surprise when he noticed that the German fighters bore in on the formation right through their own flak, "I had never seen this before! Normally, they wait just outside the barrage until we fly through it. But today they can't wait to get at us. As I watch, a Fortress from the 91st and then one from the 351st fall out of the sky. No parachutes come out of either one." Then he notices one of his own squadron's B-17s slip off on one wing and then fall out of formation, a *coup de grâce* follows an instant later when a direct flak hit ripped off the right wing.

The flak apparently had gotten the 532nd Squadron's range,

for a moment later a burst exploded under *The Joker* tossing the big bomber up more than a hundred feet, and consequently spoiling Murphy's aim on an oncoming Me-109. The concussion lifted the plane into the prop wash of the leading 351st Group and Baultrisitus and co-pilot First Lieutenant Arthur Sample have their hands full keeping the Fortress from flipping over onto its back. They heave and pull on the bucking control columns and finally force the plane back into formation.

By this time the German fighters have begun lining up for more attacks. "I have an Me-109 in my sights and I see his wings flash as he discharges his pair of rockets. They come in on our level, just a little to our left. As they get close, I yell to the pilot on the intercom, 'Tail gunner to pilot! Pull up, quick!'"

Baultrisitus yanked powerfully on the control column by instinct, for this is a crew that functions together closely and if Murphy shouts pull up, then it was time to pull up. According to Murphy's account, the two rockets passed under *The Joker* and through the formation ahead. Bracketing in one of the 532nd's planes, the rockets burst and destroy the aircraft. The squadron, once six strong, has been cut in half. The Messerschmitt then dropped its rocket firing equipment and turned to attack with its normal guns. Busy as he had been firing Murphy found that he had inadvertently pulled out his interphone connection. To plug back into the Fortress's intercom he momentarily let his guns go and they drooped downward. To the German pilot this would appear as if the tail gunner of *The Joker* had been hit, leaving the plane very vulnerable to an attack from the rear.

The Me-109 bore in on the B-17 as Murphy plugged in his cord, then turned to see what was going on outside the aircraft. Plenty: he found himself staring directly into the nose cannon of the German fighter about fifty feet away. Grasping the gun handles, Murphy aimed point blank at the German fighter, squeezed, and "the Me-109 explodes with its pilot inside."

Everywhere Murphy could see there were signs of destruction and loss: the heavens were scarred with black, oily smoke, the orange flame of burning metal, the brilliant, brief white flash of fuel, of bombs truly bursting in air and the painful death of men. As he observed German aircraft dropping bombs on the American formations, and after seeing two German fighters appear to have deliberately rammed two Fortresses, a curious calm descended upon Murphy in the tail of *The Joker.*

"Fear leaves me entirely," he would later recall. "I know this is my last day on earth. I have never seen the Germans give up their lives to ram us before. If they have the guts to do that to stop us, I don't see how we can survive."

But survive he did, as did the entire crew of *The Joker* that day, the plane suffering only a puncture through the left elevator. *The Joker* bombed with the 381st Bomb Group formation, the last of the 101st Combat Wing planes over the target. These were followed by the fifty-nine aircraft of the Composite Wing, the last of which, *Lucky Thirteen,* carried the wounded Miller.

Within a minute after *Lucky Thirteen* passed over Schweinfurt, the first bombs of the 3rd Air Task Force began hurtling toward the ball bearing factories. These were the projectiles of the lead group, the 306th, led by Major William S. Raper flying the first plane. The group provided thirty B-17s for the day's mission—all aircraft bombed and—certainly another of the day's miracles—all returned. The first paragraph of the S-3 Narrative prepared by the group's Operations Officer, Major Robert C. Williams, summarized the mission: "At 1150 hours 17 August 1943, thirty aircraft of this group took off to bomb industrial installations at Schweinfurt, Germany.

"The first nine to take off joined with nine ships from the 305th Bombardment Group (H) and two ships from the 92nd Bombardment Group (H) to fly high Group in the Composite Wing attached to the Second Air Task Force [to add to the administrative confusion, this collection of aircraft and crews from the 92nd, 305th, and 306th Groups was called the 306th Composite Group to round out the 2nd Air Task Force, while the remainder of their squadron mates flew with the 3rd Air Task Force]. The other twenty-one aircraft formed the lead Group of the 102nd Combat Wing, leading the Third Air Task Force. Of these thirty aircraft, none aborted, all bombed and all returned to base, landing after 1806 hours."

Raper, leading the twenty-one Fortresses, took off at 11:55 and two minutes later swung the formation in a 180-degree turn "to avoid aircraft from nearby fields." Formed up, the 306th planes moved to the first rendezvous point where they were joined by twenty B-17s of the 305th Bomb Group coming in from the north to fly in the high group position and, a little later, another twenty aircraft of the 92nd Group, which would fly low, came in from the south. These sixty-one Fortresses constituted the 102nd Combat Wing.

The formation was executed with great skill and, in his report, Raper noted that "our fighter escort was excellent"; undoubtedly these were two good reasons why the 306th suffered no losses that day. Second Lieutenant D. H. White, a pilot who doubled as tail gunner in Raper's plane, kept a wary eye on the group's formation, noting its condition in a running commentary through the entire mission. At 12:23, for example, his remarks pertaining to the form-up read: "Base [Thurleigh] High sqdn slow join up. Entire group in formation at 1220 except 603 and 959 [these are aircraft numbers, the last three digits on the tail]. High and low [squadrons] didn't use collision course for join up consequently had hard time rejoining. 714 out too far from Base to Northampton [this aircraft, from the low, 423rd Squadron, would be mentioned frequently in the commentary for various formation problems. Eventually it was seen, after Schweinfurt, with a feathered engine and ultimately in a later report as 'Not refueled due to battle damage']. 603 [another trouble maker] pulled up and dropped back but came back in. 2nd element of low squadron having trouble [it might be mentioned that No. 2 plane in the second element was 42-5714]."

Raper officially described the mission thus: "Upon reaching Eupen on time at 21,000 feet a course was set for 49°45′N—

08°20′ E. Fighters were continually attacking our Wing. Only part of the attacks were pressed home and those had little effect due to the excellent Combat Wing Formation. We arrived at our DR [Dead Reckoning] position on time and set course for our IP. About half way along this leg the other Task Force was sighted toward the target area. At the IP there was a little congestion but an interval was taken and a perfect bombing run was effected on the target at 155 m.p.h. at 21,000 feet.

"After the bombing run a turn to the left [i.e. north] was started and airspeed reduced to allow the Combat Wing to join as soon as possible. Our Radio Operator [Technical Sergeant J. C. Bocelli] sent a Bomber Strike Message which was acknowledged. A very quick join-up was effected and upon hearing several radio calls from crippled ships, it was decided to hold the airspeed at 150 m.p.h. We were flying about 20 miles south of the other Task Force, converging toward the rendezvous point. The navigation was excellent [the work of Captain George D. Bennett and First Lieutenant O. B. Tillery]. On our course out the altitude was reduced to 19,000 feet to allow the High Group [the 305th] to stay under the clouds. All this time we were under fighter attacks and all large towns along the route were skirted. Our Second Combat Wing had moved up close and we had a very good defensive Air Task Force.

"Upon reaching Eupen our fighter rendezvous was effected and very effective cover was given by them. We left the Coast at 19,000 feet and a let-down was started about five minutes earlier than briefed to allow the men in the Task Force, who were low on oxygen and gas, a reprieve. After reaching the English Coast a course was set for home."

The group's Intelligence Report, prepared by Captain John A. Bairnsfather, had this to say about the Luftwaffe: "Between 100/150 E/A encountered, mainly FW190s. Attacks began at 1410, tapered off before IP. Our Group not bothered by fighters from IP to target and for some distance beyond. On way back encountered fighters again, attacks continuing until 1610. Tremendous dog fights reported between P47s and E/A. P47s beyond praise. New tactic, E/A came in up to 20 at a time, from high above in front, out of sun, our top turrets getting most of shots. Some tail attacks from 6 o'clock level. Colors green, grey, some black and white. Night fighters were up, attacking composite especially. Up to 50 attacks on our Group. We have 24 claims [for enemy aircraft shot down]. At least 12 E/A seen to break up in air, a number of enemy pilots bailing out."

There were also a few final observations: "3 FW190s came in close and were reported by two men as having British markings. Both reports positive. 3 FW189s reported. Intense activity, mostly barges on the Rhine between Bonn and Cologne. Smoke screens at Antwerp, Bonn, Cologne, Mannheim, and at Target."

And so all of the aircraft of the 306th Bomb Group went to Schweinfurt, fought in, bombed, fought out and all landed at Thurleigh. The two remaining groups that had made up the 102nd Combat Wing, the 305th and 92nd, each lost two B-17s. The latter lost one plane going in to Schweinfurt and one on the way home. The 305th lost both aircraft on the way back to England. The 92nd Group's Narrative emphasized the efficacy of the "pack attacks" and the fact that the Luftwaffe was more ferocious on the way in than out—there being more than twenty Fortresses lost before Schweinfurt. As usual the low squadron of the formation bore the brunt of the attacks: "Shortly after entering the enemy coast going in to the target, a pack of seven FW-190s attacked the low squadron from the tail. They approached firing steadily their 20-mm. and small caliber tracer.

"When at 750 yards, a very large flash emanated from the center of each E/A obliterating it from view. The E/A then dove under the formation. A second or two after the flash, several large black bursts appeared in the formation about one and a half times as large as the ordinary flak burst. The projectile from the E/A following the big flash could be followed with the unaided eye and appeared to be about three inches in diameter. The projectile burst in air and not on impact. This attack crippled two aircraft so that later attacks brought them down. One FW-190 was observed to have a large gun on the under side of the fuselage." These were the rocket-armed fighters of V/JG 11 and, although they did not destroy the two B-17s lost by the 92nd (a Lieutenant Stewart and a Captain Sargent, pilots), they did set them up for the attack that came from the more conventionally armed FW-190s.

The Group Engineering Report Enumerated the Battle damages suffered by fourteen of the twenty aircraft that returned to the base at Alconbury (not including one that accomplished the mission with an engine that ran away, necessitating flying on three to Schweinfurt and back). The usual reasons for damage are given—some flak, 20-mm. cannon, smaller caliber punctures and so on. But in the report supplied by the group's Engineering Officer, Captain James J. Boutky, a generally unrecognized hazard of the air battling emerges. The damages to a single plane, B-17F No. 42-29653 of the 327 Squadron, points this up (with italics added):

(1) Left wing tip pierced by flak. No internal damage done.
(2) Leading edge of right wing damaged between numbers three and four nacelles *by falling brass.*
(3) Upper surface of right outboard wing panel damaged several points by flak. No internal damage resulted.
(4) Right wing tip damaged *by falling brass.* Wing tip must be replaced.
(5) Right horizontal stabilizer pierced by one Cal. 50 bullet and damaged *by falling brass.* The stabilizer must be replaced. The right elevator was torn in several places, but can be patched.
(6) Vertical stabilizer damaged by one 20 MM cannon shell. The vertical stabilizer must be replaced.
(7) Upper surface of left horizontal stabilizer damaged at several points *by falling brass and linkage.*
(8) Flak damaged the fuselage just above the main entrance door. One stringer was damaged and the plexilglass window in the door must be replaced.

(9) Flak entered fuselage at a point between stations six A and six B, struck the ball turret top support bracket, passed through the radio compartment floor and out through the camera door. Extensive sheet metal repair will be necessary.

Of the fourteen battle damaged aircraft, at least ten were damaged by falling brass, the spent shells from other B-17s in the formation. Pilot's windshields, fabric on horizontal tail surfaces, even a propeller blade required replacement after the battle revealing yet another peril to the low group.

The final Combat Wing—the 103rd—over the target consisted of fifty aircraft from the 379th and 303rd Groups (the latter being the only other unit, which like the 306th, suffered no aircraft losses on the mission).

The lead aircraft of the wing was piloted by Lieutenant Colonel Maurice A. Preston of the 379th Group (527th Squadron); the 303rd flew in the low group position, the most vulnerable and yet inexplicably lost no aircraft. An explanation was supplied in a Memorandum issued the following day as prepared by Captain W. Robert Thompson, who stated that "evasive action was taken to good advantage." The high group of the wing was made up of aircraft from both the 303rd and the 379th and was called the Composite Group; it was out of this formation that the 379th lost four B-17s. The comments of various members of Preston's crew detailed the loss of these Fortresses:

1445 hours a B-17 was hit by E/A on tail. He was in vertical dive going down, no chutes. Saw the ship explode when it hit ground. No chutes. Came out of high Squadron of Composite Group.

At 1450 hours—Another B-17 from high Squadron of Composite Group was shot down by fighters. The plane broke apart and saw four delayed jumps. No chutes.

At 1500 hours a ship from the Composite Group high Squadron under control was seen to go down. Four chutes seen. Two minutes later it turned back with one engine on fire and fighters were around it.

> Over target—From Composite Group a B-17 went into smoke and clouds over the target. Disappeared into smoke and clouds. Was still flying.

Preston, in his later report, did note that the "Target was obscured from previous group bombing . . ." which made it difficult for bombardier Captain Joseph A. Brown to discern the aiming point for a moment. Preston brought the plane in over Schweinfurt at an altitude of 21,000 feet on a level run of less than a minute; then at "1510½" Brown released sixteen 250-pound incendiaries into the mushrooming frenzy of Schweinfurt. Within a minute the 303rd followed also with incendiaries to enflame the havoc caused by the high explosives of the preceding Combat Wings. Before he turned northward for the wing Rally Point, roughly over the city of Meiningen, Preston looked upon the target area and decided that the bombing had been "Good."

The battle at this moment, however, was only half over; what really counted now was Getting Home.

Although the crews had witnessed several B-17s in various stages of distress, no one in the formation—from General Williams up ahead with the 91st Group to the tail gunner in the Fortress bringing up the rear of the 303rd—knew the extent of their losses, which by the turn to the Rally Point numbered twenty-one. The crews of fifteen B-17s still flying who felt immense relief when their aircraft lurched upward upon "Bombs Away" and knowing they had bombed "as briefed," were prematurely if cautiously (for they knew well what was yet to come) optimistic.

Fate, blind, indifferent and unyielding, had decreed that those fifteen crews would never make it home either.

NINE

Mere numbers rarely reveal the absolute truth. The 303rd Group, which was the last over Schweinfurt and at the end of the long and massive formation of Flying Fortresses, according to statistical tables dispatched twenty-nine B-17s of which a total of twenty-seven bombed. One of the two errant aircraft did not bomb because of mechanical problems; the other had left the formation in serious trouble after being struck by flak in the vicinity of Antwerp. Pilot Lieutenant F. H. Thompson was fortunate in that he did manage to get the plane back over Holland and the Channel, but he could not wheedle the big, wounded Fortress all the way back to their home base at Molesworth. Thompson crash-landed at Sutton Heath. Technically the aircraft was not "missing," but it would never fly again.

In the 303rd's lead plane, piloted by Major Kirk R. Mitchell, inexorable fate struck during the bomb run. As he sighted on the aiming point First Lieutenant Lawrence McCord, the bombardier, was knocked out of his position by a piece of flak that had ripped through the Plexiglass nose. The bombing was then taken over by the navigator, First Lieutenant Richard E. McElwain. When questioned by a newsman after the mission what he thought of his improvisation, McElwain replied, "It was Okay, I guess. I had to do the bombing. Poor Mac was in pretty bad shape and after I threw the bombs out, I went back to take care of him." This was a statistic, too, that would not appear on paper.

The lead plane of the Composite Group, also from the 303rd, was named *Satan's Workshop,* and was piloted by Major Lewis E. Lyle, who summed up the mission by saying, "I won't say it was the roughest, but it was more action than I have ever seen before." The mission was Lyle's twentieth and he had flown it practically all the way and back on three engines, one having been knocked out soon after *Satan's Workshop* crossed over into Germany.

Gunnery Officer, Captain Kenneth Davey manned the tail gun as an observer in Lyle's Fortress and was somewhat less sanguine. "Those fighters were just coming in and coming in," he told the newsmen. "I thought they would never stop. For a while there I really thought we had it. They knocked one of our motors out and I started looking for my parachute, but we kept right on going and I kept on shooting." Navigator Nathan J. Rosenblum supplied the reporter with what they considered the most eloquent comment: "Gulp."

But *Satan's Workshop* had returned also to become a positive statistic. So did the aircraft of Lieutenant C. M. Olsen of the 427th Squadron—only in the right waist Staff Sergeant L. A. Kesky lay dead, yet another statistic (he was one of the three known dead who would be brought back to England; the dead aboard the fallen B-17s would be listed as "Missing in Action"). Getting Home would mean nothing to Sergeant Kesky.

To the living it meant everything and, once the bombs had fallen, returning to England became paramount. The formations were tightened for mutual protection—everyone knew that the Luftwaffe would return—and air speed was diminished to enable the damaged Fortresses to remain within the protective reaches of the formations. The crippled B-17s and the men in them, the injured, the untouched and the dying, compelled by a strong will to live, strained to "come safe home."

For a brief time, as the Fortresses turned and assembled, there was a hopeful—and false—peace. It was an unreal lull as damages were assessed (and probabilities weighed as to the chances of making it in a heaving, slightly smoking plane) and preparations made for the next phase of the battle. It was a time, too, of accumulating tension.

The Germans had missed the rendezvous over Schweinfurt, for Ground Control had radioed to a formation of eight Me-110s, "Raiders over Wurzburg" (decidedly to the south of the true target and which had by that time already been bombed). Control then dispatched them to Schweinfurt where they arrived to find nothing but a massive, ugly, column of smoke—and no Fortresses. Twenty minutes later, unblooded, the Messerschmitts were ordered to land.

Some twin engined fighters that did observe the returning American bombers were ordered not to attack, but to keep them in view and to await the arrival of the Me-109s and the FW-190s. Not that the lull remained pure; Fortresses continued to fall—three between Schweinfurt and Meiningen, from flak, from previous attacks. There were intermittent attacks before the real onslaught and they took their toll also. The early history of the Eighth Air Force, *Target: Germany* (anonymously written by Arthur Gordon) recounts the adventure of the anonymous (also) crew of the Fortress known as *My Prayer* (song titles inspired the names of a great number of aircraft).

"In a Fortress named *My Prayer,*" Gordon wrote, "fire broke out and the ship went into a dive. All crew members bailed out except the pilot, copilot and the top turret gunner, whose chute was so damaged by flames that he was unable to jump. The pilot finally brought the bomber out of its dive and the gunner, painfully wounded by a shell fragment in the leg, managed to smother the blaze with the help of the copilot. The gunner then took over the nose guns, the copilot the waist guns, and they held off enemy fighters until the Fortress was down to house-top altitude and the fighters gave up the chase."

The pilot then took up the story: "We came home at 210 miles an hour, buzzing cities, factories and airfields in Germany. It was the first legal buzzing I've ever done. We drew some fire, but I did evasive action and we escaped further damage. The people in Germany scattered when they saw us coming, but in Belgium the people waved and saluted us . . ." Gordon continued in an optimistic vein: "Over Belgium, the copilot started jettisoning everything that could be spared. He came across a pair of shoes and, seeing a Belgian standing in a field cheering enthusiastically, tied the laces together and dropped the shoes to him. Running low on gas and without a navigator to guide them, the three men brought their plane across the Channel and landed it safely on an R.A.F. airdrome."

(According to Air Force records in the National Archives this incident occurred to the plane piloted by Second Lieutenant James D. Judy of the 322nd Squadron of the 91st Group. The Group Narrative reports its arrival this way: OUR A/C #712 CRASH LANDED AT MANSTON A/D [AIR DROME] AFTER SEVEN OF CREW BAILED OUT OVER ENEMY TERRITORY. AND IS NOW A WRECK.)

Within minutes after the Rally Point and with all the noses of the Fortresses pointed toward home, the refueled and rearmed German planes began the attacks, lightly at first but then in packs. From Meiningen to roughly Eupen, where the first Thunderbolts were due, a distance of more than 200 miles, the bombers were on their own. The hardest hit 381st Group underscored one of the problems of defense when the more aggressive Luftwaffe pilots employed the harrowing head-on attack; "there were many nose attacks," Major Linn S. Kidd, the S-2, reported, "in which the E/A continued to fly on level right through our formations in such a way that many of our gunners could not fire because they were afraid of hitting their own aircraft."

In the vicinity of Bonn, before Eupen, Technical Sergeant Lawrence H. Reedman, engineer-top turret gunner in the lead squadron (527th) of the lead group (379th) of the last (103rd Combat Wing) watched a twin engined Messerschmitt just slightly above and behind turn for an attack. The plane was about 1500 yards distant and made an approach almost directly into the sun.

With the sun to his back, Reedman had a fine view of the approaching plane. He waited until the Me-110 came within 800 yards and then began firing—and continued until the plane was roughly 300 yards away, using about 500 rounds of ammunition "in middle of cockpit and engines. He kept coming in with tracers entering his ship; then he fell straight down."

In the ball turret, Staff Sergeant Walter J. Gray saw the big Me-110 go past him, chillingly close, in a vertical dive. "For curiosity's sake I followed him and really saw him crash—a big flash of fire came up." Thus with Gray's confirmation was Reedman given credit for one enemy aircraft destroyed.

By then the German fighters had begun to appear in greater numbers in "mass attacks from two sides, from high. T/E [twin engine] aircraft from beneath—and around the clock," as reported by First Lieutenant C. H. Sackerson, who led the 365th Squadron of the 305th Group. After bombing Schweinfurt, the 305th had lost one aircraft "going down burning with five chutes observed, and observed hit the ground."

Another casualty, *Smilin' Thru'* (song title again) was piloted by First Lieutenant Rothery McKeegan the group's Operations Officer and flying that day's mission of his own volition. The Fortress had lost two engines somewhere along the way and the formation leader Major J. C. Price throttled back to enable McKeegan to keep up with the rest and to afford him some protection from the Luftwaffe until the American fighters arrived.

A formation of three twin-engine German fighters moved in on the 305th's formation. Leading was an Me-110, the two others were Me-210s equipped with rockets. The three aircraft moved around Price's Fortresses to attack from a level position and slightly to the left. Gunners nervously gripped their weapons as hundreds of eyes followed the menacing trio of black crossed aircraft. As if by sudden magic help arrived; a Thunderbolt dived out of the sun to attack the lead Messerschmitt. The German pilots were apparently unaware of the P-47's approach for the

Me-110 was hit square by the full blast of the Thunderbolt's guns.

The Me-110 literally came apart in the air as wings snapped off, engines flipped away burning and smaller bits and pieces scattered, leaf-like, through the air. Just at this time other elements of the 305th flew into the scene of combat and proceeded to fly under and through the falling debris. Some pieces struck Fortresses, raining down on the planes nicking away bits of metal, paint and fabric. The slower flying *Smilin' Thru'* was among those hit by pieces of the Me-110. Then an FW-190 swept in, fired and ran pursued by a P-47. For some moments, as Price watched, *Smilin' Thru'* continued to fly, then came the flame—followed by eight parachutes, one of which caught fire and plummeted down uselessly with the crewman helpless.

Two men remained in the doomed Fortress as it flared, dipped and shuddered. Whether these two men were alive, no one knew—the plane appeared to be responding to human control, so it was possible that young "Roth" McKeegan was still at the controls. In a great bursting flash the plane vanished from the sky.

The first Thunderbolts, forty-six in number from the 56th Fighter Group, again led by Colonel Hubert Zempke, made the first contact with the bombers east of Eupen at 4:21 in the afternoon—Schweinfurt had been bombed by the 91st about an hour and twenty minutes before and since then the combat boxes had been mauled. Seven Fortresses had fallen between Meiningen and Eupen. Zempke noted stragglers—and "50-60 E/A . . . making attacks on the bombers." He deployed two squadrons, the 61st and 62nd, to cover the rear box (Turner's 3rd Air Task Force) and the 63rd Squadron to protect the lead (Gross's 2nd Air Task Force). This strategy was explained in a Tactical Commander's Report: "One squadron was placed on the front box and two were taken back to the rear box where one squadron was utilized as high cover and the other sent down in front of the bombers to break up many attacks that were forming up. Within a few minutes the entire sky blew up into dog fights with flights, pairs and singles fighting to defend themselves or avert head-on attacks on the bombers."

It was in this bomber-fighter rendezvous area (to which later would come the 353rd Fighter Group with forty P-47s and even later, eighty-five Spitfires from the R.A.F. squadrons) that the great fighter battles erupted. The Germans flying Messerschmitts and Focke-Wulfs were determined to destroy the bombers and the Thunderbolts and Spitfires equally determined to prevent this. While the massive Jug packed a great deal of wallop and was most effective in disrupting the German fighter attacks, the Fortresses too, bearing men eager to get home, were capable of putting up a fight.

The redoubtable Heinz Knoke, despite the hole in the wing of his Me-109, took charge of a number of battle strays, Me-109s and FW-190s, that had landed for a number of reasons at Hangelar and led them up to intercept the returning bombers. He chose to trail the formation, sending in his charges one by one and, considering the condition of his own plane, wisely selected for himself a straggling B-17 that had fallen slightly behind and to the left of the main box.

Knoke handled his *Gustav* gently, from time to time glancing at his left wing to see if it remained intact. "At a range of 500 feet I open fire in short bursts. The American defenses reply: their tracers come whizzing all around me, uncomfortably near my head. The usual pearl necklaces become thicker and thicker. Once again there is altogether too much of this blasted metal in the air."

He was unable to maneuver his Messerschmitt out of harm's way and he was ever conscious of possible disaster should his wing give way in a sharp turn. He remained on a predictable line for too long. Fifty-caliber bursts smashed into his fuselage and Knoke, somewhat surprised that his engine continued to function, squeezed up behind it for protection from the hail of fire. He had come within 300 feet of the Fortress and opened fire again and the bomber began to burn. As he watched four parachutes blossomed below the now savagely burning plane; by the time two more fell from the Fortress, Knoke was too occupied to notice.

For a moment he had been caught up in the afterglow of his victory, had come in closer to the main bomber stream and became the target for more 50-caliber gunfire. Great pounding noises filtered through his helmet—"like a sack of potatoes being emptied over a barrel in which I am sitting"—and then worse: "Flames come belching out at me from the engine."

Gasping, eyes watering, Knoke opened the side windows in the canopy for air; that only made it worse and the smoke grew denser. His first instinct was to get away from the bombers to prevent further damage to his plane. He made a wide, gentle, swing to port and, though his instruments showed his oil and coolant were boiling, the fire in thc engine appeared to go out. He jettisoned the canopy and the sudden blast of air took his breath away; in an instant his scarf went whipping off in the wind. He considered the wisdom of getting out of the *Gustav*.

With engine off and propcller feathered he attempted to stretch a glide back to Hangelar. His altimeter informed him he was at 12,000 feet, but shortly after he had lost 2,000 of those feet. He was reminded that an Me-109 was not a glider.

With little more to lose he decided to see if there is "any life left in the engine." He set the propeller pitch, nosed down to gain a little speed and turned on the engine. Despite some unnerving clatter and thumping, he managed to get it going and lifted the plane back up to 12,000 feet. So far so good, but not for long. The smell of something burning wafted back to him and a wisp of smoke warned him to turn off the engine again. He was transformed once again into a glider pilot.

Determined as he was, Knoke realized he'd never get back to the base and that switching on the engine again could bring disaster. But the plane lost altitude so rapidly that he sought out the nearest field of any size for a place to set down the Messerschmitt. He would belly in he decided, but in order to get to the field he would have to make some tight turns and decided to risk the engine again. That really did it: he managed to achieve airspeed to the point of being able to make a few turns toward his chosen sanctuary, but then the engine seized-up and the propeller ground to a dead stop. The heat had fused the engine—he couldn't even feather any longer.

The Messerschmitt dropped in a stall to the left; Knoke found the controls stiff and heavy but managed to get the nose down to get some control. But to do this he found he had gained high speed; at near treetop level he was rushing along at 200 miles an hour. He succeeded in subtracting eighty miles of that as his wingtips brushed through the branches. One quick glance told him that he would come in at around a hundred; not at all good. Hunched behind the engine Knoke felt the thump as he struck the ground, plowed through a couple of fences tearing up posts and splinters of crossbars. Then he bounced upward and as he braced himself against the belt with feet braced on the rudder bar, saw looming in front of him an unyielding dike. The Me-109 came to an abrupt, grinding halt against the side of the dike. After that all Knoke heard was absolute silence. He unfastened his belt, crawled out of the plane and saw it was a total wreck; there "was nothing left intact except the tail-wheel." He also noticed that his right sleeve was bloodied where he had been hit by shrapnel. The following day Knoke and other pilots who had lost their planes were picked up by a patrol plane sent from Weihe; they called it "the flying garbage truck."

There was plenty of aerial "garbage" falling from the sky. Knoke may have accounted for the last of the B-17s that crashed to earth; the final two would splash into the Channel. The grand climax of the fighter battles occurred during the withdrawal in the vicinity of Liège and continued on to Antwerp when the 56th Fighter Group, primarily, contended with the crack pilots of JG 1, JG 2, Knoke's group, JG 11 and JG 26. The 353rd Fighter Group would appear during a slight lull and then the Spitfires would finish up the escort and engage in several skirmishes also.

But it was the 56th that would earn the accolade, "P-47s beyond praise."

The Fortresses were surging toward England and westward into the soon to be setting sun. At 20,000 feet the sun was still well above the horizon and over Belgium, where the most intense battles took place, the sky was clear—an intense blue; the air was sharp and brilliant flashes of sunlight glittered off windscreens, and bullet-exposed metal. It was an ethereal setting for poets, not warriors.

Not that all went well for the 56th. Belly tank problems continued to plague them, some breaking up on takeoff; one hung up and when the pilot (Lieutenant Leroy A. Schreiber) found he could not detach it over Holland he was forced to return to Halesworth accompanied by his wingman (Lieutenant Joseph R. Curtis), thus subtracting two P-47s from the force. Another fighter had already returned with a faulty tachometer.

To his chagrin Major Francis Gabreski, leading the 56th's 61st Squadron, found that *his* auxiliary tank had not been filled—so he was forced to return taking, so the rule went, a wingman with him. His position was then filled by Captain Donald D. Renwick.

Not that Gabreski hadn't participated in the opening of the battle. It was only when he had led his section (he was Keyworth White Leader that day) in an attack on two Me-109s coming in on the bombers from astern that he discovered a shortage of fuel and was forced to turn for home. Since two P-47s had already aborted from the flight, it was left rather shorthanded. Keyworth Red Leader, Captain Gerald W. Johnson, pulled in his section to tighten the formation. Shortly after they met the bombers and crossed over to take a position on the left side of the last box.

Johnson describes what followed: "As we came out on the left side north of Liège [at] about 25,000 feet, I saw a twin engine plane almost solid white, or very light gray, flying across the front of the B-17s in the last box at about 20 degrees to their course. He was flying at about their speed and about 1,000 feet above them. I immediately rolled over and went down on him from dead astern and at about 30-degrees angle. At about 150 yards I opened fire and could see strikes all through the center of the plane. After about a two second burst he exploded with a flame about 40 feet in diameter and little pieces seemed to just hang in the air burning. It is my opinion from his position and action that he was preparing to drop bombs on the B-17s and that my bullets exploded his bombs because I don't believe anything else could have caused such an explosion." This was probably the 110 that had disintegrated and fell into the 305th Bomb Group's formation.

Johnson's Number Two man, First Lieutenant Justus D. Foster, had also participated in the attack but with different results. He had been the first to call out the plane and dived on it with Johnson, but when he tried to fire his guns nothing happened. By this time Johnson had opened up and the Messerschmitt exploded, as Foster described it, "with such a blinding flash it led me to believe that it was carrying bombs for an air to air attack. Oil from this ship splattered on my canopy."

The same Messerschmitt 110 was to appear in the Combat Report of First Lieutenant Frank E. McCauley, from Gabreski's Keyworth White flight. McCauley had spotted the plane at "21,000 feet, about 1,000 feet above the bombers, and I was 500 feet above him. I got to within 300 yards of him and then pulled around dead astern. I closed to 150 yards and fired a two second burst. He exploded. I pulled up but couldn't completely avoid the flames."

McCauley's Thunderbolt swept through the flame and debris without harm and he found there were other problems: he spotted three FW-190s flying below him parallel to the bombers. The tactic had already been noted: they would then sweep around to the front of the formation and race through it head on.

"Going into a steep dive I came up dead astern of them," McCauley continued. "I chose the right wing man and fired a burst at 300 yards hoping that maybe I could get him and one of the others. I saw strikes and pieces flying off. There was also white and black smoke coming from the engine. He did not leave the formation immediately so I gave another burst at 200 yards and more pieces flew off and the pilot bailed out. In the meantime the other two broke for the deck.

"I pulled up again to about 22,000 feet and saw another FW-190 below at about 19,000 feet off to the right of the lead bombers. I dove and ended up astern of him about 400 yards back, and fired a burst. I fired another burst at about 300 yards and saw tracers going all around him and believe there were strikes on the left wing. He broke right immediately after the tracers were fired. I could turn with him so pulled up to 21,000 feet. Two of my starboard guns were out of ammunition. If I had closed before firing at this last FW-190 I believe I could have had another destroyed." McCauley was credited with the first FW, with damaging the second and shared the destruction of the Me-110 with Johnson.

Johnson, meanwhile, led his element "up toward the sun to about 23,000 feet and upon leveling out saw a single Me-109 going in head on to the bombers. We came down on him at a steep angle and opened fire at about 200 yards. I could see hits and flashes on the fuselage and wing roots. At this point he started to turn left and a full burst seemed to hit between the cockpit and engine. There was a large flash of flame and smoke as he started to go down in a slow spiral. As I pulled back up in a climbing turn I saw the pilot bail out and the chute opened immediately.

"We then pulled back up to about 1,000 feet above the bombers and to their left and was [sic] approaching the rear of the front box when I saw another single Me-109 coming in from about 10 o'clock to the bombers. I couldn't get within range until he broke away from the bombers. I then easily closed to 100 yards without being seen by the enemy aircraft. I fired about a three second burst, seeing strikes all over the fuselage, and smoke and flame coming out. Without any evasive action he slowly rolled over to the left and went straight down. As I pulled up in a tight climbing turn, I saw the Me-109 hit the ground in a cloud of smoke. I then found that I was by myself (my number two man and second element had chased two Me-109s off my tail during my last attack) and started for the coast at 17,000 feet." Johnson was near Antwerp by then and found that two Me-109s had come up behind him, slightly to the side. He kicked his rudder and turned into their approach, a maneuver that disconcerted them and the two planes dived away toward Antwerp. Johnson continued on home without further incident. In his Combat Report he attributed the success "of this flight on this mission to the splendid cooperation and teamwork of my wing man, Lieutenant Foster, and my second element, Lieutenant [Paul A.] Conger and Lieutenant R. S. Johnson."

Foster's cooperation and teamwork were contributed to that success under a tremendous handicap. The fact was he should not have even been there.

Following his, McCauley's and Johnson's attack on the Me-110, Foster pulled up again, his windshield splattered with oil, to rejoin the flight with Johnson at their original altitude. It was then they spotted the first lone Me-109 and Johnson led the dive on the fighter to intercept the head-on attack on the bombers. "Captain Johnson and I attacked this plane," he reported later. "Flame and smoke started pouring from the cockpit and the pilot was seen to bail out; again my guns didn't fire."

When he and Johnson dived on the other Me-109 which broke off its attack with Johnson in pursuit, Foster remained slightly behind to cover his leader. It was then he spotted the two Me-109s that had flown through the bomber formation and moved in on the preoccupied Johnson. Foster kicked the big Thunderbolt around and came in straight at the German planes. The two pilots were unaware of the fact that Foster was incapable of firing his guns at them. All they saw was that hulking mass of a P-47 (which was armed with from six to eight 50-caliber machine guns) and it was time to get out of the way. Immediately the two planes flipped apart and over, dived for the ground and out of the battle zone.

Foster climbed back up to 23,000 feet and found himself alone;

the battle had moved a few miles westward. Unable to locate Johnson, with one of his instruments malfunctioning and no guns he decided "I had better get out of there." Over Antwerp he encountered a pair of Me-109s which closed in and made passes at him until he again turned the big nose of the P-47 at them. He split-S'd down to 15,000 feet and soon learned that the pair had followed him. When "I reached Walcheren Island I had to repeat the same tactics. They gave up and returned inland." Foster proceeded on to land at Halesworth without having fired a single shot in the day's battles.

The tactic of flipping over into a vertical dive to escape did not always work. Such an incident was witnessed by Second Lieutenant Donavon F. Smith, also, of the 61st Squadron, a member of Captain Renwick's Blue Flight. "As we reached 23,000 feet four bandits were sighted at about 11 o'clock to the number three box of bombers and it looked very much to me as though they were contemplating a head on attack on the last box of bombers," Smith later reported. "I immediately called them in. Captain Renwick then started positioning us for an attack and we proceeded to dive at them from about 4 o'clock. As soon as we started our attack, all four Me-109s rolled over and dove away. The one that was closest to me passed almost directly to my side and below.

"I watched him as he kept up a nearly vertical dive thinking to myself all the time that he is either going to pull back up on our tails or come up under the bombers as several planes had done before, using the loop method of attacking the bombers from below and then diving away. The Me-109 kept right on diving and just as he was almost out of sight I saw him hit the ground resulting in a puff of smoke and a large flash at the exact spot where I was watching him attempting to recover from his dive. It is my belief that violent evasive action due to our attack was the cause of this casualty." Smith claimed the victory for the squadron, not himself and it was accepted as "Confirmed."

Meanwhile the 63rd Squadron had become embroiled with the Luftwaffe over the lead box of Fortresses. Postgate Red Flight that day was led by Captain Walker M. Mahurin. It had been an active one and he expended 1,247 rounds of 50-caliber ammunition before it was over. In the first few moments of combat he caught two FW-190s attempting to get into position for an attack on the bombers; he moved in behind the first and at a range of about 300 yards opened up and saw it explode. Mahurin then led his flight "up to the right and into the bombers. We completed our orbit and found ourselves in the same position with an FW-190 ahead of us. We followed him until he started to make a turn into the front end of the bombers, when I took a deflection shot at him at about a hundred yards, and watched him blow up."

First Lieutenant George F. Hall, Mahurin's number two man, relates the next incident: "We again completed a right turn over the Forts. This time we saw an Me-109 starting a right turn to make a head on attack on the lead bombers. Captain Mahurin and I started with him. But as I was turning inside of Captain Mahurin the 109 came into my sight. I fired a fairly long deflection burst; saw the 109 flip over into a spin [Mahurin had also fired at the Messerschmitt but apparently made no hits]. I followed him down firing. When I last saw him he was going down, making a trail of black smoke."

As he pulled up to rejoin Mahurin, Hall came under attack by an FW-190 from astern. Mahurin had seen this and dropped down to come up behind the German fighter and fired. "My tracers were behind him so I pulled them through the fuselage of the 190 and took a lead on it. It flipped into a half roll, rolled back again, flipped the other way and then went into a spin without firing on my number two man." By this time the Focke-Wulf was within 100 yards of Hall, easy firing range, but no doubt unable to fire because the pilot himself had been hit.

Hall concluded his Combat report with a simple sentence: "Captain Mahurin and I then joined up and came home." Mahurin, who would become one of the leading "aces" of the war, added two definites to his tally that day; the FW-190 he knocked off Hall's tail was not accepted as a definite, however. The 63rd was credited with eight "destroyed" in the afternoon's fighting (as well as a number of "probables" and "damaged"), but lost one P-47 flown by a Lieutenant Arthur Sugas.

Mahurin described, in his report, the general tactics for the day when he noted that "most of the attacks on the Forts came from the nose, the German fighters flying about five miles from the bombers and parallel to them, then when about five miles in front of the Forts, attacking them from eleven to one o'clock, flying through the formation, coming back out to the side and repeating."

Zempke, leading his 56th Group and flying with the 62nd Squadron, found that it was nearly impossible to get at the German fighters once they had initiated this tactic. He assembled a section of eight P-47s and moved forward to the lead box of Fortresses to protect the front. He was soon proved correct. Within moments he found himself flying over an Me-110 heading in the same direction, undoubtedly for the head of the bomber formation. Zempke quickly placed a few rounds in the engines of the enemy plane, beginning at the starboard and slicing to the left. The plane, which had been climbing slightly, leveled out and Zempke released another fusillade, raking again from engine to engine. Pieces began chipping off the plane and were carried away into the slip stream; smoke began puffing out of both engines.

But the Messerschmitt continued flying so Zempke put another burst into it "with good effects" causing the plane to roll over and snap into a steep dive.

"I watched this aircraft go down smoking badly and to my surprise he levelled off [at] about 10,000 feet to go into a shallow dive inland. Soon thereafter the right engine caught fire and the aircraft was seen to go into a steep dive for the ground. No parachutes were seen to open as it went down."

First Lieutenant Voorhis H. Day, leading Red Flight of the

62nd Squadron, had spotted the Me-110s about the same time as Zempke. He called out, "O.K., boys, let's go after 'em!" (these quotations are transcribed verbatim from intercepted radio conversations). Day and his number two, Lieutenant Robert Stultz, bounced two of the unsuspecting Messerschmitts while the two other Thunderbolts headed for three more. Red Three, First Lieutenant Charles R. Harrison, briefly saw Day as he overtook one of the 110s and opened fire. A few seconds later Day's voice was heard again. "I got a 110!" he shouted. Then Harrison, busy himself, lost sight of his leader.

Soon after Day's exhilarated voice was heard again. "Yippee," he exclaimed, "I got another one!"

"Good show," Stultz was heard to shout, "beautiful show!" This was followed by a brief silence and Stultz's voice was soon heard again, "Come on, Daisy," he said using Day's nickname, "you've already got two, let's get the hell out of here."

More silence and then Stultz's warning cry, "Look out, they're shooting at you!" And then a final silence. Neither Day nor Stultz returned that day. Out of respect for Day's work, the Squadron S-2, Captain William J. Chase, requested that Day be credited with the two Me-110s, but without witnesses other than the voice of Stultz on the radio these were not confirmed. Harrison reported them in favorable proximity to the Messerschmitts but he did not witness any of the battle, nor the one in which both Day and Stultz were lost. Harrison, incidentally, destroyed one of his Me-110s and so did Red Four, Lieutenant Caleb Reeder. (Besides Sugas, Day, and Stultz there were two additional fighter losses suffered during the withdrawal phase, these were Flight Lieutenant Conrad and Flight Sergeant Shouldice of No. 403 Squadron, R.A.F. The Spitfire forces claimed four Me-110s and an FW-190 in exchange for these two English fighters.)

Radio interception, such as that which recorded the victories and loss of Day and Stultz, literally jammed the air. It crackled with the warnings, shouts, cries, and curses of men under exciting tension. Around 4:30 (1630) in the afternoon as the great battle drew to a merciless close, it was almost impossible to record all the voices—American, British as well as German, that filled the battle scarred air. At 1630 and the next three minutes, for example, these were heard:

I got a 110! [Undoubtedly Lieutenant Day]
O.K., take them
Good show, beautiful show! [Lieutenant Stultz]
O.K., let's go home gang.
What's at six o'clock? Can't identify it.
That's a 47 all alone—pick him up.
They're making head-on attacks on the 17s!
Let's get those guys!
There's another bunch going into them.
Come on up!
I can't get any more out of it.
They're getting under us.
O.K., watch out, they're coming around behind and off to the right.
Two at three o'clock left.
I got you covered, boy.
I'm out of ammunition.
Let's go home, we've been here long enough.

In Britain the R.A.F. and U. S. Air Force monitors picked up the enemy conversations also. At 1634, for example, there was word of a German pilot wounded in the right arm and thirteen minutes later further word of a belly landing, probably by the same pilot. This was, chances are, Heinz Knoke coming in with a badly shot-up Messerschmitt 109G. There were other reports of German aircraft attacking the bombers, of bombers on fire, going down, crashing and reports of parachutes. At the same time that American voices crowded the airwaves, German voices were heard also.

Close up.

Look out, formation coming up behind!

Fighters to starboard.

What is your position?

[Silence]

Hope he hasn't crashed.

The hounds have arrived.

Parachute!

Ha! Down you go you dog.

Herr Gott Sakramant!

(The last, not necessarily a dying pilot's last words, can roughly be translated as "Jesus Christ!")

By five in the afternoon the great battle was practically over except for a few stray skirmishes. The battlefield again had moved on—it was never stationary, of course. Some German pilots pursued the bombers and even fighters over the Channel, but quickly realized how imprudent that was. Besides, German Control was calling in the strays and once again the skies, luminous in the approaching twilight, were unblemished by the actions of men.

The fighters began landing by 5:30, the slower bombers came in as much as an hour later. Three had fallen during the heavy fighting over Belgium and two more would not make it across the Channel. One of these was Flight Officer G. R. Darrow's Fortress of the 381st Bomb Group which splashed into the water at 11:30 that night (already mentioned). Darrow and his crew then spent the night with their R.A.F. hosts before returning to their base the next day.

The second ditching was made by a Fortress from the mission's lead Group, the 91st. This plane, piloted by First Lieutenant Eugene M. Lockhart, was initially reported on the unit's roll as officially missing until its crew turned up the following day.

Battle damage—to left wing tip and right horizontal stabilizer—plus a malfunctioning supercharger on No. 3 engine placed a serious handicap on the plane, although Lockhart elected to remain with the formation to Schweinfurt. However, ten minutes before David Williams placed them over the Initial Point it became obvious that if the Fortress were to remain with the group something would have to be thrown out. So Lockhart ordered the ten 500-pound bombs salvoed and the two boxes of "nickels" (propaganda leaflets) tossed out.

This decision may have been the reason for a curious note in one crew's report (305th Bomb Group): "A B-17 salvoed on RR train entering tunnel—direct hit and terrific expl. indicating might have been munitions train." If the bombs from Lockhart's troubled plane accomplished this he and his crew were not aware of it and did not claim credit for "one train destroyed."

The crew was too preoccupied by then with keeping the Fortress aloft, what with the ragged edges of the wing and tail spoiling their configuration and the trouble with No. 3 engine which simply would not deliver power even wide open. Still Lockhart managed to remain with the 91st all through the battling to the coast of Holland. It was not easy and later he would observe that a speed of "160 miles per hour is too fast on these long trips as a damaged A/C has a tough time keeping up and will run out of gasoline." As he would learn.

Once they had reached the Channel and the German fighter attacks lessened and then petered out, Lockhart began letting the plane down, leaving the formation and sending out an SOS and making certain the IFF (Identification, Friend or Foe) was on so that the English radar could spot them as a Friend. As they approached the water all possible equipment that could be was ripped out and thrown from the plane. Even that, Lockhart realized, would not do it. They would have to ditch.

With the rest of the crew in ditch position in the radio room he and the co-pilot, Second Lieutenant Clive Woodbury, remained in the cockpit. They would nurse the plane as long as they could, the closer to England the better. No. 3 engine was of no use; then No. 2 sputtered out followed by No. 4 and finally, No. 1. They were coming in deadstick and with full flaps, slightly downwind. Speed was about 80 miles an hour; they were then about 50 miles off the English coast and the time was 5:20 P.M.

The Channel, tricky as always, proved to be rougher than they had thought and instead of sailing in with nose not too high, their Fortress struck the water tail first. With a splashing thump it hit at the midsection and the nose dipped down, splashing a wave over the nose. Water quickly began filling up the plane as everyone in the radio room scrambled out of the roof hatch. Lockhart and Woodbury squeezed out through their cockpit windows. Within a half minute the water-logged Fortress sank.

The dinghies had come out with the men and were quickly inflated and the ten men clambered into them. They were out of the water but not out of trouble; they soon learned that their radio would not work properly because the kite which was to have lifted its aerial would not go up because of too strong a wind. They huddled in their dinghies hoping for the best, that someone had heard their SOS.

They drifted for nearly two and a half hours when they heard the roar of aircraft engines coming from the direction of Britain. When they were certain of their aircraft identification—the planes were Spitfires—they shot up flares to attract attention. The Spitfires gracefully swooped down and dropped some objects at them. These turned out to be three smoke pots. From then on, for the next thirty-five minutes, Spitfires remained over them, in shifts, until an Air-Sea Rescue Walrus arrived. Seven of the men transferred to the amphibian's cabin; the remaining three, their dinghy tied to the rear of the plane, trailed behind. Thus overloaded and encumbered, the Walrus taxied homeward over the waves.

En route they met with an Air-Sea Rescue launch which took the three men out of the dinghy which improved matters, but not enough to permit the Walrus to become airborne. It continued taxiing until it arrived at Ramsgate, on the east coast in the Straits of Dover. This was roughly nine hours after the Walrus had picked them up. The seven airmen, who had come by plane (in a manner of speaking) were chagrined to learn that the other three, who had come by launch, had arrived three hours before. This crew officially returned from the Schweinfurt mission of August 17 at 1:00 (1300) P.M. August 18. There were no complaints; they had come home.

So did the Fortress named *Ex-Virgin,* which came in skidding on its belly at Grafton Underwood. Considering the shape of the ship, it was a successful landing, but pilot First Lieutenant David A. Tyler was not pleased. A ex-Trinity College (Hartford, Connecticut) athlete, Tyler had regarded the war as a great adventure and he loved flying. He was a typical young veteran of several missions, but it was Schweinfurt that rammed home a lesson in hate and war for him.

He had one of those classic war film crews with men whose names and home towns spelled out A-m-e-r-i-c-a. The crew's composition had not been planned by Central Casting for Warner Brothers, it had merely come together according to the inexplicable law, as had all others, of the Air Force. They were a good crew and after coming over together in several Fortresses were eventually united in one named *The Vanishing Virginian.* No one was happy with that name; there was no Virginian in the crew (nor any Southerner, the only slip by Central Casting; it was a rare Fortress that did not carry a Southerner, most generally a Texan). Nor was the word "Vanishing" of attractive connotation. They had seen a flak-hit Fortress literally do that.

A little paint changed the name to *The Virgin,* which suited everyone's fancy. But upon returning from a mission they found a flak hole had deflowered the plane just over the letter "V." The name was then changed to *Ex-Virgin,* which all agreed was apposite.

On the Schweinfurt raid, the fighter escort had barely left when the German fighters swept through, striking the low squadron where Tyler held *Ex-Virgin* in place in the center of the low squadron. Two 20-mm. shells hit the port side of the plane, killing the waist gunner Sergeant Wayne Frye, ripped out the intercom and shot up the oxygen system. When the oxygen went, the entire tail section instantly filled up with a "strange white smoke," and the first man to leave the plane was the isolated tail gunner. "I guess," Tyler commented, "he remembered the time we saw a Fortress go screaming by us after everybody had bailed out except the tail gunner, still blazing away at the fighters on his tail. A few minutes later the Fort went into a spin. The first thing that happens when a Fort spins is the tail snaps off. I guess our tail gunner figured he didn't want that to happen to him. Don't blame him."

The tail gunner was followed by three other members of the crew soon after before anyone realized that the plane was not afire. This left the dead Frye in the waist and Tyler, his co-pilot Wayne Hendricks, navigator Malvern Sweet, bombardier Louis Nelson and engineer-top turret gunner Fred Boyle still inside *Ex-Virgin*—exactly one half a crew.

Tyler philosophized: "I couldn't tell them to stick to the ship, and I don't know what I would have told them if it had been put up to me. There wasn't enough oxygen for all of us to live and get to the target and then get home at altitude. And if we broke formation and tried to get home on the deck by ourselves, well, that would have been curtains for all of us."

Taking stock of the oxygen in emergency bottles and cutting down as much as possible (by setting the indicator on the regulator at Normal and keeping movement to a minimum). And so they flew in formation to Schweinfurt in their tattered *Ex-Virgin,* with the tail fabric flapping in the slipstream—that of it which remained. When they arrived over the target they found that battle damage had jammed the bomb release mechanism and they could not bomb. After all that had happened to them, this was the ultimate outrage. The wounded Boyle snatched a screwdriver and began working on the hung-up bombs, prying them free of the jam and then when he had accomplished that kicked them out of the bomb bay. They were scattered rather willy-nilly over Germany between Schweinfurt and Meiningen, but they were out and the crew felt better for it. (Could they have fallen on a munitions train?)

"When we left the target," Tyler recalled of the rest of their flight, "we started hoping we'd reach the coast. When we reached the coast, we started hoping we'd reach mid-Channel so the British Air-Sea Rescue would get us instead of the Jerries. When we got to mid-Channel, we started hoping we'd reach the beach, and when we crossed the beach, then we started hoping we'd reach home.

"But we didn't."

And so each hopeful phase of their return from Schweinfurt was eked out, despite the red warning lights, the loss of power the churning and heaving of the damaged Fortress—and the German fighters, all too willing to exploit the cripples. But somehow because of that will to get home and the miraculous airworthiness of *Ex-Virgin* they passed from one phase to the next, grateful for each extension. Even so, they were unable to make the last fragment of the miracle. With their fuel practically gone, Tyler knew he would have to set the plane down before they ever got to Grafton Underwood—and he would have to come in wheels up for the gear would not work either mechanically or manually. The first and most convenient spot was a small fighter base near Nartledram where he brought *Ex-Virgin* in as smoothly as possible, with a screeching as he skidded along the runway, the engines trailing smoke. It was bumpy until the plane swerved to an askew, clamorous stop. Well, they had made it. Tyler unbuckled his belt and stumbled back to the waist where Frye lay. Gently he picked up the dead gunner—the shell, Tyler later said, had "just tore hell out of" [him]; "he never knew what hit him.

"I didn't start to hate the Germans until I lifted" [Wayne Frye] "out of our ship when we got back home."

Tyler had always been adamant on the subject of shooting enemy airmen dangling in parachutes and would never permit anyone to remain in his crew if ever that were to happen. But the mission to Schweinfurt awakened in him a philosophy of war and a burning enmity. "I feel this way about hating the guys we're fighting," he said a few days later. "They aren't the ones that made me leave my wife and my home and come all the way over here to fight. Those guys, we never get a chance to shoot at. Just let me get my guns on Hitler or Goering and then I'd have fun killing, because I hate those guys. They're the ones that made me leave Hartford."

And so they returned in the descending twilight, with their dead and their wounded, their battle damaged Fortresses straining to make home, with the red lights blinking on to warn of the vanishing fuel supply. Those that could not make it all the way fluttered into the nearest haven. The vanguard Fortress carrying lead pilot Wurzbach, lead navigator Lieutenant David M. Williams, and lead bombardier Slayton, arrived over the 91st's base at 5:50 in the afternoon and touched down at 6:06, six hours and forty-three minutes since takeoff that day. Next to arrive was the plane piloted by First Lieutenant Maurice A. Berg, who landed a minute later—precisely the interval between the planes' takeoffs at the opening of the mission. The next plane which should have landed, theoretically, would never land: Bill Munger's ship had blown up over Germany.

To the stay-at-homes, the early returnees, the ground crews and operations people, the arrival of the planes with their crews brought home the full significance of the day's heated radio intercepts.

Of the six planes that the 324th Squadron had sent up that day (eliminating one abort), only three came in at the estimated time of arrival; all the rest were technically "Missing," including Captain Richard Weitzenfeld's *Lady Luck* carrying the mission's commander, General Williams.

The other squadrons were equally decimated; of the seven planes of the 322nd that had flown to Schweinfurt (though one had come home early), three were marked "Missing" and one, Judy's, was a wreck at Manston. Of the four the 323rd had dispatched, only one returned—with a dead radio operator in the waist. The 401st Squadron began the day with five operational aircraft: two had been forced back early, one was reported as definitely missing, another, tentatively "Missing," would finally arrive at 9:15 that evening. The other, Lockhart's, had sunk in the English Channel.

Eventually some of the strays were heard from, either after a crash-landing, or after dropping in at the most convenient airfield to take on fuel. This is what occurred to *Lady Luck,* whose name, it began to seem, had come to the end of the line. "We were so low on gas," General Williams recalls, "there was some question of our making the English Coast." But Weitzenfeld nursed the plane along until they managed to cross over the Channel coast northeast of London, at Martlesham Heath—where they noted the presence of a tiny fighter strip: no paved runways, and those short. Nor was it a real active airdrome, but merely an auxiliary base. Except for its questionable size for a B-17, it looked most welcoming.

Weitzenfeld and Williams studied the field and the General, whose experience (like LeMay's) went back to the days of the first Flying Fortresses, offered to "take it in for him if he wanted me to. He said he would do it and made a perfect approach and landing."

While the plane was being refueled by R.A.F. ground crews, Williams checked in with Eighth Bomber Command and informed them he would eventually arrive at Bassingbourn. He had already begun formulating new training procedures: "During the flight back to England, when I wasn't otherwise engaged, I was making plans to do something about our bombing accuracy" (this was for the training of crews in Italy, away from English weather).

With *Lady Luck* gassed up, Williams, Weitzenfeld, and his crew boarded the plane and headed back for Bassingbourn, where they touched down at 7:04 P.M. Williams rather jauntily stepped out of the aircraft carrying a swagger stick and headed for his headquarters. It was Weitzenfeld who revealed that when the General was "otherwise engaged," he had been manning a machine gun during the height of the fighting. This had reached such intensity that the gun's barrel had been burned out. As the General strode away, slapping his stick, Weitzenfeld was heard to say, "We sure would like to keep him in our crew."

That long day, and that long, frightful battle were over.

IV

CODA

When the London *Daily Herald* appeared the morning after the missions to Regensburg and Schweinfurt the headline declared: BIGGEST DAY RAIDS OF THE WAR in great black letters across the top of the front page. A subhead added AIR PINCERS GRIP HITLER'S EUROPE FROM BRITAIN AND MEDITERRANEAN, the latter referring to the bombing of two German-held airfields near Marseilles in southern France.

The only American losses mentioned by the *Herald* were two Fortresses (one from the 100th, the other from the 390th) that had landed in Switzerland, where the crews had been interned. The British loss of three Spitfires was noted by the paper. Not that the *Herald* was dissembling—the full extent of the double strike losses was not yet known when the paper was put to bed. There was a quote, honest and to the point, from the 384th's Frank Celantano who, still shaken after the experience of getting the seriously wounded Miller home from Schweinfurt, said, "It's a lot of ballyhoo [at least that's the printed word] to say that Germany's first-line fighters have been shot down. They came at us four abreast and they fought like hell."

A more official, less colorful, statement on the day's missions was issued by General Frederick L. Anderson who said, "The recent attacks into Germany have surely caused the enemy to doubt the safety of any part of Axis Europe. Germany is now wide open. Today she has received two blows at vital units deeper into her territory than ever before . . .

"We do not know the results of today's attacks, but we do know that the destruction of the two targets will have very serious effects upon the enemy's war machine.

"Although we cannot say that the end is actually in sight, the ultimate collapse of German resistance is obvious and inevitable.

"Our airmen go into the battle of Germany knowing that each airman lost saves thousands in ultimate cost on the ground. They realize that the very savagery of the German opposition indicates the extent of the hurt from our attacks . . ."

As soon as he was able after his arrival in Africa LeMay had informed Anderson that the objective was "believed to be totally destroyed." He and his men then heard enthusiastically from Anderson, who wired:

> CONGRATULATIONS TO YOU, YOUR COMBAT CREWS AND YOUR MEN ON THE COMPLETION OF AN EPIC STAGE IN AERIAL WARFARE FOR THE U. S. ARMY AIR FORCES. ALTHOUGH I HAVE NOT YET RECEIVED REPORTS ON THE DESTRUCTION OF THE TARGET, I AM SURE THE FOURTH BOMBARDMENT WING HAS CONTINUED TO MAKE HISTORY. THE HUN NOW HAS NO PLACE TO HIDE.

The early reports from the Schweinfurt forces was not as positive as LeMay's: "Considerable damage has been done to all three plants plus the town of Schweinfurt. Smoke from lead elements makes observations difficult. Concentration seen on marshaling yard between plants. Also large barracks [in] area severely damaged." These barracks housed the workers of the Todt Organization, a flexible, traveling, labor force (some times made up of prisoners) conscripted into critical war work. It was named for Dr. Fritz Todt, the great engineer who had been Albert Speer's predecessor in the Ministry of Armaments and Munitions.

General Robert B. Williams, commander of the Schweinfurt

forces, however, "was not satisfied with our bombing accuracy although there was considerable damage to the ball-bearing plants." The bombs, in fact, tended to fall short although none concerned could determine why excepting, as was brought out by Colonel Gross later, that "there was a little discrepancy in the settings of the altimeters." Williams, too, was mystified: "I can't understand why the bombs fell so short with such a perfect [bomb] run. In spite of this, I still think the bombing was better than good and we accomplished our mission."

Speer concurred. Years after the event he did say that he believed the American forces had been dissipated by employing them in a double strike mission. Had both forces attacked Schweinfurt—ideally that would have made it some 376 Fortresses—the mission might have been decisive in August and might not have required another trip in October—another even more deadly one that no one thought would have to be made.

In fact, the raid had a decided effect, for production at Schweinfurt fell off 38 per cent after the August 17 mission. This concerned Speer, despite the jubilance in the Luftwaffe's high command—the Eighth Air Force had lost no less than sixty Flying Fortresses and their crews, 600 men—for he foresaw its true significance. It *was* true: there was no place to hide. Schweinfurt turned out a little over half of all of Germany's ball-bearing production and the raid forced Speer to fall back on the reserve supply, which lasted about two months. What production that still could be done in the factories "was carried daily to the assembly plants, often in knapsacks."

Despite its vulnerability, the Schweinfurt plant had to be put back together for the simple reason that an attempt at relocation would disrupt production for "three or four months." Even so, Speer realized, that would have to come eventually, for the Allied bombers had come once; they could come again.

As for Regensburg, Bomber Command Intelligence Report No. 3639, issued two days after the mission—LeMay was still in Africa—and after photographs had been made, stated that the photos revealed "heavy damage to the Fighter Assembly Factory of Messerschmitt A. G. Among the buildings destroyed or damaged are:

All of the six main workshops (five severely damaged).
Final Assembly Shop.
Gun Testing Range for Aircraft.
Large new shop (½ destroyed).
Boiler House.
Main store and workshops (severe damage).
Office Blocks.
Workshops at N. E. end of factory (largely destroyed)."

The Third Division had accomplished its mission with very good results (unknown to them). According to Roger A. Freeman in *The Mighty Eighth,* "the raid destroyed most of the jigs for a secret jet fighter, the Me262." Disrupting the advent of this aircraft was an added achievement for the day and a considerable bonus. For its contribution to the day's efforts, the Third Air Division's seven participating groups were awarded the Distinguished Unit Citation, "in the name of the President as public evidence of deserved honor and distinction."

The two air divisions had accomplished, despite ferocious opposition, their missions and they had both caused serious destruction to the targets, particularly at Regensburg. The frustrating reality was that in order to make these raids mean something, larger forces attacking with regularity, as Eaker maintained, were imperative. But, at this time, they were also impossible. Had Schweinfurt been followed up soon after, as Speer has written, disaster to the industry—and to the German war production—would have been inevitable. As it was, a second Schweinfurt mission could not be scheduled until October 14, again with terrible bomber losses, but with even more devastating effect upon Schweinfurt. This second mission, its results and portent distressed Speer and he quickly appointed a special commissioner to oversee the ball-bearing industry. Thus with husbanding, vigorous control, imports from Switzerland and "peace loving" Sweden, whose representatives played both ends against the middle: the Allies paid to block the sale of ball bearings to Germany, who paid to import them. Such is war.

But equally helpful to the German cause was the Allied Air Forces' inability to continue bombing such targets as Schweinfurt at so high a loss rate. Still, the damage wrought by the October mission to Schweinfurt was cause for momentary optimism and many honestly agreed with General Arnold when he said, "Now we have got Schweinfurt." Attention, then, could be turned to other important targets.

There was that other factor: the cost in men and aircraft. In his report to Anderson, Williams cogently stated that, following the August 17 mission, combat crew morale fell very noticeably. One of the reasons, Williams noted, was no attempt was given to reward these crews with extra time off after, literally, days of tension and then the battle itself. They were disappointed, too, because the R.A.F. had not been able to follow their mission with one of its own to add further damage to the target. It was difficult to explain that the R.A.F. was incapable of carrying out such a mission—and, besides, Bomber Commander Harris did not believe in it.

Williams had an even more cogent observation: "Four Groups in this Air Division were so decimated by losses during this week that a total of only six combat boxes can be flown until suitable replacements are made operational."

Sixty Flying Fortresses had been lost over Holland, Belgium, and Germany—in the English Channel and the Mediterranean Sea. These planes with these men were off the Air Force rolls for the duration (all of the planes and many of the men forever). There were roughly thirty planes that had to be abandoned in Africa, and of those that returned to England, twenty-eight were placed on the "major damage" list and 148 on the minor. Those in the first category could only serve as a source of parts for the others. The Luftwaffe's bomber score for the day would then add up to more than a hundred B-17s.

What had happened to the Luftwaffe in the day's fighting? Bomber crews claimed no less than 288 German fighters, the Allied escort claimed 19. This would total 307, which was just about the number of German fighters that had actually participated in the battles. The true figure, according to Adolf Galland, was 25.

The discrepancy was not an Allied attempt to deceive, to feed a concerned public large figures to take the sting off the heavy bomber toll. So much occurred during the day's complex battling that many crews undoubtedly claimed the same plane. Knoke, for example, was knocked down twice that day—there was nothing decisive and final about his exits from the battle for he would return again to challenge the bombers, a statistic that simply had not stuck.

Regensburg-Schweinfurt's most obvious tactical truth was the need for a long-range escort fighter that had been so forcibly demonstrated. Where the Thunderbolts had been able to function, most notably during the withdrawal phase of the Schweinfurt forces, they had, indeed, performed "beyond praise." Or rather the men who flew these winged monsters had done so; so had the Spitfire pilots, but their even greater restricted range had precluded participation to the extent of the Thunderbolts. But even these, equipped with their belly tanks (which were a source of problems) were forced to turn back long before the targets had been reached, leaving the B-17s to stave off the Luftwaffe with their combat boxes. These formations helped, but were not foolproof—nor safe from penetration by an especially determined and aggressive German fighter pilot. And there were a great number of those out on August 17. Where the Thunderbolts could intervene—that is, when close enough to disrupt the German pilots' attacks—they were effective. They were not, simply, effective "all the way" and back.

Such a fighter was, even in August 1943, under construction, although it would not arrive in England until December. By this time the second Schweinfurt mission had been flown—with a loss of more than sixty bombers and crews—which underscored the need (not that anyone in the Eighth Air Force denied that need). This was, of course, the North American P-51 Mustang, which eventually was capable of flying to Berlin and back. But it was not available when the double strike mission was flown—and missions had to be flown, long-range fighter or not. No amount of postwar armchair generalship can ignore these facts.

But had the Regensburg-Schweinfurt mission, and the subsequent second Schweinfurt, proved the British advocates of night area bombings correct and the American advocates of day bombing—with reasonable "precision"—wrong? That the blows struck that day were effective cannot be denied. And, within the license that war-making implies, specific targets were attacked and not, except accidentally, homes and other structures not directly concerned with the war. A modicum of common sense, however, would inform us that it is extremely difficult in wartime, particularly in a "world" war and all it implies, to determine just which people who get in the way of the falling bombs are innocent and which guilty.

Whatever the ethics of this argument, the precision method of bombardment was the least destructive to the lives and property of the innocent, the near-innocent, and even the guilty who lived in civilian areas. To the victim, of course, the degree of innocence, and the intent of the bombing forces, was academic, even immaterial—except as a lesson in the meaning of war. The impact of a bomb concentration on a military target was undoubtedly of greater effect on that target than a scattering of bombs in some general area, with the hope that the specific target would suffer along with the rest.

That the bombing was more efficient and effectual by day than night cannot be denied. But this leaves the question of excessive losses unanswered. Statistically 19 per cent of the Fortresses which attacked Regensburg-Schweinfurt did not return from those targets (not all of those, however, even got to the targets). That is, nearly a fifth of the attacking force was lost that day, a loss ratio that could not have continued. The answer to that lay in the long-range escort fighter.

Both LeMay and Williams believe that had the mission been executed as planned it would have been as successful (militarily) and that there would have been fewer losses. The post-mission critiques presided over by these two men reveal that an honest, hard, and realistic attitude was taken in assessing the missions. There were no accusations made, no excuses; what had happened had happened. They would have to attempt such missions again and what had been learned, at so great a cost, from Regensburg-Schweinfurt would be applied in the future. Meanwhile, chances would have to be taken, there being nothing truly predetermined in war.

The need for well-worked-out fighter protection was a major point brought out; so was the importance of tight formations. As for flying shuttle missions, LeMay found little to commend in that idea. Working away from home bases and your own ground crews was risky—as demonstrated by the mission to Bordeaux on the return flight. His opinion was not contravened by two more such missions to Russia later in the war.

The critiques over, the various commanders scattered to their several stations. Despite its many epochal qualities, Regensburg-Schweinfurt, by the morning after, though never forgotten by those who had flown it, had become just another mission.

There was the next one to think about.

Appendix

ORDER OF BATTLE, 3RD AIR DIVISION

17 August, 1943—Regensburg

1ST AIR TASK FORCE

403 Combat Wing

(Lead) 96th Bomb Group	21 a/c
(Low) 388th Bomb Group	21 "
(High) 390th Bomb Group	20 "
Total=	62 a/c

401 Combat Wing

(Lead) 94th Group	21 a/c
(Low) 385th Group	21 "
Total=	42 a/c

402 Combat Wing

(Lead) 95th Bomb Group	21 a/c
(Low) 100th Bomb Group	21 "
Total=	42 a/c

3rd Air Division (1st ATF)=146 a/c

ORDER OF BATTLE, 1ST AIR DIVISION

17 August, 1943—Schweinfurt

2ND AIR TASK FORCE

101 Combat Wing

(Lead) 91st Bomb Group	18 a/c
(Low) 381st Bomb Group	20 a/c
(High) Composite Group: 306th B.G.—7 a/c; 91st B.G.—6 a/c; 381st B.G.—6 a/c	19 a/c
Total=	57 a/c

Composite Wing

(Lead) 351st Bomb Group	21 a/c
(Low) 384th Bomb Group	18 a/c
(High) "306 Composite Group": 306th B.G.—9 a/c; 305th B.G.—9 a/c; 92nd B.G.—2 a/c	20 a/c
Total=	59 a/c

3RD AIR TASK FORCE

102 Combat Wing

(Lead) 306th Bomb Group	21 a/c
(Low) 92nd Bomb Group	20 a/c
(High) 305th Bomb Group	20 a/c
Total=	61 a/c

103 Provisional Combat Wing

(Lead) 379 Bomb Group	18 a/c
(Low) 303 Bomb Group	18 "
(High) Composite Group: 303rd B.G.—11 a/c; 379th B.G.— 6 a/c	17 "
Total=	53 a/c

1st Air Division { 2nd ATF—116 a/c; 3rd ATF—114 a/c } =230 a/c

FLYING FORMATIONS EMPLOYED IN REGENSBURG-SCHWEINFURT RAIDS

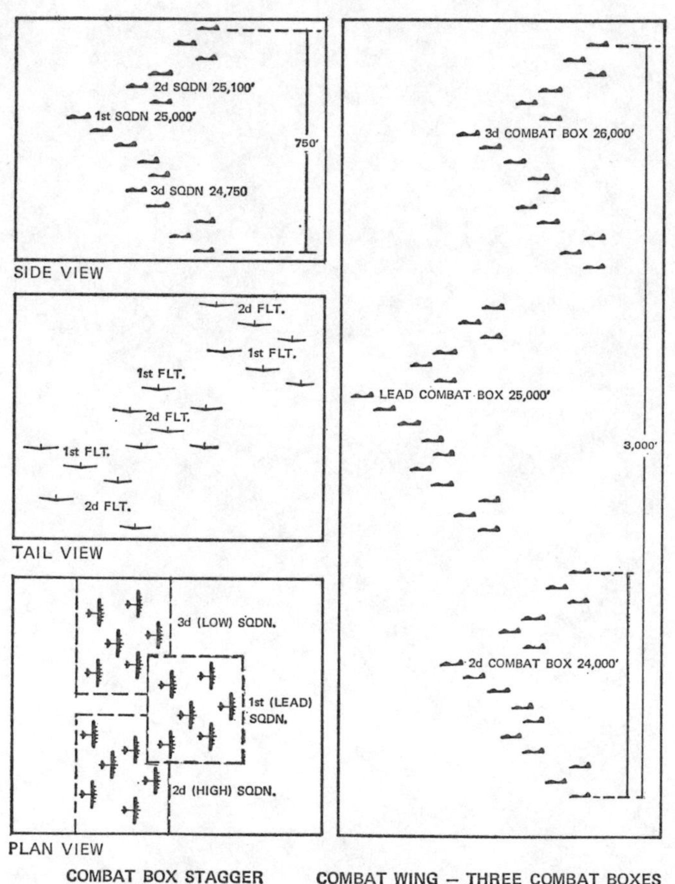

COMBAT BOX STAGGER COMBAT WING – THREE COMBAT BOXES

DOCUMENTS

This section contains several of the original Air Force documents preserved in the Modern Military Records Division of the National Archives, reproduced verbatim for those interested in the raw material of history. These represent but a fraction of the documents drawn upon for this book. These papers afford a valuable glimpse at the view of the mission, without the advantages of hindsight, held by those responsible for the execution of the double strike as well as by those who participated. There is some duplication, as some of the documents are quoted in the main text, but these are generally brief and there is a minimum of repetition. The original military classifications appear at the head of the various documents as samples of the categories at the time; all have since been declassified.

DOCUMENT 1

Col. Curtis E. LeMay's Report to Brig. Gen. F. L. Anderson:

SECRET

SUBJECT: Tactical Report of Mission, REGENSBURG, 17 August 1943

TO: Commanding General, VIII Bomber Command, APO 634

1. SUMMARY OF MISSION.

A. *Data.*

(1) Date of Mission—17 August 1943

(2) Primary Target—REGENSBURG (Messerschmitt factory).

(3) Secondary Target—ALLACH (Aircraft factory).

(4) Last Resort Target—MUNICH (City center).

B. *Narrative.*

(1) Combined Planning.

a. The plan for this mission was originated by the VIII Bomber Command Combined Operational Planning Committee. It was received by this headquarters about two weeks prior to the expected execution date.

b. After a thorough study of the plan all group commanders were called into conference and informed of the intended operation. At the same time, lead crews were selected and briefed intensively upon photographs of the target and surrounding area, without divulging names or routes. Also a memorandum was published covering maintenance and billeting arrangements at advance bases in North Africa.

c. The original combined plan included the use of medium bombers and fighter-bombers for diversionary raids on both sides of the intended 4th Wing route in, with a diversionary mission into the Ruhr Area by the First Air Division. A change in this plan was made in the Bomber Command Field Order, which called for the First Air Division to follow closely behind the 3rd Air Division forces and attack Schweinfurt while the 3rd Division was attacking REGENSBURG.

d. When this change was received, the selected lead crews and group commanders were called into conference for a final and complete briefing on the revised plan which was scheduled for execution the following day.

(2) 3rd Air Division Planning

a. The 403rd Combat Wing with the 390th Group attached was scheduled to lead the 3rd Air Division. The 96th Group was scheduled to lead the combat wing, with the 388th Group in No. 2 position and the 390th Group last. The 401st Combat Wing, with the 94th Group leading and the 385th Group second, was to follow the 403rd Combat Wing and attack the target three minutes later. The 402nd Combat Wing, with the 95th Group leading and the 100th Group second, was to attack the target three minutes after the 401st Combat Wing.

b. To insure the proper defensive formation at altitude before penetrating the enemy fighter defense, it was planned that the division would reach bombing altitude 20 minutes before the proposed time of departure from the English coast.

c. Because of its high priority, its extreme distance into Germany, and the element of surprise in the withdrawal to Africa, the destruction of the target on the first attempt was of prime importance. For this reason an IP was selected which resulted in a bombing run with very little drift. For the same reason lower than normal bombing altitudes of from 17,000 to 20,000 feet were chosen to increase the probability of good bombing results. The lower altitudes also were decided upon to increase the efficiency of both aircraft and personnel on the extraordinarily long route at altitude. This was thought to be not too dangerous since the AA defenses on the proposed bomb run were predicted to be moderate.

d. Since fighter opposition was expected to be slight in the vicinity of the target, provision was made to execute a second bombing run if for any reason the sighting was faulty on the first run. Along the withdrawal course, two Air Division rally points were selected; one north of the Alps to be used in case of a second bombing run by any unit, another south of the Alps to be used if adverse weather over the mountains should separate the formation. The presence of 200 fighters on Corsica and Sardinia required good defensive formation in the area.

(3) Execution.

a. The mission was flown by the 3rd Air Division as planned, with the following exceptions:

1. Because of fog and low ceilings which persisted at the bases at take-off time, the zero hour was advanced 1½ hours. This was the maximum delay permissible to allow a safe margin of daylight for landing in Africa. The difficulties of assembling over the overcast resulted in the division arriving at the fighter rendezvous five minutes late.

2. As the 94th Group, leading the 401st Combat Wing, turned from the IP to attack, bomb bursts and smoke from the attack of preceding groups completely obscured the target. The leader of the 94th Group therefore decided to make a second run on the target, and with this in mind proceeded to make a sweeping 360° turn to the left. In the meantime, the 402nd Combat Wing bombed the target. This maneuver placed the 402nd Combat Wing second on the rally, with the 401st last. This order of combat wings was held for the remainder of the mission.

3. In order to conserve fuel the two combat wings that bombed first immediately proceeded southward after their rally and circled to pick up the 401st Combat Wing at the southern rally point.

4. After leaving the coast of Italy, the formation was not good because of a shortage of fuel. However, all ships were sufficiently stacked in altitude to enable them to dive into defensive positions in case of attack. The coast of Africa was reached about 18 miles east of the intended landfall, with four aircraft making emergency landings here out of gasoline. Forty-four ships landed at Bône short of fuel. At least four ships ditched off the African coast and their crews were picked up. The remainder of the aircraft landed at Telergma and Berteaux as briefed.

5. There was some confusion at the airdromes because of ambiguous instructions issued by the enlisted control tower operator. The liaison officer from N.W.A.A.F. had failed to arrive because of late notification of our arrival and interference of other duties. All ships landed safely, however, in spite of heavy dust and thunderstorms in the area.

2. DETAILS AND ANALYSIS.

A. *Assembly.*

(1) Because of two layers of stratus cloud which persisted at bases at take-off time, assembly of groups was difficult. The combat wing assembly was not effected on time between splashers 5 and 6 as planned, but the combat wings attained a good defensive formation by the time of departure from the English coast.

B. *Rendezvous with Fighters.*

(1) Six squadrons of P-47's were to rendezvous with the bombers at intervals starting at 5143-0342E and provide escort as far along the route as possible. Some P-47's effected assembly with our formation, but they stayed to the rear and their numbers were insufficient to be effective. The support was poorly given.

C. *Bombing Tactics and Results.*

(1) The division reached the IP on time, finding the weather excellent and the target area completely clear. AA fire and enemy fighters, although present, did not hamper the bombing run.

(2) The 401st Combat Wing made a second run on the target because on the first run up the aiming point was obscured by smoke and dust which prevented the lead group from dropping their bombs.

(3) Bombing Data:

Order of Groups	Direct of Run	Length of Run	Time of Run	True Alt.	AFCE Used	ABC Used	No. Sighting Deflect. & Range	For Range	Dropped on Leader
96	94°	3 Min.	1143	18,550	Yes	Yes	1	0	18
388	90°	3′20″	1145	17,400	Yes	Yes	1	0	20
390	93°	3 Min.	1150	19,280	Yes	Yes	1	0	17
385	96°	6 Min.	1152	16,500	Yes	Yes	1	1	18
95	97°	90 Sec.	1154	18,000	Yes	Yes	1	2	8
94	98°	90 Sec.	1207	17,600	Yes	Yes	1	3	11
100	91°	3 Min.	1145	17,000	No	No	1	0	13

(4) Reconnaissance photographs were taken within 4 hours of the attack. These photographs show heavy damage over the entire plant area, nearly all of the buildings being affected in some degree. All six of the main workshops were hit, five of them being almost completely demolished. At least 125 strikes can be seen on key buildings, as well as numerous direct hits on subsidiary buildings. This is one of the finest examples of high altitude precision bombing yet produced by the 3rd Air Division.

D. *AA Gun Fire.*

(1) AA fire along the entire route to the Brenner Pass and Italy were meagre but accurate. AA fire was put up by numerous defended places, although our aircraft were not in range. Such fire was used as an air beacon to facilitate assembly at the first rally point north of the Brenner Pass. Other places where this fire was seen were Nurnberg, MUNICH and Antwerp. Over

these cities barrage fire control was used. Elsewhere, continuous fire control was reported.

E. *Enemy Aircraft Encounters.*

(1) Approximately 275 fighters were encountered from the Belgian coast to the Alps. The intensity of the attacks increased from Antwerp to Frankfurt, but fell off from that point to the IP. There were practically no attacks at the target. From the target to the Alps the attacks were resumed with moderate intensity.

(2) Attacks came from all levels and directions but some groups were more heavily attacked than others throughout the mission. Reports indicate all known enemy tactics were used, and that they were better planned and executed than on previous missions.

(3) The following types and numbers of enemy aircraft were encountered:

FW 190—103	Me 110—28
Me 109—89	Me 210—3
Ju 88—29	He 111—1

(4) Claims are as follows:

ROUP	DESTROYED						PROBABLE						DAMAGED					
	FW	109	88	110	210	HE	FW	109	88	110	210	HE	FW	109	88	110	210	HE
94th	4	1	5	2	1	0	0	0	0	1	0	0	2	0	0	3	0	0
95th	14	14	0	0	0	0	1	0	0	0	0	0	2	4	0	2	0	0
96th	3	2	0	0	0	0	1	0	0	0	0	0	0	0	0	0	0	0
00th	30	13	0	0	0	0	3	7	0	1	0	0	1	7	0	2	0	0
85th	12	8	16	10	2	1	2	2	1	1	0	0	0	1	1	3	0	0
88th	5	2	2	0	0	0	0	0	0	0	0	0	1	3	0	0	0	0
90th	3	7	0	0	0	0	1	1	0	0	0	0	0	8	0	0	0	0
otal	71	47	23	12	3	1	8	10	1	3	0	0	6	23	1	10	0	0
GRAND TOTAL		157							22						40			

(5) In addition to the usual wide variety of color markings, unpainted twin-engined and single-engined fighters were seen.

(6) Reports mentioned that some enemy aircraft were equipped with rockets attached to underside of the wings.

(7) In addition to the new armament just described, crews observed planes thought to be armed with 37 or 40 mm cannon.

F. *Abortives.*

(1) *a.* 95th Group.

1. A/C #42-30045 returned early; took off late could not catch formation.

2. A/C #42-3266 returned early; engine failure.

3. A/C #42-30276 returned early; low oil pressure.

4. A/C #42-30288 returned early; prop governor drive shaft snapped.

5. A/C #42-30377 returned early; fuse burned out in upper turret circuit.

6. A/C #42-3273 returned early; oil relief valve stuck.

b. 96th Group

1. A/C #42-30172 returned early; leak in oxygen system.

2. A/C #42-30412 returned early; prop governor failed.

c. 100th Group

1. A/C #42-30059 returned early; engine RPM out, oil pressure high, manifold pressure out and fuel pressure low.

d. 385th Group.

1. A/C #42-30096 returned early; radio equipment inoperative.

2. A/C #42-30094 returned early; RPM's increased to 2300 and manifold pressure from 39″59 to 40″ during climb. Oil pressure normal, oil leaked out past accessory cowling on engine. Smoke seen, engine cut and prop feathered.

3. A/C #42-3335 returned early; oil leaking from under intersection of wing and engine due to engine oil temperature regulator defect.

e. 390th Group.

1. A/C #42-30308 failed to take off; ship broke through hard stand prior to take-off.

2. A/C #42-3312 failed to take off; ball turret inoperative.

(2) Other Equipment and Personnel Failures.

a. The following engineering failures were reported, with the number of cases reported in parentheses:

1. Information not yet received.

b. The following armament failures were reported, with the number of cases indicated in parentheses:

1. Information not yet received.

c. The following communications failures were reported, with the number of cases indicated in parentheses:

1. Interphones weak or out (7), radio compasses (2); pilots mike buttons (2).

G. *Communications.*

(1) Radio Procedure

a. The command set was on 6440 kc/s for air-to-ground communication, and 5065 kc/s for air-to-air R/T. The command set worked satisfactorily, except that certain sets experienced interference over the Ruhr.

b. Liaison W/T communication was on 4370 kc/s and 3485 kc/s with the 4th Bomb Wing ground station. Two channels were used to overcome skip, but the effort was not successful. After leaving target, liaison channel was changed to 3310 kc/s for control by N.W.A.A.F. Hqs. Advance information was incorrect and the N.W.A.A.F. Hqs. had changed to 4595 kc/s.

Communication was established by zero beating the transmitter with the receiver.

c. In the African area considerable interference was experienced with MF D/F stations being crowded with distress calls.

(2) Radio Aids to Navigation.

a. Eight splasher beacons were turned on as an aid to navigation and for assembling. "GEE" was used with good results for approximately 250 miles. Enemy beacons at Bordeaux and Rennes were used with satisfactory results. VHF was used with good results by several aircraft in obtaining D/F assistance in Africa. Seven QDM's and three fixes were obtained.

3. REMARKS.

(1) This mission, one of the longest ever flown by this division at altitude and the first "shuttle" raid ever made by American forces in this theatre, was exceedingly successful. Not only were the bombing results outstanding; but the navigation, maneuver at the IP and formation flown until reaching the Italian coast were all excellent.

(2) Because of the adverse weather at take-off the details of the assembly were not good, but under the existing condition it was almost miraculous that the entire division succeeded in getting into the proper formation. Smoke signals were used for the first time during assembly, and while not perfect were generally regarded as helpful.

(3) Had it not been for the excellent formation flown on the way in, our losses would undoubtedly have been even heavier. It is believed, however, that battle losses could have been reduced still further if the combat wings had been closer together, although closer formation would have increased the gas consumption somewhat and possibly increased the loss due to ditching.

(4) Maintenance and supply difficulties experienced at the advance bases in Africa have been covered in a separate re-

port submitted to VIII Bomber Command, 29 August 1943, and are not discussed in this tactical report.

CURTIS E. LEMAY
Colonel, Air Corps
Commanding

The two items marked "Information not yet received," namely engineering failures and armament failures, were supplied soon after the Report was submitted. These covered, in double columns, about a foolscap-sized page. Thirty-two items are enumerated under Engineering Failures, with the greatest number being sixteen supercharger regulators which lagged. Five aircraft suffered from excessive oil consumption and two from engine failure. There were two window-wipers inoperative, and so on. The greatest number of Armament Failures occurred because of faulty feeding (3); one station of the bomb rack was inoperative; one gun had its charging handle broken—and so on, through ten items. Under Miscellaneous Failures there are only six: 1 GEE; 2 Liaison receivers; Command transmitter, 11 interphones (four more than the original report's); 4 Radio compasses (an additional two) and the original two Pilot Mike buttons. This report also was marked Secret.

DOCUMENT 2

Brig. Gen. Robert B. Williams's Report to Brig. Gen. F. L. Anderson

SECRET

HEADQUARTERS
1ST BOMBARDMENT WING
APO 634

23 August, 1943

SUBJECT: Report of Operations,
SCHWEINFURT, Germany, 17 August, 1943.

TO: Commanding General, VIII Bomber Command, APO 634.

1. Summary of Mission.

a. Data.

(1) Date of Mission—17 August, 1943.

(2) Primary Target—Ball Bearing Works, Schweinfurt, Germany.

(3) Secondary Target—General Engineering Works, Frankfort, Germany.

(4) Third Choice Target—R.R. Marshaling Yards, Aachen, Germany.

(5) Fourth Choice Target—Instrument Factory, Bonn, Germany.

(6) Units Participating—The 91, 92, 303, 305, 306, 351, 379, 381 and 384 dispatched a total of 230 aircraft on a maximum effort on this operation of which 187 aircraft bombed the primary target.

b. Narrative.

(1) Normal Combat Wing formations were scheduled, but due to the composition of the force, it was necessary to form at least one squadron in each Group into a composite formation. One Group each of the 102 C. W. and 103 C. W. was attached to the 101 C. W. to form the second Air Task Force of two Combat Wings at 5 minute intervals. The third Air Task Force was composed of the remainder of the 102 C. W. leading the 103 C. W. at an interval of 5 minutes, both in normal C. W. formation. This resulted in 3 composite Groups and 1 composite C. W. formation. Assembly of all of these heterogeneous units was a tedious task to which considerable planning was devoted.

(2) At take-off time, the weather at all First Air Division bases was heavy fog, ceiling zero, and visibility varying from 50 to 100 yards. Several delays were authorized by Bomber Command which made final take-off 5 hours later than originally planned. This made an afternoon attack rather than a morning attack as originally planned, necessitating a change of axis of attack due to the position of the sun. Orders effecting the change were issued over the broadcast system on the operations telephone and caused no undue confusion. At final take-off time, the clouds had become broken, and the formations assembled as briefed and departed from the English Coast as scheduled.

(3) General Williams was designated Air Division Air Commander. Colonel Gross was designated as Second Air Task Force Air Commander, and Colonel Turner was designated as Third Air Task Force Air Commander. V.H.F. call signs were assigned to each Commander in the Air Division Field Order for authentication and identification. All three Commanders made important decisions in the air and contributed to the success of the

mission by relieving the lead pilots of all responsibilities except those of piloting and leading the large formations.

(4) The route to the target was closely adhered to by both task forces. The Air Commander of the Second Air Task Force had trouble with clouds and reduced his altitude from 21,-000 as planned to 17,000 feet on the route to the target. Due to the fact that he had no friendly fighter support as expected, he closed his two combat wings to a closer interval than the 5 minutes prescribed for the penetration of the fighter belt. Sustained and vicious enemy fighter attacks were experienced from the French Coast to about 10 minutes west of the IP. Navigation was superb and formations were superior.

(5) The Third Air Task Force, following at an interval of 12 minutes found it possible to fly the course at prescribed altitude. Navigation was made simple by the trail of burning Fortresses and parachutes from the preceding task force. Due to the altitude differential in speed, this force closed on the preceding task force by the time the IP was reached. Due to the excellent visibility, this caused no trouble at the IP and the leader of the Third Air Task Force was able to maneuver his formation so as to get an unobstructed bombing run. This turned out to be a fortunate circumstance, as the enemy did not start his smoke screen until after the first bombs had fallen, and the last formation across the target did not find the aiming point obscured by the smoke screen.

(6) On the return trip, the leader of the Second Air Task Force again descended to 17,000 feet in expectation of the cloud formation. The leader of the Third Air Task Force was able to maintain an altitude of 20,000 feet without difficulty. The return route was planned to close all four Combat Wings into a close column of Combat Wings by the time the Ruhr area was reached. As flown, the formations formed into task forces flying abreast by the time fighter rendezvous was reached. Shortly after fighter rendezvous, the Air Commander of the Third Air Task Force gave the order to his formations to reduce speed in order

to allow a crippled group leader to maintain formation. At the same time, the leader of the Second Air Task Force continued to lose altitude, resulting in an eventual 10 mile interval between Task Forces. Otherwise the route back was as planned.

2. Details and Analysis.

a. Assembly.

(1) Assembly was accomplished above broken clouds in accordance with a carefully prepared plan. One task force departed the English Coast at Orfordness with Combat Wings at 5 minute intervals and C. W. leaders at same altitude. The other task force departed at Claxton 12 minutes later, also with C. W.'s at intervals of 5 minutes and leaders at the same altitudes. The two points were selected about 20 miles apart for departure points and nearby splasher beacons were assigned to each task force in order to reduce confusion and recognition difficulties in so far as possible. Normal C. W. formations were employed, and by an extremely commendable effort on the part of all concerned, the total number of A/C was within 7 of the number previously planned, after all units had sustained severe losses and heavy battle damage on two days of the previous five. Combat Wing and Air Task Force Commanders are to be especially commended for the success of the various assemblies.

b. Fighter Rendezvous.

(1) 4 Squadrons of Spitfire IX's were scheduled to rendezvous with the bombers at bombing altitude at 5135-0340E on the route to the target and escort them to 5115-0435E. At this point, 6 Squadrons of P-47's were to take over the escort and accompany the bombers to Eupen. The bombers were to be without escort from this point to the target and back that far. On the route back, 6 Squadrons of P-47's were to escort them from Eupen to Antwerp where 8 Squadrons of Spit IX's were to escort them to the English Coast.

(2) On the route to the target the group of P-47's detailed to escort the lead task force was 9 minutes late taking

off, and was unable to catch the proper bomber formations. No Spitfires were seen. The result of these unfortunate circumstances was the loss of at least 15 B-17's along the route where fighter escort was scheduled. The lead task force performed the entire mission without any help from friendly fighters.

(3) The Group detailed to protect the following task force was on time, and with the help of the late group of P-47's rendered superb support to the bombers to the designated point.

(4) On the route back, the P-47's were on time, but were hopelessly outnumbered by enemy fighters. Again the leader of the Third Air Task Force received practically all of the support, and attacks continued on other formations to Spit IX rendezvous. The Spit IX's were on time and flying very high above the bombers. Although they were not seen to come down to engage, the enemy attacks ceased abruptly with their appearance.

(5) Timings were as planned. The support rendered by the P-47's was not as planned. The bomber formations were disposed to take advantage of the usual P-47 tactics of sweeping over the bombers in a column of squadrons at 2 or 3 minute intervals, furnishing a corridor support. The P-47's on this mission retained their group formations and remained with only 1 C. W.

3. Conclusions and Recommendations.

a. This Headquarters has only the greatest praise for all lower echelons for the successful accomplishment of this vital mission. Air Commanders and leaders used good judgement and executed their assigned tasks with precision and skill. The bombing, although not perfect, was good and the targets received severe damage. Formations were the best any of the experienced leaders had ever seen, and due to the unprecedented ferocity of enemy attacks along the entire route, resulted in the mission being effective, and a tremendous number of claims against the enemy.

b. It is recommended that an immediate conference be held with the fighter commanders to find what type of support can be expected in order that we may dispose our formations in the way which will take maximum advantage of the limited support available at present.

c. There was a noticeable sag in combat crew morale after this mission due to:

(1) Crews expected to be given some extra liberty privileges after maintaining such a long period of alert for this particular mission. The necessity of continuing the offensive after the Germans had shot down over 100 allied heavy bombers during this 24 hours was explained to them, but to little avail.

(2) Crews had been briefed in the past that the RAF would follow our raid with a maximum effort. It could not be explained to them why this was not possible on the particular day of the attack, and crews felt that they had been let down after their bloody fight to pave the way.

d. Four Groups of this Air Division were so decimated by losses during this week that a total of only 6 combat boxes can be flown until suitable replacements are made operational.

e. The length of the route for this mission is the maximum distance our forces can fly. A large number of A/C were forced to land at the English Coast on return for gasoline before proceeding to bases.

f. The abortion average on this mission was only 4% of the A/C scheduled. In view of the heavy operations during the preceding week, this is a remarkably commendable performance.

ROBERT B. WILLIAMS,
Brigadier General, U. S. Army.
Commanding.

DOCUMENT 3

Brigadier General Frederick L. Anderson's Report to Major General Ira C. Eaker

SECRET

HEADQUARTERS VIII BOMBER COMMAND
APO 634

SUBJECT: Report of Operations, 17 August, 1943.

TO: Commanding General
Headquarters Eighth Air Force, APO 633.

1. IDENTIFICATION.
   a. Mission No. 84.
   b. Targets Planned.
      (1) 1st Bomb Division—Ball Bearing Works, Schweinfurt, Germany.
      (2) 3rd Bomb Division—Messerschmitt Aircraft Factory, Regensburg, Germany.

2. PLANNING.

a. It was planned to dispatch eight (8) forces, four (4) from the 1st Bomb Division, and four (4) from the 3rd Bomb Division.

b. The four (4) forces from the 1st Bomb Division were assigned the three (3) Ball Bearing Works at Schweinfurt.

c. The four (4) forces of the 3rd Bomb Division were assigned the Messerschmitt Factory at Regensburg.

d. The 1st Bomb Division forces assigned to Schweinfurt were to penetrate enemy territory approximately 10 minutes after the 3rd Bomb Division forces assigned to Regensburg. This was planned because the 3rd Bomb Division forces were slightly slower than the 1st Bomb Division forces due to long-range tanks, and also because of the necessity for the 3rd Bomb Division forces leaving the Schweinfurt area before the 1st Bomb Division forces arrived there.

e. It was believed that the 3rd Bomb Division, by preceding the 1st Bomb Division into enemy territory, would receive the preponderance of the enemy fighter opposition and was therefore assigned the majority of the fighter escort.

f. It was planned that after attacking the target at Regensburg, the forces of the 3rd Bomb Division would then proceed to advanced airdromes in North Africa. The 1st Bomb Division forces, due to their limited range, were obliged to withdraw over the reciprocal of their route in to the target at Schweinfurt.

g. Due to extremely adverse weather over the bomber bases in England, it became necessary to advance the zero hour one (1) hour. Since a further delay would cause the 3rd Bomb Division forces to arrive at bases in North Africa at dusk or later, the decision was made to dispatch the 3rd Bomb Division and to make available all the fighter escort originally assigned to both Bomb Divisions.

h. A new time schedule was set up for the forces of the 1st Bomb Division which gave them a take-off time approximately 3½ hours after the 3rd Bomb Division had crossed the enemy coast in order that the fighter escort would have been able to land, refuel, rearm and be available to escort the 1st Bomb Division forces on their penetration.

i. One additional factor affecting the decision to carry out the plan as outlined above was the fact that weather conditions over the entire route and at the target areas were the best which had been forecast for a period of over two weeks. Inasmuch as the importance of these targets increased almost daily, the risk involved in dispatching the two Bomb Divisions individually was felt to be commensurate with the results which the destruction of these two targets would achieve.

3. EXECUTION.

a. Targets Bombed.

(1) 1st Bomb Division—Ball Bearing Works, Schweinfurt, Germany.

(2) 3rd Bomb Division—Messerschmitt Aircraft Factory, Regensburg, Germany.

b. 1st Bomb Division.

(1) The 1st Bomb Division dispatched four (4) forces of three (3) Groups each to attack the targets at Schweinfurt. Despite adverse weather and heterogeneous units, assembly was as planned, and the forces departed from the coast of England on schedule.

(2) The route to and from Schweinfurt was flown as planned.

(3) Fighter rendezvous was not accomplished as planned. Although the fighters were met, the escort was reported as not being fully effective by all forces.

(4) Bombing results at Schweinfurt were good. The three roller bearing factories have suffered damage. In the Kugelfischer Werke, direct hits and severe damage were scored on four (4) large machine shops, an office building (gutted by fire), canteen building (destroyed by fire), and a stores building (destroyed by fire). The new central administration buildings were damaged. In V. K. F. Werke I, an unidentified building was destroyed, and another unidentified building severly damaged by direct hits and fire. In the V. K. F. Werke II, a pressing shop was partially destroyed, a large machine shop suffered extensive roof damage, and another machine shop suffered damage. Additional bomb damage was as follows:

In the Fichtel and Sachs A. G. (Aircraft Components Factory), a building gutted by fire, a building destroyed, extensive roof damage to machine shops, severe damage to an unidentified building and two shelters;

In the fruit preserving factory, two medium buildings were gutted by fire, one medium and two small buildings destroyed;

In the Ultramarine factory, two medium buildings and one small shed destroyed;

In the malt factory, one unidentified factory and several small buildings severely damaged;

In the railway marshalling yards, the station buildings gutted, platforms and roofs half destroyed, hits on all tracks through the station, a train severely damaged, the station footbridge destroyed in two places, maintenance and engine sheds damaged by direct hit, and an unidentified building severely damaged.

In the military post, two barracks blocks were destroyed and 17 blocks were damaged.

In the city of Schweinfurt, one wing of the town hall gutted by fire, the town bank damaged, many business and residential buildings destroyed or damaged, several unidentified commercial premises damaged, and two streets damaged by direct hits.

c. 3rd Bomb Division.

(1) The 3rd Bomb Division dispatched three (3) forces, two (2) composed of two (2) Groups each, and the third composed of three (3) Groups, to attack the target at Regensburg. The forces assembled into good defensive formation although difficulty in assembly, due to adverse weather conditions, caused the forces to depart the English coast five minutes behind schedule.

(2) The route was flown essentially as planned for the entire mission.

(3) Fighter rendezvous was accomplished even though the bomber forces were five minutes late at rendezvous point. Fighter escort was reported to be ineffective, however.

(4) Photographic reconnaissance taken four hours after the attack showed bombing results at Regensburg to be excellent.

In the Messerschmitt factory hardly a building remains undamaged. Out of a total of 62 installations damaged, those destroyed or severely damaged include 13 workshops, 5 office buildings, 19 unidentified buildings and 17 other structures, including the final assembly shop, gun testing range, 3 buildings of the light metal works, hangar for engine installation, a new unidentified building under construction, and 10 living quarters. Other buildings suffering blast damage were 1 workshop, 5 unidentified buildings, 1 living hut, and the hospital. Photographs revealed 51 single engine aircraft on the airfield and near the factory buildings, of which 37 were probably destroyed or severely damaged.

4. Enemy Opposition.

a. 1st Bomb Dvision.

(1) Anti-Aircraft: Reported meagre to moderate with accuracy varying from poor to excellent at Schweinfurt. Reported meagre and inaccurate from Noord Beveland, Antwerp, Aachen, Bonn, Mannheim, Antwerp Hannuef, Eupen, and Knocke. Intense fixed barrages were observed at Frankfurt, Koln and Bonn. Slight evasive action was taken.

(2) Enemy Aircraft: The forces of the 1st Bomb Division reported 300 encounters which began at 1347 hours as the forces penetrated the enemy coast and continued until 1703 hours as the forces departed from the enemy coast on return. Attacks were from every position of the clock with the majority from six o'clock, high, low and level. Attacks were mostly in formation and carried out aggressively. Use of large-bore cannon and rocket guns by the enemy was reported.

b. 3rd Bomb Division.

(1) Anti-Aircraft: Reported meagre and inaccurate over Regensburg. Reported meagre and inaccurate to accurate elsewhere along route. Barrage type used over Nurnberg, Munich and Antwerp.

(2) Enemy Aircraft: The forces of the 3rd Bomb Division reported 174 encounters which began at 1000 hours as the forces penetrated the enemy coast, and continued until 1430 hours

as the forces crossed the Alps on route to Africa. Attacks were from all levels and directions, and all known tactics employed and were well executed.

5. WEATHER.

Poor visibility and low ceilings over England caused delay and difficulty in assembly. No difficulties were experienced on the remainder of the mission.

6. BATTLE LOSSES.

a. 1st Bomb Division—(36) Aircraft lost; (1) to antiaircraft, (26) to enemy aircraft, and (9) to reasons unknown.

b. 3rd Bomb Division—(24) Aircraft lost; (15) to enemy aircraft, (4) to accidents, (5) to reasons unknown.

7. BATTLE DAMAGE.

a. 1st Bomb Division—Major damage (27), minor damage (95); (49) by anti-aircraft, (52) by enemy aircraft and (21) by miscellaneous causes.

b. 3rd Bomb Division—(These figures include battle damage also for return mission to attack Bordeaux on 24 August, 1943, since the nature of the case made separate compilation impossible): Major damage (1), minor damage (53); (27) by antiaircraft, (5) by enemy aircraft, and (22) by miscellaneous causes.

8. RADIO AIDS.

a. 1st Bomb Division—Splasher beacons were employed for assembly and navigation, and multi-group beacons were employed for navigation. Sixty-one (61) aircraft were equipped with "Gee."

b. 3rd Bomb Division—Splasher beacons used for assembly and navigation, and enemy beacons also employed effectively. "Gee" used effectively for 250 miles.

9. COMMUNICATIONS.

a. 1st Bomb Division—V. H. F. employed effectively for bomber-to-bomber and fighter-to-bomber communication. Liaison used effectively for strike and ETA messages, and for D/F fixes.

b. 3rd Bomb Division—V. H. F. used effectively for D/F fixes, and liaison also used effectively for D/F fixes although difficulty was experienced in establishing contact with North African ground stations.

10. COMMENTS.

a. As mentioned Paragraph 2, PLANNING, it was expected that some, or all, of the enemy fighters which had been called into the area through which the 3rd Bomb Division force passed, would have been ordered to return to their normal defensive bases by the time at which the 1st Bomb Division would be departing the English coast. Had this expected procedure been followed by the German fighter controllers it is felt that the 1st Bomb Division units would have received very little fighter opposition enroute to the target. However, it was apparent that the German fighter controllers were either expecting an additional force to penetrate their territory or were expecting the 3rd Bomb Division to withdraw on a reciprocal of their route in. The result of this expectation was that a large number of enemy fighters were in a position to attack the 1st Bomb Division force enroute to and in the target area. Range limitations imposed by this operation required that all forces should follow the most direct routes to and from their targets.

b. There were many conflicting reports as to the effectiveness of our fighter support. Again, these reports are based on the idea that to those units which are hard hit by fighters and suffer excessive losses the fighter support is poor, and that to those units which are not hard hit the fighter support is good. As the number of friendly fighters operating in this theater are not sufficient to protect all of our units directly, it is necessary that they attempt to cover units which are under attack in order to disperse the enemy fighters or to cause them to break off engagement of a particular unit. When all factors effecting this operation are taken into consideration, it is felt that the fighter support afforded our units may be classed as excellent!

c. The original plans for this operation prescribed that our daylight attack on Schweinfurt would be followed almost immediately by a night attack of heavy bombers of RAF Bomber Command. This Command was in a position to carry out this operation from approximately 1 August and from that date on weather conditions were watched very closely for an opportunity to attack this target. However, weather conditions did not present themselves as feasible for an attack upon this target until 17 August. By this time the moon was full, causing the nights to be light enough to the point that the R.A.F. Bomber Command could not afford an attack on this target.

F. L. ANDERSON
Brigadier General, U.S.A.
Commanding.

DOCUMENT 4

Bomber Command Narrative of Operations, Mission No. 84

CONFIDENTIAL

HEADQUARTERS
VIII BOMBER COMMAND
A.P.O. 634

Bomber Command Narrative of Operations
Day Operations—17 August, 1943
Mission No. 84

PART I—SCHWEINFURT

Two Air Task Forces, composed of two Combat Wings each, of the 1st Air Division, were dispatched to attack three ball-bearing plants at Schweinfurt in central Germany. The target was bombed with good results. Strong e/a opposition was encountered along the route from near the Dutch coast to the target and back to the French coast. Penetration and withdrawal support was provided by VIII Fighter Command P-47s and RAF Spitfires. 36 B-17s are missing. Claims against e/a are 148-18-63.

UNIT	NUMBER OF A/C						PERSONNEL CASUALTIES		
			Failed						
	(Dis-	*At-*	*To*						
1st Wing	*patched*	*tacked*	*Bomb+*		*Lost)*	*Claims*	*(Killed*	*Wounded*	*Missing)*
			A.	*B.*					
91	24	9	3	12	10	13-1-3	1	1	97
92	22	21	0	1	2	17-3-1	0	1	20
303	29	27	1	1	0	20-7-9	1	4	0
305	29	27	2	0	2	17-1-4	1	1	24
306	30	30	0	0	0	16-1-3	0	0	0
351	28	26	0	2	2	25-2-21	0	0	20
379	24	18	2	4	4	11-3-2	0	1	40
381	26	18	1	7	11	21-0-14	0	1	101
384	18	12	1	5	5	8-0-6	0	3	50
	230	188×	10	32	36	148-18-63	3	12	352

+ Failed to Bomb—A—Mechanical and Equipment Failures.

B—Other than Mechanical and Equipment Failures (includes weather, recall, enemy action, etc.)

× 183 A/C on Schweinfurt, 1 on Frankfurt and 4 on Opportunity Targets.

BOMBING RESULTS: 183 B-17s dropped 1017×250 British incendiaries, 719×500 G. P. fused 1/10 sec. nose and 1/100 sec. tail and 235×1000 G. P. fused 1/10 sec. nose and 1/40 sec. tail from 19,000–22,600 feet at 1459–1511 hours on industrial plants in Schweinfurt. The B-17s had as aiming points, three ball bearing plants which contribute approximately 50 of total output of ball bearings available to Germany. Bombing results were very good. Considerable damage was inflicted on a number of buildings of the *Kugelfisher Works* (ball bearings), *Fichtel & Sachs* (aircraft components) and the *Vereingte Kugellager Fabriken* (ball bearings) Works I and II. Communications, including the main railway station, also suffered very heavy damage as well as a number of residential areas in *Schweinfurt and Oberndorf*. At the *Kugelfisher Works* the power house, a single-story machine shop, a multi-story machine shop and a large group of office buildings and stores received hits. At the *Fichtel & Sachs* Plant at least two bombs burst directly on a single-story machine shop, with three more on adjoining buildings. Direct hits were scored on two machine shops of the Works II plant of the *V.K.F.*, and other buildings received blast damagc. At Works I of the *V.K.F.*, part of the manufacturing buildings were destroyed. A barracks in a military establishment northwest of *Schweinfurt* was also damaged by a concentration of bombs.

REASONS FOR FAILURE TO BOMB: 42 a/c failed to bomb—10 because of mechanical and equipment failures, 2 because of personnel failures, 1 because of flak damage, and 29 which are missing.

ENCOUNTERS: E/a opposition was extremely strong. Up to 300 e/a were reported encountered, with attacks beginning at *Antwerp* and continuing in intermittent waves to *Schweinfurt* and back to the French coast. Attacks came from all directions with those from nose and tail—high and level—predominating. At times as many as 20–25 e/a would attack in line astern, with many other attacks being made by groups of 2–5. Many attacks came from above and out of the sun, with e/a diving on high squadrons and continuing through formation to strike the low squadron. Twin-engined e/a were reported as staying farther away from formations and generally showing poor tactics. Most of the e/a seen were FW-190s, Me-109s, Me-110s and JU-88s, with a few reports of Me-210s, DO-217s, HE-113s and FW-189s. Some single-engined e/a were reported resembling P-47s, being painted green with white cowlings and tails.

CASUALTIES: *Personnel*—3 killed, 3 seriously wounded, 9 slightly wounded and 352 are missing. 2 crews were picked up by Air Rescue Service.

Equipment—36 B-17s—1 by flak, 26 by e/a and 9 by reasons unknown.

Estimated Battle Damage—73 category "A," 9 category "AC" and 3 category "E."

ANTI-AIRCRAFT FIRE: At *Antwerp* meagre to moderate fire of the predicted concentration type was reported as fairly accurate.

Moderate to intense fire of a barrage type, largely inaccurate, was met at *Schweinfurt.* Intense fairly accurate fire came from *Darmstadt,* with moderate fairly accurate flak being encountered at *Bingen, Hasselt* and *Maastricht.* At *Diest* flak was meagre and fairly accurate and at Bonn moderate and inaccurate. Meagre inaccurate flak was reported at *Koln, Frankfurt* and *Aachen.*

ROUTE: *Clacton* (102nd C.W.) and *Orfordness* (101st and 103rd C.W.), to 51°35′ N—03°40′ E, to *Eupen,* to 49°45′ N—08°20′ E, 50°04′ N—09°41′ E, to *Schweinfurt,* to *Eupen,* to 51°20′ N—03°20′ E, to *Felixstowe.*

WEATHER: Nil to 3/10 cumulus and 4/10–6/10 alto cumulus encountered on route out over North Sea, decreased to nil over continent where 6/10–9/10 high cirrus was reported. Over the target there was 5/10–6/10 cirrostratus above the bombers with traces of cumulus and stratocumulus at 3000 feet. Visibility was 15–30 miles, although some of the groups were bothered by smoke screens. On return route conditions were similar as those on route out.

FIGHTER SUPPORT AND DIVERSIONS: 18 squadrons of VIII Fighter Command P-47s and 16 squadrons of RAF Spitfires provided penetration support for 1st and 4th Wing formations and withdrawal support for 1st Wing bombers. The escorting P-47s destroyed 20 e/a, and the Spitfires destroyed 13. In conjunction with these operations VIII Air Support Command B-26s attacked *Bryas/Sud* and *Poix* Airfields, RAF Mitchells bombed *Calais* Marshalling Yards, and RAF Typhoon bombers raided the airfields at *Poix, Lille/Vendeville* and *Woensdrecht.* These attacks were supported by RAF fighters which destroyed one e/a. From all these operations 3 P-47s, 3 Spitfires and 1 Typhoon are missing.

OBSERVATIONS: Smoke screens were observed at *Antwerp, Bonn, Koln, Mannheim* and five miles southwest of the target. Approximately 40 single-engined e/a were reported on airfield at *Schweinfurt.* On 4 occasions flashes from the ground and smoke puffs about 5000 feet high appeared on course about 20 miles ahead of the formation. Heavy barge traffic was noted in the Rhine between *Bonn* and *Koblenz.*

PART II—REGENSBURG

An Air Task Force composed of three Combat Wings of the 4th Air Division was dispatched to attack the Messerschmitt A. G. plant at Regensburg. The aircraft after attacking with excellent results, proceeded to bases in North Africa. The formations encountered strong oppositions from e/a. Fighter escort was provided by P-47s of the VIII Fighter Command. 24 B-17s are missing. Claims are 140-19-36.

UNIT	NUMBER OF A/C						PERSONNEL CASUALTIES		
4th Wing	*(Dispatched*	*Attacked*	*Failed To Bomb+ A.*	*B.*	*Lost)*	*Claims*	*(Killed*	*Wounded*	*Missing)*
94	21	20	0	1	1	13-1-5	0	1	10
95	21	14	4	3	4	25-1-8	0	0	40
96	21	19	2	0	0	5-1-0	0	0	0
100	21	14	0	7	9	36-10-7	1	2	90
385	21	19	1	1	3	48-4-4	2	1	20
388	21	21	0	0	1	7-0-4	1	3	0
390	20	20×	0	0	6	6-2-8	1	2	40
	147	127×	7	12	24	140-19-36	4	9	200

+Failed to Bomb—A—Mechanical and Equipment Failures.

B—Other than mechanical and equipment failures (includes weather recall, enemy action, etc.)

×—1 a/c bombed a target of opportunity.

BOMBING RESULTS: 126 B-17s dropped 971×500 G.P. fused inst. nose and 1/100 sec. tail, and 448×250 British incendiaries from 17,000–20,000 feet at 1148–1207 hrs. on the important fighter assembly factory of *Messerschmitt A. G.* which contributed a large percentage of the total output of Me109s to the G.A.F.

P. R. U. [Photographic Reconnaissance Unit] cover taken at 1530 hours on 17 August shows that the bombing was accurate and results are excellent. Except for a concentration of bursts close to the northeast corner of the Messerschmitt Works, practically all of the bombs fell either within the factory boundaries or on the airfield. Heavy damage was inflicted on the factory and nearly all the buildings were affected in some degree. Five of the main workshops were seriously damaged and four other large workshops were partially destroyed. A hanger probably used for engine installation was more than half destroyed. A main store and workshop was three-fourths destroyed and was still burning at the time the P.R.U. cover was taken. Office buildings, shops, sheds, canteens and miscellaneous buildings were damaged. Photographs show 37 e/a fighters close to the factory, and it is probable that these were damaged although smoke over the area prevented any definite assessment.

REASON FOR FAILURE TO BOMB: 19 a/c failed to bomb—7 because of mechanical and equipment failures and 12 were lost before reaching the target.

ENCOUNTERS: Enemy fighter opposition was extremely strong, with 200 or more e/a reported making attacks which started just after crossing the Belgian coast and continued until formations had reached the Alps. Types of e/a reported included a large percentage of Me109s, FW-190s, Me-110s, Me-210s, and JU-88s, with a few He-113s, FW-189s, FW-200s and Do-217s. As the formation penetrated deeper into Germany, attacks by single engined a/c decreased while those by twin-engined e/a increased. All known enemy tactics were employed, with attacks being made from all directions and angles. The essential pattern of attack was for groups of 5–11 e/a to come in simultaneously at 2 and 10 o'clock, with an attack at 6 o'clock being made at the same time. Pilots appeared experienced and extremely daring, with reports of many instances in which e/a attacked the high squadron and then dove through the group formation. There were several reports of 1 or 2 e/a staying alongside the formation as decoys while others attacked from nose or tail. Frontal attacks were described as from slightly above and slightly below. Stragglers were smothered by e/a, and there were reports of parachutists being attacked. Individual attacks were chiefly out of the sun, regardless of angle. For the most part the attacks seemed better planned and executed than any encountered on previous missions.

Some Me-109s were reported firing heavy cannon from under each wing, with bursts resembling flak. Several crews reported e/a firing rockets. Other e/a were reported pulling up sharply and dropping clusters of 20–30 black or brown objects which would sail toward the formation and explode.

CASUALTIES: *Personnel*—4 killed, 7 seriously wounded and 200 are missing. Two complete crews are in Switzerland where 2 B-17s landed.

Equipment—24 B-17s are missing—19 from e/a and 5 from unknown reasons.

Estimated Battle Damage—not available.

ANTI-AIRCRAFT FIRE: AA fire was not a deterrent and for the most part was sporadic and inaccurate all along the route. Two Groups reported AA fire from Regensburg and one of the two stated it was meagre and accurate during the second bombing run. Meagre accurate AA fire was reported from Woensdrecht, Wiesbaden, Rosenheim and Brenner Pass. Meagre inaccurate AA fire was encountered at numerous places along the route.

ROUTE: Bases to Lowestoft to 51°43′N—03°42′E to Eupen to 49°45′ N—08°20′ E to 49°15′ N—11°05′ E to 49°02′ N—11°29′ E to target; to 48°50′ N—12°10′ E to 47°52′ N—12°13′ E to 45°53′ N—11°03′ E to Italian coast (44°13′ N—09°30′ E) to 42°30′ N—08°00′ E to 41°00′ N—07°20′ E to 36°55′ N—07°45′ E to Telergma.

WEATHER: *Route out*—9 to 10/10 stratocumulus over England breaking from English coast, becoming 5 to 7/10 at 1500 to 2000 feet over Channel and becoming isolated patches over continental coast, becoming nil amounts of low cloud just inland. No low cloud remainder of distance to target. Patches of isolated medium at 10,000 ft. over England decreasing to nil over Channel except small patch of altocumulus at 10,000 feet in mid-channel. Visibility increased to 10-plus miles on English coast and over 20 miles over continent. *Target:* Regensburg—1145 hours. Clear of all cloud. Visibility 25 miles. *Target to African Base:* Clear to Alps with cumulus developing over Alps to 3 to 4/10 with little vertical development. Becoming clear of low cloud over Italy and then 2 to 3/10 cumulus over Mediterranean, base 2000 ft., tops 7000 ft., continuing to vicinity of bases. Visibility 10-plus miles decreasing to 5 to 7 miles over Mediterranean in haze and locally 1 to 2 miles over Africa in blowing dust. *Bases in Africa:*—1800 hours —3 to 4/10 swelling cumulus, base 2000 ft., tops 7000 ft. Visibility 10-plus miles except locally 1 to 2 miles in blowing sand.

FIGHTER SUPPORT AND DIVERSIONS: See Part I.

OBSERVATIONS: Smoke pots were reported at Mannheim, Nurnburg, Darmstadt, Regensburg and Wurzburg. Balloon barrages were observed at Mannheim, Aachen, and to the right of the course at Brenner Pass. 50–75 twin-engined enemy fighters were observed on a large airfield approximately southeast of Regensburg.

DOCUMENT 5

Typical Group Report (Regensburg):

HEADQUARTERS
NINETY-FOURTH BOMBARDMENT GROUP, (H), AAF
Office of the Operations Officer
APO 634

26 August, 1943

SUBJECT: Report of Operations, Mission of 17 August, 1943.
TO: Commanding Officer, Headquarters, Station 468.

1. *a.* Narrative: Twenty-four aircraft of the 94th Bombardment Group took-off from this Station at the scheduled time, assembled over the field and flew as the lead group of the 401st Combat Wing, which was the second wing of the Fourth Air Division [sic.] Three aircraft of this Group returned from the English Coast when they were not needed to fill in the Formation. The route was flown as briefed. Enemy aircraft attacked the formation immediately after our fighter support had departed. These attacks continued until shortly before the target was reached and was resumed again after the bombs were dropped until the Brenner Pass was reached. One of our aircraft was destroyed before the target was reached. The 401st Combat Wing made two bomb runs on the Target. Bombs were dropped on the second run and the reports indicate that bombing results were very good. Heavy inaccurate flak was encountered on the route to the Target. Accurate moderate flak encountered in the Bren-

ner Pass, especially at Bolzano, caused some damage to our aircraft.

b. Abortives: No aircraft of this Group aborted. Three aircraft returned from the English Coast as instructed when they were not needed to fill in the Formation.

c. Bombing: Twenty aircraft of this Group dropped bombs on the target on the second bomb run with excellent results.

d. Air Combat: Over three hundred enemy aircraft made attacks on this formation between Antwerp and the Brenner Pass. When our fighter support turned back the attacking aircraft were mostly FW190's and ME109's and the attacks were pressed home vigorously. As the formation proceeded further into enemy territory, more twin engine aircraft were encountered. The attacks broke off shortly before the target was reached and resumed after the formation had left the target. The attacks made after the target was passed were by twin engine fighters but these attacks were not pressed home. After the Formation crossed to Italy only a few aircraft were seen and these did not attack. One of our aircraft was lost to enemy fighters shortly before the target was reached.

e. Flak: Meagre, inaccurate, heavy calibre flak was encountered on crossing the coast at Antwerp and at the target, chiefly continuous following fire. Barrage type noted at Munich. Accurate, moderate flak at the Brenner Pass. Meagre inaccurate flak at Lake Gorda, Verona and near La Spezia, Italy.

GALE E. SCHOOLING,
Major, Air Corps,
Operations Officer.

DOCUMENT 6

Typical Group Intelligence Report (Schweinfurt):

CONFIDENTIAL

381ST BOMBARDMENT GROUP (H)
Office of the Intelligence Officer
APO 634

17 August, 1943

SUBJECT: S-2 Interrogation Report—Mission August 17, 1943.
TO: Commanding Officer, 381st Bombardment Group (H), APO 634.

1. Twenty-six (26) A/C took off from Base at 1210, crossing the English Coast at 1314 at Orfordness. Twenty (20) A/C composed the 381st Group which was the low group in the 101st Combat Wing. Six (6) A/C of this Group were in the lead squadron of the composite group which was the high group in the 101st Combat Wing on this mission. The course was as briefed to and from target. The enemy coast was crossed 51°35′ N—0°34′ E at 1339. The target was attacked at 1459 from a true heading of 100° by the 381st Group and at 1500 from a true heading of 96° by the composite group. The English coast recrossed at Orfordness at 1733 with landing made at base at 1745. From observations of crews, five (5) A/C of the 381st group and two (2) of the composite group went down before reaching the target and therefore are assumed not to have bombed. A/C 999 returned with one (1) bomb to base due to mechanical difficulties. A/C 941 returned to base early at 1313 from 13,000 feet over 52°02′N—

01°36′E due to leaks developing in fuel transfer system and gas fumes in plane with fire in ball turret. Ten (10) bombs were returned to base. Visibility at the target was reported at 8 miles—CAVU on the route to and from the target.

2. Between 250 and 300 E/A were encountered, but due to the duration of the mission over enemy territory it is probable that a considerable number of these E/A refueled and returned to the attack. The majority of the enemy fighters were Me-109's (E, F and G), a large number were FW 190's, and half a dozen were T/E (Me-210 and Ju-88). The following colorings were observed: Noses—yellow, red, orange, black and white checked; Spinners—yellow, white, red and black; Fuselage—slaty grey, dull blue, mottled green and white; Wings—dull blue, mottled green, white, and one wing white while the other black. E/A began their attacks a few minutes after the enemy coast was crossed, although attacks were not numerous either on the route out or the route back while we had fighter support. Combats continued until the enemy coast was reached on the route back, with attacks diminishing in number in the vicinity of the target. Attacks began at 1340 hours and continued to 1625, a total of 2 hours and 45 minutes. Enemy attacks were exceptionally determined, persistent and savage, and E/A frequently closed to within spitting distance. Attacks were mainly from 11 o'clock—high and level—but there were many from 5–7, as well as from 3 o'clock; also there were many nose attacks in which the E/A continued to fly on level right through our formations in such a way that many of our gunners could not fire because they were afraid of hitting their own aircraft. Attacks were singly, in pairs, by squadrons, and at times by from 15 to 20 E/A at a time, sometimes in line abreast. No new or unusual armament or tactics other than those set forth above were reported.

3. AA fire going into and coming out from target was meagre, inaccurate for deflection but very accurate for altitude at the following points—Knocke, Noard, Beveland Islands, Rhine River, Mannheim, Bonn, Aachen, Antwerp, and Diest. At Jossa, fifty

(50) red bursts were reported, altitude 20,000 ft., continuously pointing, but inaccurate for deflection. Very accurate fire was reported at Darinstadt in bursts of 4 to 8 at 22,000 ft. and with very accurate deflection. Koln put up AA fire, although 4 miles from formation and therefore inaccurate, however it was moderate in intensity. At the target AA fire was meagre to moderate, extremely accurate for altitude and deflection with two reports of predicted concentrations and three reports of continuously pointed fire. Fire seemed to be coming from the southwest part of the town. The consensus that fire was experienced in both large and small towns all along route which was very accurate for altitude.

4. The Ruhr had many smoke screens. Smoke screens were observed over Bonn, Germany and Liege, Belgium and at the Target area. Considerable river traffic was observed on the Rhine below Koln—mainly loaded barges. Fifty (50) 2-engine bombers were observed at an airfield near Schweinfurt, Germany. Six hangar size buildings and a group of large Gray buildings were observed in wooded area 50°11′N—10°08′E.

5. Statistics:
 a. A/C lost to AA fire —1
 b. A/C lost to E/A —6
 c. A/C lost by reason unknown—3
 d. Casualties —1
 e. Claims 17-6-4

6. No particular comments were made on fighter cover except that it effectively stopped enemy attacks.

LINN S. KIDD
Maj., Air Corps,
Intelligence Officer

DOCUMENT 7

Excerpt from Fighter Command Narrative

CONFIDENTIAL

DESTROY OR FILE

HEADQUARTERS VIII FIGHTER COMMAND

NARRATIVE OF OPERATIONS

8 FC F.O. 106 AS AMENDED—65th FW F.O. 38 AS AMENDED
8 BC F.O. 213—2 GP A.O. 321, 322, 323—11 GP RAMROD
206

17 August, 1943

Statistics—American Fighter Groups.

4th Fighter Group	1 Mission	41 Offensive Sorties
56th Fighter Group	2 Missions	86 Offensive Sorties
78th Fighter Group	1 Mission	41 Offensive Sorties
353rd Fighter Group	2 Missions	72 Offensive Sorties

Claims and Casualties.

Enemy Casualties—19 destroyed, 3 probably destroyed, 4 damaged.

Our Casualties—3 P-47's lost, 3 pilots missing.

1. GENERAL NARRATIVE.

On 17 August, 1943, VIII Bomber Command's first task force consisting of 3 combat wings, bombed a target at Regensburg in South Central Germany. VIII Bomber Command's second and third task forces, consisting of two combat wings each, bombed Schweinfurt in North Central Germany. The operation as originally planned was to have had the second and third task forces entering enemy territory from 9 to 17 minutes later than the first task force so that our fighters furnishing first task force penetration support could offer general support to the second and third task forces as the fighters withdrew. The second and third task forces were not able to take off on schedule because of weather at their home airdromes, so the plan was altered to have the second and third task forces enter enemy territory shortly after 1200 hours. This was to allow 2 of our groups, escorting the first task force on penetration, time to return to their home bases, install belly tanks and to return to Eupen to pick up the second and third task forces on withdrawal. The final plan was as follows:

The 353rd Group, equipped with belly tanks, was to rendezvous with the first task force at Haanstede and escort them to Diest. The 56th Group was to rendezvous with the first task force at Herenthals and escort them to Eupen. This part of the plan was carried out as scheduled.

The 78th Group was to rendezvous with the second and third task forces at Antwerp and escort them to Eupen. The 4th Group was to rendezvous with the second and third task forces at Diest and escort them to Eupen. The 78th Group was 8 minutes late for rendezvous; otherwise this part of the operation took place as scheduled. Investigation is being made to determine the reason for the 78th Group being late.

The 56th Group was scheduled to rendezvous with the withdrawal of the second and third task forces at Eupen and escort them to St. Nicolas. The 353rd Group was scheduled to rendezvous with the second and third task forces at Malines and escort them back to St. Nicolas. The 353rd Group on this part of the mission was not equipped with belly tanks. The second and third task forces were to be escorted from St. Nicolas to the English coast by 11 Group Spitfires. This part of the operation took part as scheduled. It should be noted that most of the fighter claims was made by the 56th Fighter Group on furnishing withdrawal support for the second and third task forces from Eupen to St. Nicolas.

This was too great a distance for one group to furnish such a large bomber formation adequate protection, but it was impossible to put another group in to help them because of supply difficulties and time involved.

DOCUMENT 8

Tactical Commanders Report, 56th Fighter Group:

SECRET

HEADQUARTERS 56TH FIGHTER GROUP
OFFICE OF THE OPERATIONS OFFICER
STATION ℀365, A. P. O. ℀637

19 August 1943.

SUBJECT: Tactical Commanders Report, Amendment 4, Field Order ℀38, 65th Fighter Wing, Reg. Field Order No. 106, VIII Fighter Command, 17 August 1943.

TO: Commanding General 65th Fighter Wing, Station ℀370, A.P.O.℀637.

ATTENTION: A-3

1. In compliance with VIII Fighter Command Memorandum 55-3, dated 19 March 1943, as amended, the following Tactical Commanders Report is submitted:

a. Track flown:

(1) 1506 hours—Engines started.

(2) 1514 hours—First squadron began taking off.

(3) 1530 hours—Group assembled and on course over base at 6000 feet.

(4) 1557 hours—Made landfall on northwest tip of Walcheren Island at 20,000 feet.

(5) 1605 hours—Dropped belly tanks northeast of Antwerp at 20,000 feet and began to climb. The 61st Squadron was bounced shortly thereafter by 4 to 6 Me 109's but was able to reassemble and carry on with the Group formation.

(6) 1616 hours—Reached Bomber Fighter Rendezvous point where Group leader decided to move into enemy territory a bit further when he gave an order to orbit; altitude, 27,000 feet.

(7) 1619 hours—Saw bombers to the southeast in two very large boxes about ten miles apart. They were heading west at this time on course for England.

(8) 1621 hours—61st and 62nd Fighter Squadrons over the rear box of bombers while the 63rd Fighter Squadron was getting into position over the front box. The position was then in the vicinity of Eupen. Engagements and combats ensued from that point until the P-47s were told just north of Antwerp to return home. At this point P-47s were seen to pass going into the bombers. Shortly thereafter two squadrons of Spitfires were seen to be moving in.

(9) 1651 hours—Landfall out by singles, pairs and flights of P-47s in the vicinity of Flushing.

(10) 1735 hours—Group down at Base.

b. Previous to taking off this Group received an amendment to the Field Order stating that the bombers would be five (5) minutes early at the rendezvous point. This placed this Group at the rendezvous point at 1616 hours so penetration was made a bit deeper when the bombers were not seen. The Squadrons were just getting into good position at 1621 hours.

c. Strategy employed—One squadron was placed on the front box and two were taken back to the rear box where one squadron was utilized as high cover and the other sent down in front of the bombers to break up many attacks that were forming up. Within a few minutes the entire sky blew up into dog fights with flights, pairs and singles fighting to defend themselves or avert headon attacks on the bombers. Most of the fighter activity began to develop around or on the front box so the Group was ordered to move up to that box. This order was given with the hope that a few of the unoccupied fighters in the rear might assist the one squadron which had been going thru the thick of it in the front. Finally the strength of our fighters was dissipated so much by combat that an order was given to the remaining few to return to base.

d. Tactics—Some pilots dropped to twenty thousand (20,-000) feet to meet the fighters as they queued up several miles to the side and ahead of the bomber formation. Some retained their altitude and dove three or four thousand feet to pick off those E/A just going into the attack or about to. Others were shot at or shot down off the tails of friendly fighters or while they moved past.

e. Formation:

(1) Climb—In 4 ship Vee with Squadrons in close.

(2) Escort—In loose 4 ship string with 8 aircraft (2 flights) operating separately.

f. The enemy threw his concerted effort into the attack of the bombers from positions well ahead or to the side. He also sent pairs or singles up higher to occupy the P-47s attention and break up their formation. Whenever the enemy found himself in difficulty he ceased combat and broke off for the deck in a vertical dive.

g. Communications—"C" channel was completely jammed as to any communication with the bombers. The normal operating channel was bad with jamming until sometime after entering enemy territory whereupon it cleared to give good intercom reception. Morelight radio operated about the same save for the fact it became very weak at extreme range.

h. Several belly tanks broke on take-off. One belly tank hung up at the time the pilot tried to release it over enemy territory causing him to return to base with escort. One pilot found his airplane not completely serviced and had to return to base with escort. One aircraft returned early because of faulty tachometer.

i. Tactics against flak—At certain locations, flak was found to be most accurate from 18,000–20,000 feet. These hot spots were only found after the bursts were observed in the formation. Violent weaving together with an abrupt loss of altitude or gain of altitude was the only procedure followed.

j. Weather—Visibility good with clear and unlimited conditions in vicinity of Eupen. Haze and 5/10 clouds at lower altitudes in vicinity of Antwerp. Haze over the sea.

k. Recommendations:

(1) At least one more group could have assisted in the withdrawal support from Eupen to St. Nicolas. This added group or groups could have taken the front box or provided high cover. As is, this Group engaged in combat with an estimated 125–150 enemy fighters. We could in no way stop the many enemy attacks on the bomber formations and in some cases had to resort to defending ourselves. Such withdrawals as this will always be a guarantee to heavy fighting.

(2) With as many bombers as were on this mission better protection could have been given had the two main boxes been on a front rather than in line astern. With the two boxes on a wide front the fighter Group could have S'd in front of the formation at all times. When the bomber formations are in line astern the fighters are often unable to give any coverage to rear boxes when up forward and vice versa when with the rear.

(3) The escort cover had difficulty in seeing the enemy fighters below until they reduced their altitude from 27,000 feet to 24,000 feet. In the future this Group intends to send bouncing sections of eight aircraft

each at lower altitudes while the remaining section of each squadron gives them top cover.

For the Group Commander:

JAMES C. STEWART,
Captain, Air Corps,
Operations Officer.

DOCUMENT 9

Report on Enemy Tactics:

SECRET

HEADQUARTERS VIII BOMBER COMMAND
APO 634

ENEMY TACTICS

17 August, 1943

REGENSBURG

Time Up	*No. of A/C*	*Height*	*Seen*	RDF.
0923	Fortresses	23,000 Ft.	12 FW-190s	50 e/a
"	37 Thunderbolts (S.E. of Diest)		12 Me-109s 15/30 e/a	
0924	50 Thunderbolts (Eupen)			

German Fighter Action

Opposition estimated from available R/T to Allied bombers flight, cutting across the length of Reich territory to exit over Italy amounted to 114 aircraft, of which 100 were single-engined fighters and 14 were twin-engined night fighters. The total opposition to this operation cannot be estimated as it will be understood that on the latter stages of the flight German Fighter R/T would be too distant to be intercepted.

One Staffel up from the Woensdrecht/Glize area was first heard at 0952. At 0955 Control reported the approaching hostile formation 45 miles Northwest of Goeree. A sighting was obtained at 1011 and at 1013 the enemy was reported to be above the German fighters' own base. At 1017 there was some reference to a parachute. Further information was not forthcoming, although there had apparently been combats at this time in the Woensdrecht area. Thirty-five fighters were sighted at 1019, but from this time R/T was only fragmentary. As the order to land did not come until 1040 it is thought these fighters may have pursued the bomber formations South-Eastwards.

Four Staffeln, probably from Schipol, were involved and some of them airborne by 0955, were receiving plots of the hostile formation which at that time was placed 45 miles North-West of Goeree. Control continued to send out reports of the formation's progress South-Eastwards, estimating its height as 26,500 feet and recognizing that it consisted of bombers and fighter escort. Eupen was reached at 1037.

Contact by some German fighters were made at 1016 in the Woensdrecht area and persistent attacks ensued from this time until 1030, special points being made of head on attacks and from behind and above. Contact was maintained by at least one Staffel until 1037 and pursuit may have continued for some minutes after this. At least two withdrawals were announced between 1025 and 1030, but the reasons were not intercepted. At 1028 an aircraft appears to have been shot down, but its identity was not confirmed. Congratulations were offered at 1043 but it is thought this would refer to an earlier combat. It is evident that one, and possibly two, Staffeln will have landed in the Munchen/Gladbach area soon after 1055, one having returned to base at 1025.

Two Staffeln up from Deelen at 1034 were being vectored Southwards and ordered to fly at a height of 23,000 feet with all possible speed. Contact does not appear to have been made and it would seem that these fighters took off too late to make any effective interception of the bombers. They flew on, however, as far as Cochem, which point was reached by some fighters at 1053 after which time nothing was heard. It is thought they may have landed in this vicinity, rather than endeavor to make for Deelen.

Three Staffeln, probably from Munchen/Gladbach, were active between 1033 and 1113. At least one Staffel was airborne by 1033 and proceeding Southwards. Although Control did not plot the course of the bomber formation after 1037, the course of the pursuing German fighters was so accurately traced that a very clear picture is obtained of the route taken by the enemy formation until 1113, when German fighters were positioncd near Worms. Contact was made at 1040 and at 1042 a pilot was heard to say, "I have been hit and am bailing out." Between 1038 and 1043 another pilot was very distressed because he was unable to see through his windscreen. From 1048 to 1107 three withdrawals were announced, one because of engine trouble. At 1105 a victory was claimed; two minutes later this German fighter's position was stated to bc in the vicinity of Mains, but it cannot be certain that the casualty was in this area. A pilot being asked at 1113 the whereabouts of one of his comrades replied, "Apparently he's been shot down." It is assumed that German fighters must have landed somewhere in the Worms area.

Control of 5/F-123 aircraft was heard at 1041 warning his aircraft of Thunderbolts just West of Schouwen. This would appear to refer to the Thunderbolts returning from their escort duties.

At least eight twin-engined fighters from the Mannheim area were on patrol between 1212 and 1349. Hostiles were reported at 1224 at Linz but beyond this the route of the bombers were not reported. Probably in anticipation of the enemy formation flying back to England on a reciprocal course, some of these aircraft were ordered to patrol between Mannheim and Karlsruhe above the Rhine, at a height of 23,000 feet. They were, however, recalled to base at 1318, and all sections appear to have landed at 1350. At 1339 Control inquired of a pilot if he had scored a victory, but no reply was heard.

At least six twin-engined fighters from the Stuttgart area were heard between 1159 and 1300. At 1207 Control warned his aircraft of hostiles to the South of Regensburg and later announced that they were proceeding towards Italy. One aircraft on being instructed at 1241 to land queried the reason and was told that their target was out of range. These fighters landed by 1300.

SCHWEINFURT

Time Up	*No. of A/C.*	*Seen*	RDF.
1336	Fortresses		
	96 Spitfires IX (N. of Antwerp)	No. of FW-190s &	
	85 Spitfires IX (withdrawal cover)	Me-109s FW-190s and Me-110s	75
	181 Thunderbolts (withdrawal cover)	Me-109s, 110s 210s and FW-190s	

German Fighter Action

The extended interception area now necessitated by the scale of the Allied daylight offensive, and for which the German defenses in the West have been forced to arrange, seems at the moment to be causing German controls less anxiety than one might have expected. The development of the air situation had been evidently foreseen and prepared for. Fighter pilots themselves evince little consternation in being dispatched so far out of their normal areas. Evidently, before they set out, they have instruction to their possible area of combat and all details of landing grounds in the strange territory. The organization is complete with pilots receiving appropriate cards for the coded place names in the affected area. Controllers in France and Holland appear also to be in possession of a bird's eye view of the situation and know of the raiders' progress deep into Germany. They can, in this way, calculate well in advance, how best to fit their particular fighters into the interception scheme.

Further, arrangements seem to be made to fill in the gaps caused by the exploitation of defence Staffeln away from their own area. On this day, after a strong force of fighters from Holland had pursued the raiders to Regensburg down the Rhine, further fighters from Northwest Germany appear to have been brought down to bases in Holland, so that should the Regensburg bombers return, these fighters would be available on convenient airfields. As events turned out, they were employed not against returning Regensburg raiders, but against incoming Schweinfurt raiders.

The interception by single-engined fighters, which we can describe from the German R/T covers two periods; the inward flight from Schouwen to Aachen between 1340 and 1423, and the homeward flight from the Koblenz area to the estuary of the Scheldt between roughly 1600 and 1700. The events of the route Eastwards from the Mosel-Rhine confluence was reflected in the R/T of twin-engined fighter units.

The depth of the penetration once again stirred to action fighters from four Jafues [*Jagdfueher:* Fighter Leader]. During the operation it is estimated that some 300 machines were thrown against the raiders.

Opposition in the first stage, after landfall was made over the Dutch Isles, was drawn from a number of fighter staffeln, believed to belong to Schipol, Münster, Jever and Oldenburg, but all coming up apparently from bases between Antwerp and Rotterdam. Elements of two Schipol Staffeln were first heard. Airborne by 1339 they were informed at 1351 of heavy bombers Northeast of Antwerp, flying a course due east. These German planes may have taken off from Gilze or Volkel. By 1355, they claimed contact. A certain amount of agitated questioning was caused by Controls being unable to give exact information about the presence of Allied fighters. It was recognized at 1403 that the bombers had turned S. E. and German fighters followed them, going in to attack between Maastricht and Aachen. By 1415 these pilots had given up the chase and were apparently turned back Northwards to base.

Some 20 aircraft, half of whom were probably Münster aircraft, who had landed at about 1148 in Woensdrecht, were up by 1343 in reaction to an alarm of enemy aircraft, heavies, coming in from the direction of Schouwen. The course of the bombers was plotted every few minutes until they reached Sittard. German fighters were, by this time (1418), in a favourable position to attack. Head-on combat ensued and a running fight continued until 1425 (Southwest Bonn). Seventy heavy bombers were counted by the Hun. R/T on this frequency faded out at 1428 while German fighters were apparently still following down on a South-Easterly course.

Two Staffeln, possibly from Jever, who must have travelled down from their own base earlier in the day in almost complete R/T silence, were operating during the period 1341–1418 in an area between the Dutch Isles and East of Beverloo. One hundred bombers were counted. This was at 1345. Severe combat did not commence until about ten minutes later. Somebody claimed a shoot-down at 1357 and another pilot claimed to have seen a second one go down immediately afterwards. Nothing more was heard after 1415.

Also taking part in this combat in the Beverloo area were fighters believed to belong to Oldenburg, but coming up apparently from Antwerp direction. Possibly two Schwarme were involved and these made contact at about 1407 and continued active until 1421.

Thus, the main burden of the interception on this inward route was taken by fighters belonging to bases in Germany. As the bombers penetrated deeper inland it is unlikely that many of these fighters followed across the Rhine.

Preparation for interception of returning raiders was early initiated. At 1300 Jafue 2 collected the best part of his fighter force under the leadership of Wutz, Matoni, Sternberg, Naumann and others and brought them up to Lille Nord and landed them there.

At 1605 these were up again, together with further formations under Rudi, Brille and Brenndiger and all, possibly 40–50 aircraft, were sent to Brussels. This command was corrected one minute later to Namur.

Meanwhile Jafue 3 Control had decided to send part of his fighter strength, possibly three Staffeln and a Stab formation, up Northwards. They were assembled at 1550 over Evreux and received, three minutes later, the instruction to proceed to Cambrai. He added that a large force of heavy bombers was approaching from the East towards Cambrai. This was a very early deduction, for the Allied raiders were still travelling across Central Germany, possibly in the neighborhood of Giessen. At 1610, Control told aircraft that the enemy was 200 Km. to the East of Cambrai, course Cambrai, height 23–26,000 feet. At 1620 this force was sent on to Brussels and further on to Antwerp. The flight does not appear to have been particularly successful; there had been several withdrawals, and one pilot at 1624 complained that he was flying alone, having lost the formation enroute. Control, however, persisted in his determination to attempt to make contact. The bombers at 1630 were plotted north of Charleroi. German pilots' language at this time suggested either contact or more likely intense aggravation with comrades or Controller. The last reports of hostiles until 1648 gave their position over Brussels.

Jafue 2 aircraft were more successful, as indeed they had the better chance of being. As early as 1616 Control considered that bombers were to the North of his wing and inquired whether they had been sighted. The wing leader replied, "No." They were vectored North-North-East and ordered to wait North of Namur. At 1621 enemy aircraft were reported having passed Liege and flying straight in their direction. Combat followed immediately. There was a moment of tension when at 1627, after heated engagements during which Wutz Gallard had been issuing imperative warnings to "close up, look out, formation coming up behind; fighters to starboard," etc. [so] that Brenndiger asking

Wutz his position could get no reply. Comment from another pilot was, "Hope he hasn't crashed." Engagements increased in intensity. The signal, "The hounds have arrived" at 1636 did nothing to alleviate the situation. Claims of strikes and kills, mingled with cries of "Parachute," "Ha! Down you go, you dog," and after almost half an hour's combat, a final gasp, "Herr Gott Sakramant!" By 1700, aircraft were landing at nearest possible airfield.

Holland/Ruhr opposition on the withdrawal came from six Staffeln probably up from bases at Venlo, Munchen-Gladbach, Aachen area. It will be appreciated that as fighter units had landed at scattered airfields after the preceding engagements it is difficult at this stage in the study of the R/T to determine exactly where they came up from again.

Serious interception by these fighters were not undertaken until after 1600 hours. The main centre of the interception was again the Aachen-Liege area and the peak period of combats around 1620. Great stress was laid on the arrival of the fighter covers and running fights developed with both fighter and bomber activity finally ceasing at about 1640.

Nightfighter units took a significant part in this day's defensive activity. Altogether some 60 twin-engined machines were airborne in reactions, though not all of them made contact.

The first to be aware of the bomber penetrations were apparently from the Florennes area. The enemy were reported to be too far off at 1355; but nevertheless three were sent at 1410 towards Aachen, but no contact was established and they were ordered back at 1424.

At least a Schwarme from the Metz area was asked at 1422 whether they were still in contact. At 1444 enemy aircraft were reported to be over Giessen and Frankfurt. This information of the progress of the raid, coming through twin-engined fighter R/T is a feature of the day's raid. The messages must have been intended more as a guide to pilots of the whereabouts of the raiders in case they might find themselves opportunity in the line of flight, than as a warning of immediate significance. At 1450, stragglers apparently coming Northwest from South Belgium were noted, but again there is no evidence of contact.

Some eight twin-engined planes of the Stuttgart area were heard first at 1423. At this time Control urgently ordered them to land, refuel and rearm and be at complete operational readiness. At 1500 they were up again and ordered to wait, for, as yet, the course of the enemy was still uncertain. At 1517 the signal "Raiders over Wurzburg" came through and followed by the enthusiastic reply, "O.K.—we are setting off in the direction of the enemy." At 1533 bombers were reported above and around Schweinfurt, but by 1540 when aircraft reported having arrived over the city the pilots asked where were the enemy as they could not see any. These aircraft were in receipt of landing orders at 1602.

A schwarme operating East of Venlo, between 1505 and 1515, were ordered at 1525 to Dortmund to await bombers coming from the Southeast. At 1556 bombers were reported between Marburg and Cologne.

Possibly two Staffeln of units not yet identified, operating on V.H.F. with call-signs which suggest twin-engined fighters were heard between 1544 and 1644. They were sent against the bombers in the Liege area. Great insistence was laid on the instructions to these fighters to avoid at all costs combats with Allied covers and to attempt attacks on bomber planes only. At 1615 aircraft were ordered not to pursue any further to the West as fighters were coming up.

Some eight T.E. fighters, probably of Enschede, were heard between 1545 and 1736. Nothing of interest came through until 1614, when warning was given to be on their guard against enemy fighters. At 1633 pilots were hoping to find some lone Allied fighters. By 1700 they must have been in combat for they were discussing whether they had seen anyone bail out, and, apparently, referring to an Allied aircraft, they said they had seen one on fire, shot down by an Me-109.

Perhaps the most effective opposition of twin-engined aircraft appears to have been put up by about eight planes from Laon-Athies area. At 1619, 170 bombers were reported over Malmedy, corrected at 1624 to 100 bombers. They had by this time crossed the German/Belgium frontier. Fighters were instructed to gain height and at 1630 they reported being in the midst of air battle. By 1650 the Allied raiders were said to have departed.

Note to the above: Luftwaffe Units that Participated in the Battles of Regensburg/Schweinfurt, 17 August 1943.

Units stationed in Holland, Belgium and France:

Jagdgeschwader 1
Jagdgeschwader 2
Jagdgeschwader 3
Jagdgeschwader 26

Units stationed inside Germany:

V Gruppe Jagdgeschwader 11 (V JG 11; brought down from Jever)
111 Gruppe Jagdgeschwader 54 (brought down from Nordholtz)
Zerstörergeschwader 26
Jagdgeschwader 25
I Gruppe Jagdgeschwader 27
II Gruppe Jagdgeschwader 27
Jagdgeschwader 50
II Gruppe Jagdgeschwader 51
Jagdgeschwader 300 (Wilde Sau, nightfighters)
Nachtgeschwader 101 (nightfighters)

BIBLIOGRAPHY

Besides the various documents from the Washington National Records Center (National Archives) which were consulted (a small portion reproduced above), contemporary newspapers and letters from a number of participants (listed in the Acknowledgments), the following published sources were most useful and valuable:

BEKKER, CAJUS: *The Luftwaffe War Diaries,* Garden City: Doubleday & Co., Inc., 1968.

CRAVEN, W. F. & CATE, J. L., editors: *The Army Air Forces in World War II* (7 vols.), Chicago: University of Chicago Press, 1948–58.

FREEMAN, ROGER A.: *The Mighty Eighth,* Garden City: Doubleday & Co., Inc., 1970.

GALLAND, ADOLF: *The First and the Last,* New York: Henry Holt & Co., 1954.

HANSELL, HAYWOOD S., JR.: *The Air Plan That Defeated Hitler,* Atlanta: Privately Printed, 1972.

HARRIS, ARTHUR: *Bomber Offensive,* London: Collins, 1947.

HUTTON, BUD & ROONEY, Andy: *Air Gunner,* New York: Farrar & Rinehart, Inc., 1944.

KNOKE, HEINZ: *I Flew for the Führer,* New York: Henry Holt & Co., 1954.

LEMAY, CURTIS E., with KANTOR, MACKINLAY: *Mission With LeMay,* Garden City: Doubleday & Co., Inc., 1965.

MCCRARY, JOHN R. & SCHERMAN, DAVID E.: *First of the Many,* New York: Simon & Schuster, 1944.

MAURER, MAURER, editor: *Air Force Combat Units of World War II,* New York: Franklin Watts, Inc., 1963.

MORRISON, WILBUR H.: *The Incredible 305th,* New York: Duell, Sloan & Pearce, 1962.

NILSSON, JOHN R.: *The Story of the Century,* Beverly Hills: Nilsson, 1946.

PEASLEE, BUDD J.: *Heritage of Valor,* Philadelphia & New York: J. B. Lippincott Co., 1963.

SPEER, ALBERT: *Inside the Third Reich,* New York: Macmillan, 1970.

TANTUM, W. H. & HOFFSCHMIDT, E. J., editors: *The Rise and Fall of the German Air Force,* Old Greenwich: WE, Inc., 1969.

U. S. ARMY AIR FORCE: *Target Germany,* New York: Simon & Schuster, 1943.

UNITED STATES STRATEGIC BOMBING SURVEY: *Over-all Report (European War),* Washington, D.C.: U. S. Government Printing Office, 1945.

ACKNOWLEDGMENTS

Originally the intention was to place this section where it belongs: in the front of the book. However, as time went by, the numbers of individuals and organizations contributing to the work grew, rendering the plan impracticable. Thus those who so kindly made this book possible are tucked away in the back—but not by any means as an afterthought.

As with so many of my aviation projects, this one initiated during discussions with my editor, Harold Kuebler, who subsequently, and with superhuman patience, withdrew to await developments—offering suggestions and encouragement as work progressed. His editorial work which followed greatly shaped the book and, as customary with us at this point, was virtually collaboration.

Once the book got under way the next step was to approach and obtain the aid and cooperation of Air Force's Magazine and Book Branch in the location of the various documents, the myriad of Reports, Group Records, aircraft loading lists, and the other materials dating back to the moment, literally, of the Regensburg-Schweinfurt mission. In this I was initially aided (1970) by the then Chief, Commander Joseph W. Marshall, USNR; the Magazine and Book Branch was then under the Office of the Assistant Secretary of Defense. The Air Force subsequently took over again and I was guided by Lieutenant Colonel Gerald M. Holland, USAF, and especially by his successor, Major Larry K. Brown, USAF.

They in turn led me to the National Archives and Records Service, Edwin R. Flatequal, Chief (since retired). There I was rendered excellent help in acquiring the Air Force unit historical reports by Joseph Avery and especially Mrs. Edna Finch, who on several occasions had great piles of papers, maps, forms, and folders waiting for me when I arrived at the Washington National Records Center.

The interest, encouraging cooperation and, no doubt for them, tedious correspondence of the two men who led the strikes on 17 August 1943, General Curtis E. LeMay, USAF(Ret) and Major General Robert B. Williams, USAF(Ret) amounted to a good deal more than I had a right to expect. General LeMay, when he happened to be in the East, managed to find time for me to discuss his recollections of the mission—as well as other fascinating memories of the Second World War, which, happily, he permitted me to tape. This meeting was facilitated by the gracious aid of Mrs. Kathryn Nagy of the Office of the Chief of Staff of the Air Force. General Williams, residing in Texas, responded quickly and at length to my querying letters; and Mrs. Williams managed to dig out a newspaper clipping from 1943 which prevented me from making a rather embarrassing error (which proved, too, that even objective records can be wrong). I might add that the objectivity, the grasp of detail after so long a time as well as a quickness of mind in visualizing the meaning of the Regensburg-Schweinfurt mission by both these men was truly impressive.

It would be possible to continue at length about nearly all who contributed to this book, but there is a point at which sentences must stop and lists begin. So my gratitude also to the following:

David Aiken, American Aviation Historical Society, Weatherford, Tex.

Paul Andrews, American Aviation Historical Society, Rome, N.Y.

Anthony Arcaro, Brooklyn, N.Y., (91st Bomb Group).

Joseph W. Baggs, Carnegie, Pa., (384th Bomb Group).

Jean Bennett, Doubleday & Co., N.Y.

Arvin O. Basnight, Los Angeles, Cal., Federal Aviation Administration.

John M. Bennett, Jr., San Antonio, Tex. (100th Bomb Group).

Everett E. Blakely, Northridge, Cal. (100th Bomb Group).

William E. Charles, Jr., Bedford, Ind. (95th Bomb Group).

Robert C. Chapin, Villanova, Pa., (384th Bomb Group).

Kenneth S. Cohen, New York, N.Y. (322nd Bomb Group, M).

Harry H. Crosby, Newton, Mass. (100th Bomb Group).

John S. Durakov, Sr., San Francisco, Cal., (385th Bomb Group).

James N. Eastman, Jr. Chief, Research Branch, Albert F. Simpson Historical Research Center, Maxwell Air Force Base, Ala.

Virginia Fincik, 1361st Photo SQ., AAVS (MAC), Arlington, Va.

Adolf Galland, Bonn-Rhein, Germany.

William H. Geir, Woodbridge, N.J. (94th Bomb Group).

Dr. Karl Gundelach, Oberst i. G., Millitargeschichtliches Forschungsamt, Fachgruppe VI, Freiburg im Breisgau, West Germany.

Don Hayes, Stockton, Calif. (91st Bomb Group).

Edward J. Huntzinger, Perrysburg, Ohio (388th Bomb Group).

Howard Justin, Forest Hills High School, N.Y. (96th Bomb Group).

Delmar E. Kaech, Arnold, Mo. (91st Bomb Group).

Katharine Kaufman, Forest Hills, N.Y.

Frank Kegel, Forest Hills High School, N.Y. (452nd Bomb Group).

Marguerite Kennedy, Chief, Archives Branch, Albert F. Simpson Historical Research Center, Maxwell Air Force Base, Ala.

Major General and Mrs. John B. Kidd, Fairfax, Va. (100th Bomb Group).

Gene Kropf, Los Angeles, Cal., Federal Aviation Administration.
Frances Lewis, 1361st Photo Sq. AAVS (MAC), Arlington, Va.
Denny McFarland, Abilene, Texas (386th Bomb Group, M).
L. Corwin Miller, Stockton, Cal. (384th Bomb Group).
John R. Mitchell, Corona del Mar, Cal. (92nd Bomb Group).
Henry Nagorka, Washington, D.C. (388th Bomb Group).
Joseph Oravec, Clarks Summit, Pa. (Ex-USAAF, WW II).
George W. Parks, M/Sgt, USAF(Ret), Vallejo, Cal. (91st Bomb Group).
James A. Roe, New York, N.Y. (388th Bomb Group).
William G. Ryan, Bloomington, Ind. (91st Bomb Group).
Phillip R. Taylor, Alameda, Cal. (91st Bomb Group).
Horace Varian, Newton, Mass. (100th Bomb Group).
Ernest E. Warsaw, Los Angeles, Cal. (100th Bomb Group).
David M. Williams, Col., USAF(Ret), Atlanta, Ga. (91st Bomb Group).
Edward Parks Winslow, Jr., Menlo Park, Cal. (91st Bomb Group).

A closing note of gratitude: My son David, an author himself, and a full-time student, was my steadfast research assistant on this book, as he has been on others. He was especially astute in going through the piles of National Archives materials, selecting those that proved useful and avoiding much repetition. Our discussions while the book was in progress were also most helpful to me. So this brief note must suffice for a great deal of help rendered over a long period of time.

My wife, Edith, as before, Attended to Things, unperturbed by the Writer At Work, the Researcher At Bay and the Typist At Profanity. We have a busy household, generally filled with more children than I am certain we have; the walls reverberate with the music of today (and yesteryear, when I can get at the phonograph), young voices and laughter (among other sounds); these never impinged on me, thanks primarily to Edith—who, by the way, has her own writing deadlines to meet, for she is a writer-editor herself. She manages, too, to keep me off the precipices of illiteracy.

Our other two youngsters, Carla and Emily, are young ladies now so that they no longer provide the morning intrusions (I don't mind being taken from the typewriter so long as I can blame it on someone else). It was Emily's little verse-like query on war, asked so many years ago, which inspired me to see if a study of Regensburg-Schweinfurt might answer the question: "What is war?" The answer is, I suppose, now so simple only because war has become—in our time—so complex. War is, I repeat, killing and destruction; that is the ultimate and bitter truth, whatever you stand for.

Index

INDEX

GREENVILLE COLLEGE LIBRARY
940.5J11 C001
JABLONSKI, EDWARD.
DOUBLE STRIKE 1ST ED. GARDEN CIT STX
3 4511 00093 4097

86076

940.5
J11